MW01007014

THE
ENCYCLOPEDIA
OF THE
STRANGE

OTHER BOOKS BY DANIEL COHEN

FOR YOUNG READERS

THE

ENCYCLOPEDIA

OF THE

STRANGE

BY *DANIEL COHEN*

ILLUSTRATED

DORSET PRESS • NEW YORK

To Liz and Gene Honofee

Copyright © 1985 by Daniel Cohen
All rights reserved.

No part of this book may be
reproduced or utilized in any form or by any
means, electronic or mechanical, including
photocopying, recording or by any information
storage and retrieval systems, without permission
in writing from the Publisher.

This edition published by Dorset Press
a division of Marboro Books Corporation.
1989 Dorset Press

ISBN 0-88029-451-5

Printed in the United States of America

M 9 8 7 6 5 4 3 2

Contents

Introduction: The Unknown World, ix

Introduction:

The Unknown World

Practically everyone loves a mystery. All but the dullest among us are excited by the notion that all is not quite as it seems; that there are things in this world that are not only unexplained, but unexplainable, at least in conventional terms.

There are those who love mysteries, or profess to, because they really have a hidden agenda. They think that by attacking the accepted view of the world they can subtly promote their own view. It's not so much that they are fascinated by the unexplained, but that they wish to impose their own often bizarre explanations.

For most of us, however, the wonder of the unknown is its own reward. We can speculate endlessly about phenomena, but are quite comfortable with conclusions that are unsolved or unproved still. We can even accept a mundane explanation if it is well founded.

Many of the cases and phenomena that are discussed in this book might be called Fortean. The word comes from the name of Charles Hoy Fort, an American writer of the early twentieth century. Fort loved to collect odd bits of information about all man-

ner of strange things: things or people that disappeared, fish that
fell from the sky, unknown planets, unusual behavior of animals,
or what have you. If it didn't seem to make sense in terms of the
ordinary way of looking at the world, Fort was interested in it.

He haunted libraries and read prodigiously in the scientific and
popular journals. As his interest became known, he received clip-
pings and correspondence from people all over the world. Fort
took piles of notes, kept huge files, and ultimately much of the information found its way into one of his books. He wrote four famous, or semifamous, books: *The Book of the Damned, New Lands,
Lo!,* and *Wild Talents.* Actually, Fort was never really famous, but
he did have a band of devoted disciples who have carried on his
work after his death; there are today small Fortean societies in
both the United States and Britain, and Forteanlike groups in
other countries as well.

Some of his followers become quite lyrical in praising Fort.
One, John Mitchell, recently wrote quite seriously that Fort was
"the best modern philosopher and the greatest genius to come out
of America."

I wouldn't go that far. In fact, when you get right down to it, I
never really liked Charles Fort very much. When reading Fort, I
really do get the impression that he has a hidden agenda, an alter-
nate view of the universe that he is trying to get across. The trouble is that I have never been quite sure what his views were, and
neither has anyone else. He had a strange circular writing style,
and he told a lot of not-very-funny jokes. Mitchell speaks of his
wisdom being "hidden from vulgar eyes." I have never found in-
scrutability a virtue. Mitchell also says that "no idiot, bigot, dog-
matist or true believer of any brand has ever been able to
understand Charles Fort," which means, if you don't understand
him you are one of the above, so you better not admit that you
don't understand him.

Unfair, I say. There is no need to hide behind obscure and deliberately confusing language. And one should not cover one's beliefs
by pretending it's all a big joke. If you believe something, come

Charles Fort

out and say it clearly. If you don't understand or don't know, come out and say that as well. Don't elevate the wonder and joy one feels in the presence of strange phenomena into some sort of half-cracked philosophy. Forteans, whose avowed purpose is to puncture the absurdities and pomposities of orthodox believers, can become pretty absurd and pompous themselves in the attempt. I'm going to try very hard to avoid those particular pitfalls.

Still, one must give Charles Fort his due—he was a great oddity collector, and though he didn't always exercise the best judgment, he was honest. The same, alas, cannot be said for some of today's collectors of strange phenomena.

To report a mystery is one thing. To make a mystery by leaving out or distorting significant facts is quite another. Granted that in the field of the strange, reliable information is difficult to come by. Sometimes it is quite impossible to determine what information is reliable. If we had to apply a courtroom, or worse, a scientific, test to the evidence for all strange phenomena, then this would be a very thin volume indeed. So a certain amount of leeway must be allowed in presenting evidence—but making things up is not allowed. It was perfectly acceptable for Wilkie Collins to bring a group of sinister Indian avengers into his novel *The Moonstone*. It is quite unacceptable to bring them in when recounting the strange history of the Hope Diamond. The line between fact and fiction in some of the accounts in this book is difficult to locate, but I have made a good-faith attempt to try to find that line, and not just uncritically retell the most exotic version of a story available.

In two previous volumes, *The Encyclopedia of Monsters* and *The Encyclopedia of Ghosts*, I stated that it was impossible to cover the whole field, and that in the end the choice of what was included and what was excluded was personal. I put in what interested me. That goes double for this book, because the field of the strange is even more diffuse. There are "big" mysteries, like UFOs and Atlantis, and little ones, like the reality of Robin Hood or the identity of Jack the Ripper. The only requirement is that the mystery is or once was an object of speculation and wonder.

Some of these accounts, like El Dorado and the canals of Mars, are really mysteries no more. They have been "solved." Yet the stories of what happened remain extraordinarily interesting.

But enough excuses and explanations. Ultimately, a book must stand on its own. If you find what follows to be interesting, if every once in a while what you read makes you say "Wow!" or some stronger and more modern expletive—then I have succeeded in what I set out to do.

1

ANCIENT

MYSTERIES

ANCIENT HIGH TECH   In 1900, Greek sponge divers an-
chored off the island of Antikythera during a storm, located a
sunken wreck. The report of their initial investigation was enough
to bring archaeologists to the scene. They determined that the
wreck was that of a commercial vessel, probably Greek, sunk
about 65 B.C. while on its way to Rome from either Rhodes or Cos.
The cargo was mainly pieces of sculpture, but from the wreckage
they pulled what appeared to be a badly corroded piece of machinery. The object remained merely a curiosity for years until it
was studied with care by the highly respected academician and
historian of science Professor Derek de Solla Price. Professor Price
decided that the device, which had been made with bronze plates
and complicated gears, had been designed to display the positions
of the sun and moon, and possibly the planets. According to British
astronomer Colin Ronan, "It was an instrument that gave the positions of celestial bodies in figures—there were pointers that
moved over dials to indicate the results of its internal calculations.
. . . In short, this was a mechanical computer, and a complex one
at that. Internal evidence also shows that it was a contemporary
machine definitely made for everyday use, and not a treasure from
some bygone age. We are forced to the conclusion that it pays
tribute to a tradition of highly advanced technology in Greece.
. . . But if there was a tradition of an advanced technology in the
ancient world, it did not penetrate into Western Christendom."

At a scientific meeting, Professor Price told his colleagues,
"Finding a thing like this is like finding a jet plane in the tomb of
King Tutankhamen."

This astronomical "calculator" does indicate that the ancients were far more technologically advanced than we have given them credit for. Still, such a device could conceivably have been constructed by the extremely clever application of some relatively simple principles that were known to the Greeks and Romans. What is exceptionally interesting about the discovery is that it was completely unexpected. We have fairly voluminous records from this period in history, yet none of them mention this apparently common device. It was found by accident, and one wonders what other technological marvels may one day turn up in an ancient wreck or undiscovered tomb.

Somewhat more controversial than the Greek calculator is the evidence for ancient electronics. In 1938, German archaelogist Wilhelm König thought he had discovered electric batteries that were some two thousand years old. It is not altogether clear whether König dug these artifacts up himself or found them among material lodged in the National Museum of Iraq. Whatever the case, they had originally come from a settlement of the Parthians at a place called Khujut Rabu, a few miles from Baghdad. The artifacts were earthenware jars with necks covered with asphalt and iron rods encased in copper cylinders. To König, they looked like electric batteries, and he said so in an article published in 1940. But by the time the article appeared, war had broken out, and there wasn't much time for speculating over ancient dry-cell batteries.

After the war, Willard F. M. Gray of the General Electric High Voltage Laboratory in Pittsfield, Massachusetts, built some duplicate batteries based on the König discovery. They worked perfectly, and one is still on display in the Berkshire Museum in Pittsfield.

The Parthians were the descendants of nomadic horsemen who had established a wide empire in the Middle East. They were excellent fighters and occasionally fought the mighty Romans to a standstill. But they were never noted for their technological achievements. So if they had batteries, they probably got them from somewhere else. But where?

The principle of the battery was not invented, or reinvented, until the early 1900s. Were these ancient batteries an example of an isolated and accidental development? Were they batteries at all? They were not in working condition when they were found, so perhaps König and Gray reconstructed too much. Many scientists simply do not accept the battery identification. If indeed they were batteries, they probably were used for electroplating rather than producing power. The puzzle remains where it was thirty years ago because no new evidence has turned up.

Stories of eternally burning, mysterious lights have been reported from dozens of ancient societies. There is also an ancient Egyptian relief that appears on a wall of the Temple of Hathor at Dendera. According to Swedish writer Ivan Troeng, the drawing "obviously shows electric lamps held by high tension insulators." To archaeologists, the "lamps" are not lamps at all, but "snake stones," lumps of granite with pictures of snakes carved on them. Snake stones were often used in places like Dendera, where a snake cult was worshiped, and there definitely appear to be snakes rather than filaments in the middle of the "lamps." The drawings do, however, still bear a striking resemblance to electric lamps.

Naturalist and Fortean Ivan Sanderson has insisted that a small gold object found in a thousand-year-old tomb in Colombia looks exactly like a delta-winged airplane. Others say that the little golden object is really a stylized representation of a skate or ray, those flattened relatives of the shark. In fact, the object does look a lot more like a delta-winged plane than a skate or ray, no matter how stylized.

After this initial discovery was publicized it became apparent that there were quite a number of "little gold airplanes" from South America scattered about in museum collections. One in the Chicago Museum of Natural History was called a "flying fish."

Another at the Smithsonian Institution was labeled simply "cast gold ornament." Erich Von Däniken, the promoter of the ancient astronaut theory, found a couple of additional "gold airplanes," but some of these really do look like skates or flying fish, and they tend to weaken the entire ancient airplane theory.

Von Däniken also cited a "model aeroplane" in the Cairo Museum that was originally found in a tomb near Sakkara, where the famed Step Pyramid is located. Von Däniken said that it is "accepted without question" as a model aircraft. That statement itself is questionable, for although the object does look rather like a model of an airplane, it looks a lot more like a stylized model of a hawk, a common motif in ancient Egyptian art. When viewed from the side, the eyes and beak of the "model aeroplane" are clearly visible.

Sanderson has also located what he thought to be a small pre-Columbian model of a backhoe. The thing was found in Panama and is probably around a thousand years old. It is now housed at the University of Pennsylvania museum. The object is generally regarded as a model of a jaguar or crocodile, and it does look like an animal with large teeth, but for an animal it has some odd fea-

Formalized jaguar or ancient backhoe?
(From the collections of the University Museum, Philadelphia)

tures, and Sanderson thought that it was even more intriguing than the "ancient airplanes."

Here is how he described it in his book *Investigating the Unexplained:* "It is a piece of jewelry made by a consummate artist; in gold containing a huge green gemstone, and obviously intended to be a pendant. It is four and a half inches long and was described by its discoverers as a crocodile, but later by others as a jaguar. It is, however, covered with mechanical devices, including two cogwheels."

A backhoe is not particularly high tech, but if the people who lived in Panama a thousand years or so ago used or saw a backhoe or anything like it, then they had knowledge far beyond anything ever dreamed of by conventional scientists. But is the piece of jewelry meant to represent an animal, albeit a highly formalized one, or is it meant to show a piece of machinery? The answer remains a matter of opinion or prejudice.

A̤NCIENT MAPS OF THE ANTARCTIC   There is a serious scholarly dispute over the possibility that some ancient and unknown seafaring civilization discovered and mapped not only the New World, but also the continent of Antarctica, possibly even before it was covered by its present ice sheet.

The controversy started with a map drawn in the year 1513 under the direction of a Turkish admiral named Piri Re'is (Admiral Piri). The painted parchment map showed the Atlantic Ocean and its islands and the bordering lands.

The Piri Re'is map was entirely forgotten until it turned up in the archives of the Imperial Palace in Constantinople (or Istanbul) in 1929. This map, which was made a mere twenty-one years after Columbus's voyage of discovery, was claimed by the Turks to be the most accurate of the early maps of the New World. More intriguing was the claim in one of the inscriptions that the map was based on a map that Columbus himself had used on his first voyage.

There had long been speculation that Columbus already pos-

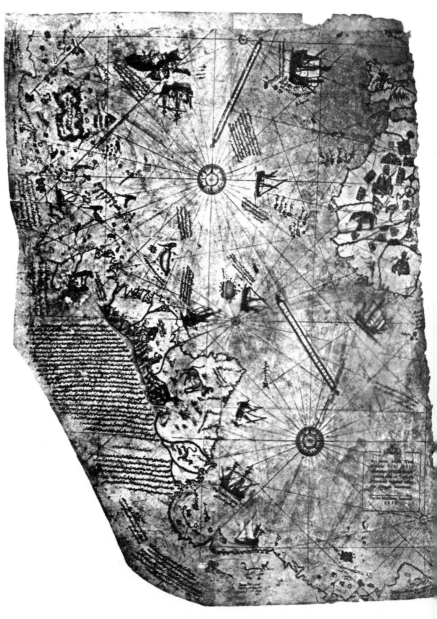

The Piri Re'is map

sessed a map of the coast of the New World before he set out on his voyage. Such a map obviously would have indicated pre-Columbian voyages. But since such a map had never been located, there was considerable doubt that it ever existed. Columbus never said anything about it. Piri Re'is's apparently authentic reference to the "lost" map was exciting. But that was just the beginning, for another inscription quotes Piri Re'is as saying that he had consulted twenty older maps, some dating back to the time of Alexander the Great, in preparing his map. Constantinople might certainly have been a storehouse of ancient maps and documents.

The Piri Re'is map created a short-lived sensation, but scholars were dubious about the Turkish admiral's claim to have possessed the "lost map of Columbus." The Piri Re'is map again slipped into obscurity until it caught the attention of Captain Arlington H. Mallery, a retired U.S. Navy officer and an avid student of old maps. But it wasn't the Columbus claim that intrigued Mallery; it was something far more sensational.

At its southern tip on the Piri Re'is map, South America appears to blend into a large southerly land mass. This looks vaguely like the continent of Antarctica. Yet as far as anyone knew, that continent had not yet been discovered at the time the Turkish map was drawn. And it wasn't just the early knowledge of Antarctica that intrigued Captain Mallery, either. His idea was more radical still. It looked to him as though the map showed the bays and islands of that part of the Antarctic coast called Queen Maud Land. Queen Maud Land is now concealed under a thick ice sheet. The ice has overlain the Antarctic coast for centuries, and in fact, the outlines of Queen Maud Land under the ice had been traced by a series of expeditions using seismographic equipment only in the late 1940s and early 1950s.

Captain Mallery proposed that Piri Re'is had in his possession maps of Antarctica based on information gathered at a time before the ice sheet covered the continent. That would have been over ten thousand years ago. Moreover, said Mallery, the accuracy of the map might indicate that the mapmakers had access to geographical information gathered from the air!

This theory was so radical, so fantastic, that it was rejected by virtually all professional geographers. But it was taken up by Professor Charles H. Hapgood, a longtime supporter of the unorthodox. After a lengthy study of the Piri Re'is map and other old maps, Professor Hapgood concluded that at one time, probably during a warm period between major ice ages, there was a worldwide civilization that possessed a technology that far surpassed anything known until modern times. He contended further that although this civilization had been destroyed, traces of it survived. Some of the geographical knowledge, for example, had been passed on, often in a garbled form, to the geographers of Greece and Rome, and had finally wound up in the Imperial Palace at Constantinople. It was from such information that Piri Re'is had obtained his picture of Antarctica before the last Ice Age.

In his book *Maps of the Ancient Sea Kings*, Professor Hapgood wrote, "The evidence presented by the ancient maps appears to suggest the existence in remote times, before the rise of any of the known cultures, of a true civilization, of a comparatively advanced sort, which either was localized in one area but had worldwide commerce, or was in a real sense a worldwide culture. This culture, at least in some respects, may well have been more advanced than the civilizations of Egypt, Babylonia, Greece and Rome. In astronomy, nautical science, map making and possibly ship-building, it was perhaps more advanced than any state of culture before the 18th century of the Christian Era. It was in the 18th Century that we first accurately measured the circumference of the earth. Not until the 19th Century did we begin to send out ships for the purposes of whaling or exploration into the Arctic or Antarctic Seas. The maps indicate that some ancient people may have done all of these things."

To bolster his theory, Professor Hapgood cites a number of archaeological sites in South America and Mexico that have been radiocarbon-dated as being many thousands of years old. Such dates are entirely out of line with the chronology of South and Central American history that is supported by most archaeologists. Of one of these sites, Hapgood says, "We may have here a relic of the people who navigated the whole earth and possessed the most advanced science necessary to make our ancient maps." Hapgood also contends that there is at least some evidence that all the people on earth once spoke a universal language, and that all peoples appear to share a common mythology.

The radical theories of Mallery and Hapgood have been given at least qualified support in studies made by Dr. John W. Weihaupt, vice chancellor for academic affairs at the University of Colorado at Denver. Dr. Weihaupt is a specialist in seismic and gravity studies and planetary geology.

Dr. Weihaupt does not endorse the most astonishing theories of Ice Age supercivilizations, but he does suggest the possibility that Bronze Age seafarers from the Mediterranean, trading along the east and west coasts of Africa, might have ventured much farther south than previously believed.

From 9000 to 2600 years ago, the world was warmer than it is today, indeed warmer than it has been at any time in the last million years, except for the period between the last two Ice Ages. Polar ice was probably reduced, tempting the seafarers to explore farther than ever before. Just how primitive navigators could have accurately mapped the Antarctic continent, even if they had reached it, is unknown, Dr. Weihaupt admits.

In his own analysis, Dr. Weihaupt did not use the Piri Re'is map, which he believes to be of questionable authenticity. In the past, others have suggested that the map is a phony, produced during a period of intense Turkish nationalism in order to raise the status of Turkey in the eyes of the world.

For the basis of his arguments, Dr. Weihaupt used the Orontius Fineaus map of 1531 and the Gerhardus Mercator world map of 1538, as well as a map of the Americas made by Ptolomaeus Basilae in 1540. He says that these maps, which contain representations of what looks like the Antarctic continent, "suggest that man's knowledge of that continent may date from a time some-what earlier than that century or at least three centuries before the continent's modern discovery."

There is some dispute about who first discovered the Antarctic continent, though most scholars believe that the discovery was made independently by the representatives of several different na-tions in the early years of the nineteenth century.

Some ancient Greek philosophers had suggested that there had to be a large continent in the Southern Hemisphere in order to balance out the continents in the Northern Hemisphere. The Greeks were great believers in symmetry. Thus, most scholars thought that southern continents on maps like that of Fineaus were merely imaginary additions used to conform to the influen-tial Greek theory. But Dr. Weihaupt believes that the correlation between what the maps show and what is actually there is too close to be the result of imagination only. "The geography of the southern continent," he says, "may thus have been known in its broad configurations before the mid 16th century. Indeed it may have been known at a prehistoric time when warmer climate had melted much of the ice sheet."

If even this tentative speculation proves to be correct, it raises a host of historical and archaeological questions that will not be easy to answer within the framework of our current beliefs about the development of civilization.

See also: LEMURIA AND MU

THE CRYSTAL SKULL   A genuinely weird-looking but beau-tifully fashioned skull, cut from a single piece of clear crystal, has been the object of a great deal of speculation and wonder for many years. *Chariots of the Gods?* theorist Erich Von Däniken cited the skull as an example of advanced ancient technology. "Nowhere on the skull is there a clue showing that a tool known to us was used!" he wrote. The lower jaw of the skull can be detached, and there

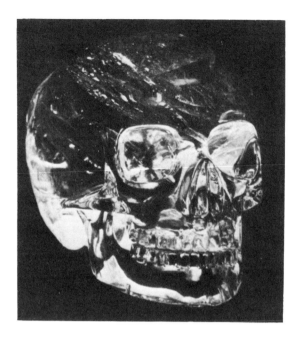

The crystal skull

are small holes suggesting that there once was some sort of mechanism that allowed the lower jaw of the skull to be moved.

The eleven-pound, seven-ounce highly polished skull is made from quartz crystal, a material that has often been believed to possess "mystical" or "psychic" powers—the crystal ball, for example. Some persons who have kept the crystal skull in their homes have reported strange noises, such as the sounds of chimes, bells, and the mewing of cats. Objects have been moved about mysteriously in its presence, and the skull has been reported to produce strange scents of various sorts.

People who scoffed at the skull's powers have reputedly been suddenly stricken dead.

The skull's origins are mysterious and controversial. It was first brought to public attention in the mid-1950s by the British traveler and adventurer F. A. Mitchell-Hedges. It had supposedly been discovered at Lubaantum, a Mayan city in British Honduras, that Mitchell-Hedges visited in the late 1920s, though all he ever said of the skull's origins in print was, "How it came into my possession I have reason for not revealing."

His adopted daughter Anna, who inherited the object, claimed that she was actually the one who first discovered the skull when she went to Lubaantum with her father. However, there is no evidence that she ever visited British Honduras.

Joe Nickell and John F. Fischer, who investigated the skull's history and published their results in a two-part article in *Fate* magazine in 1984, found that it is far more likely that Mitchell-Hedges purchased the skull at an auction at Sotheby's in London in 1944 for four hundred pounds. The previous owner was an art dealer named Sydney Burney. Prior to that, the skull had been in the possession of some unnamed collector.

Mitchell-Hedges was a well-known fabricator who told stories about how he had played poker with J. P. Morgan, roomed with Leon Trotsky, and fought with Pancho Villa. None of these stories had any basis in fact, and the origin of the skull appears to be another one of his tall tales. The accounts of the skull's mysterious powers may also be exaggerations or downright fictions.

Yet this does not entirely dispel the mystery of the crystal skull, for the skull exists, and it is a marvelous piece of workmanship—but whose? And could the skull possibly have been made by a people who did not possess machine tools?

Some think that the skull came from Mexico and is of Aztec or Mixtec origin, because the people of Mexico were known to use skulls as a common motif, and several small crystal skulls from Mexico have been found.

However, the Mitchell-Hedges skull is far more anatomically accurate than the usual skulls of Mexican origin. Norman Hammon, who examined the skull, has written: "It is a splendid object, of fine workmanship, I have always thought that it is most likely a *memento mori* [a reminder of death], of 16th–18th Century origin. While a Renaissance origin is not improbable, given the sheer size of the rock crystal block involved, manufacture in Quing Dynasty China for a European client cannot be ruled out."

H. J. Braunholtz of the British Museum, who examined the skull while it was still in Burney's possession in 1936, wrote of it: "Such realism seems beyond ordinary range of Aztec art, and gives the skull the character almost of an anatomical study in a scientific age." Comparing the skull with a known Aztec crystal skull in the British Museum, he said, "This difference of spirit seems to me to be a crucial factor and one which should be given full weight in drawing conclusions."

There is some evidence that the crystal used in the skull is similar to crystal found in Calaveras County, California—but this is by no means certain, and Anna Mitchell-Hedges has refused to allow the skull to be tested further.

While many of the wilder stories told about the crystal skull are almost certainly untrue, the skull itself remains a marvelous and genuinely mysterious object.

DISCOVERY OF AMERICA   Every schoolchild knows that "Columbus sailed the ocean blue/In the year of fourteen ninety-two" and, on his way to the Orient, bumped into the New World. It is unarguable that Columbus's voyage spread the first authentic news of the Americas to Europe and began the European colonization of the New World.

But was Columbus the first to discover America? Clearly not, for when Columbus arrived he found the New World populated with a variety of native Americans that he called Indians—because of his erroneous notion that he had reached the East Indies. The ancestors of these inhabitants had "discovered" America by the simple expedient of walking there from Asia across a land bridge that no longer exists. Just exactly when the first Americans arrived is still a matter of considerable dispute, but there is little dispute as to where they came from and how.

So when the question "Who *really* discovered America?" is raised, it generally means, What European got there first? That

subject is an amazingly emotional one, for it is not only an historical and archaeological dispute; it involves national, religious, and
racial feelings and is shot through with the fascination of arcane
lore. Even Columbus is not safe from controversy. There is dispute
over exactly where he landed first and over where the great mariner was buried. Then there is the controversy over who should
honor him. In America, Columbus Day is basically an Italian-
American festival, for Columbus was born in Italy. Many of Spanish descent, however, feel that the Italians have usurped the
honor, for Columbus sailed for Spain. "To credit the Italians with
Columbus' voyage is tantamount to crediting Germany with victory in World War II only because Dwight D. Eisenhower is of
German descent," raged one Madrid newspaper. Such a dispute
probably would have puzzled Columbus, who, like most of the
mariners of his day, was essentially a cosmopolitan figure.

The people who have the strongest claim to a pre-Columbian
discovery of America are the Vikings. The Vikings, who were superb seafarers, may have reached and even colonized North
America around the year 1000. At least that is what some of the
old Viking sagas indicated—they spoke of Leif Ericson sailing to a
land beyond Greenland that he named "Vinland" or "Vineland."
If the sagas are to be taken literally, then Vinland could really only
have been North America. Yet since the tales were so filled with
obviously legendary events, they were treated as mere fables. But
beginning in the eighteenth century, scholars' view of the sagas
began to change, until there was a very considerable body of respectable opinion that held that the Vikings had indeed discovered America some five hundred years before Columbus.

There was certainly nothing implausible about the theory, for it
was well known that the Vikings had colonized Greenland, and
the hop from Greenland to North America would have been an
easy, almost natural one for them, particularly around 1000, when
the weather was much warmer than it is today. What was lacking,
however, was material rather than literary evidence that they had
actually made the trip. A major problem was that it was impossi-

ble to tell where Leif Ericson had landed from reading the sagas, and various authorities and enthusiasts had located Vinland everywhere from northern Canada to North Carolina. Viking artifacts of all kinds were found all over the east coast and as far west as Minnesota. These were either mistakes or downright frauds.

A notable "Viking artifact" is the Newport Mystery Tower in Newport, Rhode Island. Some people think it was built by the Vikings, though archaeological investigation indicates that it is a stone mill that was built in colonial times.

The first really solid proof of a Viking presence in America came in 1960 when the Norwegian Arctic explorer Helge Ingstad and his archaeologist wife Anne Stine located what appeared to be the remains of a Viking settlement in Newfoundland. Subsequent excavations have confirmed this discovery. There is still a question of how extensive or long-lived the Viking settlements in America were, but the discovery of North America by the Vikings is now an accepted fact, well, almost accepted.

In general, the Italian supporters of Columbus did not dispute the Ingstad discovery. Nor did they raise much objection when

The Newport mystery tower

October 9 was officially declared Leif Ericson Day. But in 1965, there was a tremendous outburst when Yale University announced that it had in its possession a map of Vinland drawn before Columbus's voyage that conclusively proved the Viking discovery. The problem may have been that Yale chose to make this announcement on Columbus Day. Pure coincidence, said Yale. Insult, cried the Italian-American Historical Association. The map, they said, must be a fraud. For a while that sounded like nothing more than injured pride, but in fact the Italians were right—the map did turn out to be a fraud. That didn't disprove the Viking discovery of America, but it gave a lot of Italian-Americans a real sense of satisfaction.

It did not, however, satisfy the Spanish, for, aside from claiming credit for Columbus's voyage, the Spanish also say that an Andalusian sea captain reached the New World in 1484. Later, this captain met Columbus and gave him the idea for the historic voyage.

That's only the beginning of the list of possible discoverers. The Portuguese too have put in claims for pre-Columbian discovery. Some records indicate that two Germans and a Pole sailing in the Danish service reached Labrador in about 1470. The mariners of Bristol, England, also may have picked up some knowledge of the New World around 1480. And the Italians came back again with stories of their fellow countrymen, the brothers Zeno. These mariners, when in the service of Prince Henry Sinclair of the Orkneys, Shetlands, and Faroes, explored a western land called "Drogio" in 1398. Drogio, it is claimed, was North America. The Zenos, however, were just looking for lands already accidently found by some of Prince Henry's fishermen. Near the town of Westford, Massachusetts, about ten miles north of Concord, there is a rock carving that is supposed to be an image of Prince Henry himself. Some have said it might even be a grave marker.

The Italians, who will simply not be outdone in this area, have some additional claims. The ancient Romans seemed to have had some knowledge of lands out in the Atlantic. With a little imagination, these can be made to resemble America. Ancient artifacts inscribed in Latin have reportedly been dug up in the Tucson, Arizona, area. Using a little more imagination, enthusiasts have found signs that a party of Roman Christians fleeing the persecutions of Nero landed in Virginia around A.D. 64. An Italian linguist said that the Etruscans, early inhabitants of Italy, came to America about 1000 B.C. The evidence: some symbols of the Akawayo Indians of South America were identical with, or at least similar to, symbols of the Etruscans.

One of the most forceful claims has been put forth by the Irish on behalf of their hero St. Brendan the Navigator, who was born in County Kerry about A.D. 484. Tales of Brendan's life and adventures have him and a party of monks sailing westward, and after a wondrous voyage lasting seven years, coming upon a tropical paradise, "the Fortunate Isles," God's Promised Land. The Fortunate Isles themselves have been identified with the West Indies or even Florida.

The tales of the Irish saint are not quite as farfetched as they sound at first. The Celts of St. Brendan's time were neither primitive nor insular people. Irish monks were the finest Christian scholars west of Byzantium, and they regularly sailed to nearby islands in their sturdy hide-covered boats called "curraghs." In order to escape Viking raids, they sailed to the Shetlands and Faroes and finally to Iceland, and perhaps even to Greenland. From there, as we already noted, it is not that long a voyage to North America.

There are also loads of objections to the Brendan theories, the most persuasive being that the curraghs were not seaworthy enough for the journey to the New World. But there are also stories of white Indians speaking a Celtic dialect and one theory that some of the Irish in America today are really descendants of these original Irish settlers, and not of more recent immigrants. That idea may not have been proposed seriously and certainly should not be treated seriously.

Rough stone structures that in some ways resemble the "beehive" type of dwelling used by the early Irish monks have been found in America, but like the Newport Mystery Tower, they too may be of more recent origin.

Behind the Vikings and the Irish, the most popular European claimants to pre-Columbian discovery are the Welsh. There is a tale that Prince Madoc of Wales brought ten shiploads of colonists to the New World in 1170. Skeptics argue that this story first appeared during the reign of the Tudor monarchs, who had a good deal of Welsh blood in their background, and at a time when England was contesting with Spain the riches of the New World. A prior claim to discovery would have been useful. One Elizabethan scholar tried to include America in the realm of King Arthur.

The Arthur idea never really caught on, but the Madoc legend was repeated for hundreds of years, and it still crops up now and then today. It has been kept alive by reported encounters with white Welsh-speaking Indians, but these tales have no better foundation than any of the other "white-Indian" stories. American artist and writer George Catlin thought that the Mandan Indians of the upper Missouri River were descendants of Prince Madoc's band. No one else thought so, and unfortunately the Mandans were completely wiped out by smallpox in 1838. So there the theory of Welsh discovery rests.

Then there are those fearless, far-ranging, and rather mysterious ancient mariners, the Phoenicians. The Phoenicians really were great sailors, and if the Romans had any authentic knowledge of lands out in the Atlantic, they probably got it from the Phoenicians. But just how far into the Atlantic the Phoenicians went and what, if anything, they found is really impossible to say. The Phoenicians were traders, and in order to keep a commercial advantage they were secretive about their discoveries. Phoenician artifacts of one sort or another are frequently reported in North and South America, but the authenticity of such artifacts is doubtful.

Joseph Smith, prophet and founder of the Mormons, believed that it had been revealed to him that the true discoverers of America were Jews who migrated from Jerusalem in 600 B.C., and that these Jews were the true ancestors of the American Indians.

Although the Jews of *The Book of Mormon* were not the famous Ten Lost Tribes of Israel, many others have placed the Ten Tribes in America. Since about the tenth century, the Ten Lost Tribes have been "found" in almost every country on earth, and inside the hollow earth as well. But for a good two hundred years the Israelite-Indian theory has been popular.

Even this hardly exhausts the list of candidates for possible discoverers of America. From the East, the Japanese and Chinese have both been mentioned frequently, and there are intriguing bits of evidence that might support either theory. Then there are refugees from the destruction of Atlantis—a very popular theory, and mariners from some as yet unknown Ice Age civilization.

See also: ANCIENT MAPS OF THE ANTARCTIC; THE KENSINGTON STONE; MOUND BUILDERS

D RUIDS   We have very little firsthand information about the ancient Druids. What we do know comes from the Romans, and since the Druids were the priests of peoples of Britain and elsewhere who were conquered by the Romans, the picture they left is not a flattering one.

The most direct evidence comes from the Roman historian Tacitus, who describes "Druids, who lifted up their Hands to Heaven, pouring forth most terrible Execrations. The Horror of this Spectacle astonished our Men." Tacitus adds that after a battle, "this inhuman people were accustomed to shed the Blood of their Prisoners on their Altars, and consult their Gods over the reeking Bowels of Men."

Caesar found the Druids of Gaul also addicted to human sacrifice: "unless for a man's life a man's life may be paid, the majesty of the immortal gods may not be appeased." The gods of the Druids preferred criminals to be sacrificed, but when there weren't enough criminals to go around, anyone would do. "They resort to the execution even of the innocent." Sometimes they "used figures of immense size, whose limbs, woven out of twigs they fill with living men and set on fire, and the men perish in a sheet of flame."

Diodorus Siculus said that they "kill a man by a knife-stab in the region above the midriff, and after his fall they foretell the future by the convulsions of his limbs, and the pouring of blood."

Somewhat more restrained ceremonies were described in Pliny the Elder's *Natural History*. These took place around the sacred oak tree; "they solemnize no sacrifice, nor perform any sacred ceremonies without branches and leaves thereof." They also found mistletoe sacred.

That is really about all that is actually known about the Druids. They and their religion were totally wiped out by the Roman conquest. They left behind no books, no legends, no known artifacts.

The man who really recreated the Druids for modern times was an eccentric eighteenth-century cleric, Dr. William Stukeley. Previously, others had suggested that the Druids built Stonehenge and conducted their ceremonies there. Stukeley, who despite his oddities did some really excellent field work at Stonehenge, decided that the Druids were in reality the direct descendants of Abraham and keepers of the pure British religion that was later embodied in the Church of England. Instead of the bloodthirsty savages that they had been portrayed as by the Romans, to Stukeley the Druids were the noblest of beings, though he did admit that human sacrifice was a failing, perhaps based on a misunderstanding of Abraham's act.

Since Stukeley, the image of the Druids has never quite been the same. A semisecret Druid society organized along Masonic lines was formed in the late eighteenth century. During the nineteenth century, a bewildering variety of Druid societies, some serious, some not so serious, sprang up. Members paraded about in long white robes, often sporting long false beards. They held rituals and chanted songs in an allegedly authentic Druidical fashion. It was all part of the Victorian outburst of Celtic romanticism, fas-

Stonehenge

cination with arcane mysticism, and some high-spirited foolishness. In his younger days, Winston Churchill was a Druid.

Nineteenth-century Druidism was raised to a high pitch of eccentricity by Dr. William Price of Wales. Price was born in 1800, lived to be ninety-three, and is best remembered for his 1884 trial at Cardiff for cremating his son, whom he had named Iesu Grist, on his death at age five months. Cremation was illegal at that time, but Price was acquitted and was himself cremated in 1893. While he lived, Price did not settle for the traditional white robes of modern Druidism. One photo shows him wearing what looks like scarlet long underwear covered with green lettering. At other times he wore an elaborate fox-skin cap, and he often chanted ancient Druid songs that he had composed himself.

Today several different Druid societies exist (one could hardly say that they flourish), primarily in England. Some have become strictly fraternal societies, while others retain a strong mystical bent. They are little heard from except on the day of the summer solstice, when some of them gather to perform an "ancient" ritual at Stonehenge.

The Druid solstice ceremonies have been conducted at Stonehenge since 1905, but over the last couple of decades they have begun to attract larger and rowdier crowds. The ancient monument itself has seemed threatened by the throng of Druidwatchers who come to cheer, jeer, or just simply have a good time on a warm evening. The British government, which owns Stonehenge, would dearly love to get rid of the Druid celebration altogether, but the modern Druids have been around long enough to

23

become a recognized religion, and after eighty years they have established a good claim to Stonehenge on the summer solstice. They cannot decently be excluded, but the government does manage to keep all others out. On the day of the ceremony there is a sign at the checkpoint reading PRESS PASSES AND DRUIDS ONLY PERMITTED.

Author Christopher Chippendale describes the scene: "The press goes through the tunnel into [Stonehenge] followed by the Druids in procession with various articles of their faith, a cross, banners, a copper globe hanging from three chains, a small silver cup and a couple of oak sprigs. The rites begin, and the crowd discovers Druid worship is not diverting to the outsider. There is standing, there is walking in procession, there is more standing. Evidently Druids, like royalty, need to be blessed with sturdy legs and good bladders. Quiet words are quietly spoken. . . . The northeast sky brightens, the Druids progress down to the Heel Stone for further devotions (during which the chief Druid anxiously consults his watch). . . . The Druid ceremony drones on. . . . At last they acknowledge the dawn raising long bronze horns and blowing them, quietly." The horns, far from being yet another age-old element in an ancient ritual, were only introduced recently, when an alert off-duty Druid spotted them in a London streetmarket and snapped them up at a bargain price. They may in fact be Tibetan.

It is all very amiable, not at all like the Druidic rituals described by Tacitus.

See also: STONEHENGE

THE KENSINGTON STONE   In 1898, a Swedish-born farmer named Olof Ohman said that he had dug up an inscribed stone on his farm near the village of Kensington, Minnesota. The inscription appeared to be runes, the alphabetic characters of Northern Europe during the Middle Ages. Translated, the runes told the story of an inland expedition of Vikings during the twelfth

century. That the Vikings had reached the shores of North America during the eleventh century was considered a distinct possibility in the late nineteenth century, and today is considered a virtual certainty. That the Vikings had journeyed inland as far as Minnesota, fortuitously the home of many modern Scandinavian immigrants, including farmer Ohman, seemed remarkable, almost too good to be true. And when experts looked at the Kensington Stone, they declared that it *was* too good to be true, that it was in fact a crude modern forgery. There was no specific evidence as to who had created the fake, but people began to look suspiciously at Olof Ohman, and the embarrassed farmer took the stone home where he used it as an anvil.

The story of the Kensington Stone would probably have ended right there if it had not come to the attention of a Norwegian college student, Hjalmar Holland. No cause could ask for a more devoted supporter than Holland. For the rest of his very long life he championed the Kensington Stone with unflagging energy and remarkable ingenuity. He wrote millions of words on the subject and developed grand theories of a Viking "crusade" to America, based on the evidence of the stone. In 1948, primarily because of Holland's efforts, the Kensington Stone was actually placed on display in the National Museum in Washington, D.C., and Alexandria, Minnesota, dedicated a Runestone Memorial Park, featuring a huge replica of the stone. The influence of the stone is even reflected in the name of the National Football League team, the Minnesota Vikings.

But the experts remained unconvinced. More came forth to declare the artifact a thoroughgoing fake, and it was hustled out of Washington. Still Holland stuck to his belief. Right up until his death in 1963 at the age of ninety, he kept on fighting.

Although from time to time a few scholars have agreed with Holland that the stone is genuine, the vast majority believe that it is a modern hoax, and not a very clever one. An exhaustive examination of the history of the stone shows that Olof Ohman was not as uneducated as he liked people to believe, and that concocting a fake would certainly not have been beyond his capabilities. Holland, however, appears to have been a true believer.

Holland's death did not entirely end the controversy. Frederick J. Pohl, one of the more active supporters of the Viking exploration of America idea, has continued to support the authenticity of the stone in his books. And the stone itself was a center of attraction at the Minnesota Pavilion at the New York World's Fair in 1963–64. That honor must have warmed the last year of Hjalmar Holland's life.

See also: DISCOVERY OF AMERICA

THE LEY LINES

In 1921, a sixty-five-year-old English merchant and amateur archaeologist named Alfred Watkins rode up to the top of a hill in his native Herefordshire. Looking out over the familiar landscape, he suddenly had a near-mystic vision of a network of straight lines crisscrossing the countryside. These lines passed through ancient stone monuments, earthworks, churches, and castles.

Working with ordinance survey maps, Watkins confirmed his vision, at least to his own satisfaction. He found that straight lines could connect up many prominent natural and man-made features. This was not accidental; he believed the features marked an ancient system of straight tracks. Where the markers were chuches or crosses or other sites that were not particularly ancient, Watkins concluded that these more modern monuments had replaced ancient monuments or been put up at pagan holy places. He called these lines "ley" lines because many ancient places with names ending in -ley, -ly, and -leigh were found along the straight lines.

In 1925, Watkins published his theories in a book called *The Old Straight Track*. The book has become a classic of its type, and though Alfred Watkins is long gone, his followers have carried on and expanded his work of "ley hunting." Today there is a small but vigorous group of ley hunters in Britain, and researchers in other lands have found evidence of leys in their parts of the world.

The leys themselves are not physical roads; there are no actual lines to be found, and a straight line is not necessarily the best way to get from point A to point B, particularly in a primitive landscape. The leys do not skirt rivers, swamps, or other difficult terrain.

If the leys are not physical paths, then what are they? That all depends on who you consult. In the words of one modern ley hunter, they are part of a system of geomancy or landscape geometry, "a striking network of lines of subtle force across Britain, and elsewhere on spaceship Earth, understood and marked in prehistoric times by men of wisdom and cosmic consciousness."

Some have said that the leys mark underground "lines of force" that can actually be followed with a divining rod.

What orthodox archaeologists and prehistorians think of such theories should not be difficult to imagine; they have derided leys as "lunatic fabrications."

The professionals raise several objections. There are so many different kinds of structures and features that can be used to define a ley that simple chance will make a great many straight lines possible. Besides, some of these markers, like prehistoric earthworks, are quite large. Christopher Chippendale points out, "It would be extraordinary, for instance, if many straight lines could not be drawn near Stonehenge [one of the chief ley markers] that ran through three or more of the many hundred barrows in the area."

Another objection is that markers of so many different ages are used. Salisbury Cathedral is supposed to be an important point on one of the best-known leys in Britain. Yet the reasons for choosing the site for the cathedral in medieval times are well documented, and they have nothing to do with any kind of alignments.

Besides, many of the ley hunters do a great deal of fudging. It is sufficient for them if the ley runs near a site, rather than through it. They make the hunt suspiciously easy.

None of these objections discourage the ley hunters in the least.

As Chippendale points out, there is a "democratic accessibility" to ley hunting. "There are no university professors of ley science to quibble about methods, or tiresome paper qualifications to hold the novice hunter back. All you need is a map, a straight edge, and sufficient patience."

See also: STONEHENGE

MOUND BUILDERS

M OUND BUILDERS   Throughout the nineteenth century, a majority of the people in the United States believed that the North American continent had once been inhabited by a mysterious and mighty race who had built the many earthen mounds found scattered beyond the Alleghenies and in the Mississippi Valley.

Learned men attributed the building of the mounds to the Ten Lost Tribes of Israel, Greeks, Persians, Romans, Vikings, Hindus, Phoenicians, or any other Old World civilization that built, or was believed to have built, any sort of mound at any time in their history. The mounds were also attributed to migrants from South America, China, or to refugees from the sinking of Atlantis.

It has frequently been said that Joseph Smith, prophet and founder of Mormonism, was profoundly influenced by the speculations about a great and vanished civilization of mound builders that were so popular in his day. Mormon historians strongly deny this, but the parallels between some of Joseph Smith's writings and those of earlier mound-builder theorizers and fantasizers are striking.

The mounds themselves are often visually unimpressive, mere heaps of earth. Some, however, are colossal in size, like the Cahokia Mound in Illinois, which is over one hundred feet high and covers sixteen acres. Others are built in the shape of snakes or bears. Still, none of the individual mounds rival the great ancient monuments of the Old World or the monuments of South America. But there were so many mounds, ten thousand in the Ohio Valley alone, that the cumulative effect is impressive.

When the mounds were excavated, they were often found to be burial mounds containing bones and a small number of simple tools, weapons, and pottery. They contained no evidence whatever of Hebrew or Atlantean origin or evidence that would connect them with any other advanced civilization, real or imagined. Yet the belief in the vanished race of mound builders flourished.

Why a vanished race? Robert Silverberg, whose *Mound Builders of Ancient America* is the definitive work on the subject, finds several reasons. First, the idea of a vanished race was profoundly satisfying to the residents of the new nation of the United States. Silverberg writes, "The men of the Thirteen Colonies lamented the absence of grand, imagination-stirring symbols of vanished greatness. In all this mighty continent, was there nothing to compare with the antiquities of the Old World?

"Men in search of a myth will usually find one, if they work at it. In the fledgling Thirteen Colonies the mythmakers had little raw material with which to work; but as the colonists gradually spread westward and southward they found the mounds and the process of romantic embellishment began." The mounds could be used to connect the new land with the great civilizations of antiquity, and perhaps with people and events mentioned in the Bible.

The area in which the mounds were found was already inhabited by a variety of Indian tribes. Nothing about the mounds really connected them with the Old World, or with any people other than those who were living on the land at the time—the Indians themseves. Why didn't people conclude the obvious, that the mounds were built by the Indians or their direct ancestors?

Such a conclusion would of course have been far less dramatically satisfying, but there were other, less attractive reasons for conjuring up an unknown race of mound builders. The Indians were regarded as primitive and brutal savages; moreover, they were a people with whom the white man was contesting for land. Indian wars were still very much a part of American history.

To those of European origin, it seemed impossible that the "savages" could have built anything more elaborate and permanent than a wigwam. Never mind the pueblo cities of the Southwest; they were not well known to settlers in the Midwest, nor were they sufficiently romantic to fulfill the need for a myth.

The myth of the vanished race of mound builders served another useful function. What had happened to the highly civilized mound builders? Writes Silverberg, "The answer was obvious; they had been exterminated at some past date by the despicable, treacherous, ignorant red-skinned savages who even now were causing so much trouble for the Christian settlers of the New World."

Thus, when the settlers drove the Indians off the land, they were, in a sense, only taking back what the savages had already stolen from others, perhaps even from the white man's own ancestors.

The Indians themselves do not seem to have had any particularly strong traditions about the mounds, though most, if questioned, would say that the mounds had been built by their ancestors long ago. In fact, the Indians of various regions were still vigorously building mounds of one sort or another when the earliest European explorers came through America. If anyone had bothered to check the accounts of these early explorers, the "mystery" would have been solved. But no one bothered to ask the Indians or check the records for over a century, and tales of a lost race grew.

Finally, a series of careful investigations sponsored by the Bureau of American Ethnology proved, beyond any doubt reasonable or unreasonable, that the mounds were built not by a lost race, but by the ancestors of the Indians.

One of the most vigorous of the demythologizers was Major J. W. Powell, conqueror of the Colorado River and, later, founder of the Smithsonian Institution. In 1890, he wrote: "It is difficult to exaggerate the prevalence of this romantic fallacy, or the force with which the hypothetic 'lost races' has taken possession of the imaginations of men. For more than a century, the ghosts of a vanished nation have ambuscaded in the vast solitudes of the continent, and the forest-covered mounds have been usually regarded as the mysterious sepulchres of its kings and nobles. It was an alluring conjecture that a powerful people, superior to the Indians, once occupied the valley of the Ohio and the Appalachian ranges, their empire stretching from Hudson Bay to the Gulf, with its flanks on the western prairies and the eastern ocean; a people with a confederated government, a chief ruler, a great central capital, a highly developed religion, with homes and husbandry and advanced . . . arts, with a language, perhaps with letters, all swept away before an invasion of copper-hued Huns from some unknown region of the earth, prior to the landing of Columbus."

While the myth of the lost race of mound builders is quite dead today, it is useful to recall just how vigorously it once flourished, and why.

See also: DISCOVERY OF AMERICA

NAZCA DRAWINGS   The Nazca Desert is a high plateau about sixty miles long and five miles wide on the coast of Peru, some 250 miles south of Lima. A cold ocean current cuts through the warmer waters of the southern Pacific and brushes the coast. Moist ocean air passing over this cold water is effectively blocked from dumping its moisture until it is pushed up and over the Andes Mountains, which rise steeply from the western edge of the desert. For half the year, the sky over the desert is clear and the surface is blazingly hot. For much of the other half, the desert is shrouded in fog, but still no rains fall.

In this virtually rainless land there is minimal erosion, and etched into the surface of the desert are a series of ancient lines and figures that have excited wonder and speculation ever since they were first "discovered" in the 1950s.

Occasional travelers through the Nazca had doubtless noticed the strange and obviously artificial lines in the desert floor, but the lines were unimpressive and meaningless at ground level. How-

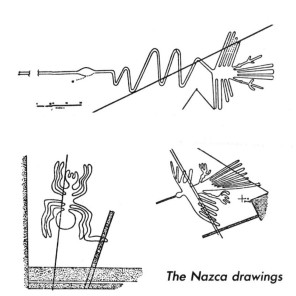

The Nazca drawings

ever, as planes began to pass over the Nazca region, air travelers saw that some of the lines really formed parts of gigantic figures whose shape could only be appreciated from the air. Aerial photographs of the region proved to be highly dramatic.

Therein lies the basic mystery and allure of the Nazca figures. Why would anyone bother to make figures that could only be appreciated from an airplane in an era when there were no airplanes? For it is well established that these drawings are at least fifteen hundred years old.

There are a variety of figures—birds, spiders, fishes, even a monkey—and a couple of unidentifiable creatures. There are also rectangular shapes and a large number of straight lines or "roads" that run apparently from nowhere to nowhere. The surface on which the figures and lines are incised is made up of gravel and pebbles. It is often called "desert pavement." To form the drawings, the rocks and pebbles were moved to expose the lighter soil beneath. The rocks are then piled up on each side of the line. From the air, the figures and lines might seem etched by a light-colored line, which itself is outlined by two darker filaments.

32

When the sun is low, the little piles of pebbles cast long shadows that make the outlines of the drawings sharper.

No one is exactly sure who made the drawings, but the best guess is that they were made about fifteen hundred years ago by a pre-Inca people called the Nazcas. Some of the figures match designs found on Nazca pottery. The Incas, who conquered the Nazcas, seem to have had no respect for the figures; they built a road that cuts right through them. Neither the Nazcas nor the Incas possessed a written language, and the Nazca themselves were wiped out after the Spanish conquest, so that piece of history is quite blank.

Though the figures would not have been difficult to make, they still would have required a good deal of time and labor, so they must have meant a great deal to the people who made them. But what did they mean? That is where the speculation takes off.

One of the first to become interested in the Nazca figures was an American scholar, Paul Koosk. He thought that the lines represented "the largest astronomy book in the world." He believed that the lines pointed to certain astronomical alignments.

Koosk died before he could expand on his theory but the work was taken up by Dr. Maria Reiche, a German-born astronomer and mathematician who pursued the theory with almost fanatical intensity. She worked out a huge number of astronomical calculations. She has shown, for example, how certain "fixed" stars rose and set over the lines and could have been used by the astronomer-priests of the Nazcas for their own calendar computations.

Dr. Reiche's conclusions have not been accepted by other scientists. The basic problem is that there are a lot of lines and an almost infinite number of possible astronomical correlations. The relationship between the rising of stars or the setting of the sun at different times of year and some of the lines may have been deliberate. But given the huge number of possibilities, these relationships may also be accidental. This is the same objection that is raised to many other "ancient astronomy" theories.

The most sensational explanation of all for the Nazca lines and figures was stated bluntly by Erich Von Däniken in his best seller *Chariots of the Gods?* "Seen from the air, the clear-cut impression that the plain of Nazca made on me was that of an airfield." He suggested that the desert was a landing field for extraterrestrial spaceships, and that the drawings were made to be seen by the spacemen.

This startling idea did not originate with Von Däniken. In *Flights Into Yesterday,* a book on aerial archaeology written before Von Däniken's book, Professor Leo Deuel notes, "For a number of years the Nazca 'sand drawings,' though by then a fairly familiar landmark, were looked upon as little but an odd curiosity. Facetiously they were dubbed 'prehistoric landing fields,' or invited comparisons with the canals of Mars. Indeed, a Martian aura clung to them for quite a while." It still clings to them.

Scientists do not take the prehistoric landing field idea seriously. Though the lines cannot be adequately explained at present, most assume that the figures were meant for the gods of the Nazcas, who presumably lived in the sky. There are many examples of societies building monuments that could only be appreciated by their gods.

Yet when the first space shuttle flight landed at Edwards Air Force Base in California, many who viewed the landing on television were struck by the similarity of the markings that covered the field on which the shuttle landed and those in the Nazca desert.

See also: STONEHENGE; UFOS

Erich von Däniken

2

UNKNOWN

PLACES

ATLANTIS   There have been uncounted millions of words written on the subject of Atlantis. The "lost continent" has been searched for and "found" hundreds of times. All of this activity has a single source: Plato.

About 355 B.C., when Plato was over seventy, he planned to write a trilogy in which the story of Atlantis was to figure prominently. The first part was called *Timaios* and contained an account of the creation of the world, the nature of man, and the most complete account of Atlantis. The second part, *Kritias*, goes into the Atlantis story in much greater detail, but the project was abandoned in the middle. The third part, *Hermokrates*, was never even begun. Plato went on to other matters and died before what might be called his Atlantean trilogy was ever completed.

Plato laid out his ideas in playlets called dialogues. A group of prominent people, inevitably led by Plato's famous old teacher Socrates, sit around and discuss various philosophical and moral questions. The discussion of Atlantis was to have taken place about 421 B.C., when Plato himself was just a boy.

The characters in the dialogues are real historical figures like Socrates. Their words, however, are Plato's creation. The story of Atlantis in the dialogue is told by Kritias, a distant relative of Plato. According to Kritias, the account had been in his family for generations. It had originally been told by the great Athenian statesman Solon, who had heard it on a trip to Egypt, traditionally the repository of all ancient knowledge. An Egyptian priest had informed Solon that there had once existed a great Athenian empire some nine thousand years previously, or, by our reckoning, about 9600 B.C. At that same time, there had been a second great empire, the empire of Atlantis, which was located on an enormous island continent to the west of the "Pillars of Hercules" (our Strait of Gibraltar), that is, somewhere in the middle of the Atlantic Ocean. The island continent was as big as North Africa and Asia Minor combined.

The Atlanteans, Kritias says, had been a great people, but they had become decadent and greedy. "But then there happened exceedingly violent earthquakes and great floods. In one terrible day and night all of your warriors in a body were swallowed up . . . and in like manner the Island of Atlantis sank into the sea and vanished. Even now the ocean at its former location cannot be crossed or explored, as there is a great shoal of mud in the way, a consequence of the foundering of the island."

On the next day, or in the next dialogue, Kritias takes up the story in more detail, describing the island continent and its circular city. When the Atlanteans got too greedy, Zeus decided they had to be punished, and he called the gods together to discuss what should be done. "And when he had assembled them, he spoke thus. . . ." And that is just where Plato's story breaks off. The destruction of Atlantis, the part of the story that has so fascinated later generations, is described only in outline in the first dialogue.

There is no mention of Atlantis in any Greek literature prior to Plato, though Plato indicates that the story was kept in his own family and was not widely known (remember that Kritias was Plato's kinsman). At several points in the dialogues, Plato says that he is recounting "authentic history," but he often made up stories in order to drive home a philosophical point. Most of the writers who followed Plato appear to have regarded the story as pure fiction. Plato's most famous pupil, Aristotle, collected facts covering almost every aspect of human knowledge, yet he mentions Atlantis only once, and his comment is ironic: "He who invented it also destroyed it."

Over the next few centuries, when Atlantis was mentioned at all

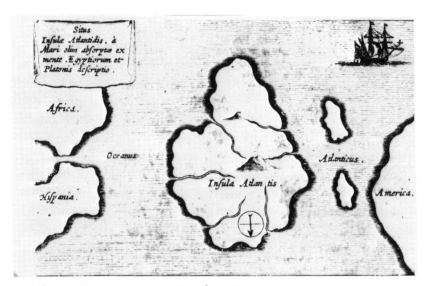

Atlantis shown on a seventeenth-century map

it was prefaced with a phrase such as "if we are to believe Plato." The Neoplatonists of the later Roman empire took Atlantis a bit more seriously. An early Christian writer said that the Atlantis story was nothing more than a garbled version of the biblical flood.

Columbus's discovery of America brought the Atlantis idea to the forefront once again. Some speculated that America was Atlantis, or at least that Plato had heard rumors of America and this gave him the basis for his Atlantis story. As late as the eighteenth century, some stubborn cartographers insisted on calling America Atlantis on their maps.

The civilizations of the Maya and Incas came as quite a shock to some Europeans, who then decided that these peoples must be refugees from Atlantis. By massively mistranslating Mayan documents, some were actually able to prove this at least to their own satisfaction.

There were lots of other strange theories about Atlantis floating around, but the man who gathered all these scattered speculations together into one massive and influential work of crank scholarship was an American named Ignatius T. Donnelly. Donnelly, a man of enormous intellectual and physical energy, had been a congressman from Minnesota and one of the founders of the Populist Party. In this time away from politics, he tried to prove that Francis Bacon wrote Shakespeare's plays, and he researched the subject of Atlantis.

Donnelly's book, *Atlantis: The Antediluvian World,* was published over a century ago but remains the bible of modern Atlantism even today. Briefly, Donnelly believed that Atlantis was the original homeland of all civilizations, from the Egyptians to the Mayans. It was the source of all the memories of a lost Golden Age. The Garden of Eden, the Garden of the Hesperides, the Elysian Fields, Olympus, Asgard, and all the rest are a "universal memory of a great land where early mankind dwelt for ages in peace and happiness," Donnelly wrote.

After the disaster, says Donnelly, a few survivors fled to the lands east and west, bringing with them "tiding of the appalling catastrophe, which has survived in our own time in the Flood and Deluge legends of the different nations of the old and new world."

In 1912, Paul Schliemann, grandson of Heinrich Schliemann, the discoverer of Troy, claimed that his famous grandfather had left him a large number of documents and artifacts that proved the existence of Atlantis. But when Schliemann was pressed to present these marvelous artifacts to public view, he first hesitated and then fell silent.

Some Nazi-influenced scholars tried to prove that Atlantis had been the original homeland of the superior Aryan race. They went so far as to move Plato's island continent from the middle of the Atlantic to the North Sea in order to get it closer to the Fatherland. Even after World War II, one German historian spent a lot of time chugging about the North Sea in a motorboat looking for sunken cities. He was convinced that he had found Atlantis, but no one else was.

There is still a moderately vigorous group that holds that Atlantis was really Britain. Not that Britain sank to the bottom of the sea, but, according to this theory, Plato had heard rumors of the "fair and noble island" and had used them in his Atlantis story.

Geologists and oceanographers regard the idea of a sunken mid-Atlantic continent as absurd. But mystics who are not bound by physical facts are quite comfortable with the thought; Atlantis became a standard part of mystical lore. Madame Helena P. Blavatsky, founder of Theosophy, wrote extensively of Atlantis. Most of her information, which was supposed to have been based on mystic inspiration or special knowledge, was in reality lifted, without credit, from Donnelly's book.

The American mystic Edgar Cayce, who died in 1945, had placed Atlantis somewhere off the coast of Florida. A number of expeditions went looking for Atlantis there and said that they had found it. One of Cayce's pet prophecies was that Atlantis would rise again by the end of the decade of the 1960s and that this would be the first event in a chain of worldwide geological catastrophes that would include the abrupt sinking of California, New York, and Japan. Those who found Cayce's Atlantis also found evidence that it was rising again. Since this prediction has spectacularly failed to come through, it has been quietly shelved by Cayce supporters.

The idea that Atlantis will rise again has become so firmly embedded in public consciousness that when, in the early 1960s, a group of British newspapermen were asked to list the most important story they could imagine, they placed the reemergence of Atlantis fourth; it rated five places ahead of the Second Coming of Christ!

This really just scratches the surface of the speculation about Atlantis. But over the last few decades there has been an accumulation of data that may have finally solved the mystery first posed by Plato so many centuries ago.

In the early years of this century, some scholars noted the similarities between Plato's description of Atlantis and what was being discovered of the Minoan civilization, centered on the island of Crete. The Minoans, a sophisticated seafaring people who were a great power in the Aegean before the rise of Greece, had flourished around 1500 B.C. The power of the Minoans had declined rather abruptly around 1400 B.C.

It was also known that somewhere around 1400 B.C. there was an enormous explosion on the volcanic island now called Santorini, or in ancient times, Thera. There had been suspicions about Thera and Atlantis, but as we have seen there had been suspicions about Atlantis and practically everywhere. Somehow, no one put all these intriguing facts together in a convincing manner until seismologists began taking a closer look at the magnitude of the ancient explosion of Thera. What they discovered was that the eruption may have been the most destructive of historic times, surpassing even Krakatoa's famous eruption in 1883. As the magma chamber under the island emptied, it collapsed, and a large portion of the ancient island simply sank into the sea.

Excavations on what remains of Thera have revealed a Minoan city virtually intact under a thick layer of volcanic ash thrown up by the explosion. This discovery ranks as one of the greatest of twentieth-century archaeology. But Thera itself was only a Minoan outpost. The explosion had other, wider effects.

The collapse of the island would have created a huge tidal wave, just as the collapse of Krakatoa did. This would have inundated most of the harbors on nearby Crete, the Minoan center. For a seagoing people, the loss of the harbors and the ships in them would have been crippling.

Archaeological investigation indicates that the harbors of Crete were indeed destroyed suddenly and not rebuilt. The thick fall of volcanic ash might have ruined Minoan agriculture as well.

Minoan civilization did not collapse completely. The inland capital of Knossos was relatively sheltered from the tidal wave. But the Minoans were badly weakened and open to invaders from Greece.

Some scholars think that Thera itself was Atlantis and that Plato's description of it fits closely with what Thera must once have been. Others believe that Atlantis was really all of Minoan civilization.

The main objection to this theory is that Minoan civilization was too small, too new, and too close to Greece to square with Plato's Atlantis. But Professor Angelos Galanopoulos suggests that Solon or some other Greek misread the Egyptian symbol for 100 as 1000 in the records, and thus every number in the Atlantis story became multiplied tenfold. Knock all the figures down to a tenth their size, and you have the sinking of Atlantis taking place nine hundred years before Solon—in the fifteenth century B.C. The size of Atlantis would be on the order of eighty thousand square miles, an acceptable estimate of the lands under Minoan domination. And Professor Galanopoulos notes triumphantly that the Strait of Gibraltar is not the only Pillars of Hercules; there are two promontories on the coast of Greece facing Crete that also carry that name.

There remain many problems and uncertainties with the Atlantis-Minoan identification. Absolute certainty in such matters can never be reached. But there now seems very good reason to believe that, while exaggerated and garbled, Plato's Atlantis story was a good deal more than a myth or a playground for crank scholars.

See also: LEMURIA AND MU; MADAME BLAVATSKY

CAMELOT   The legendary home of King Arthur and his Knights of the Round Table became famous in modern times because of a Broadway musical of that name and because of its association with the brief presidency of John F. Kennedy. But before we can examine the problem of the reality of Camelot, we must first ask whether its most famous inhabitant, King Arthur himself, was real.

The answer to that question is proabably yes, though Arthur was certainly not the heavily armored symbol of medieval chivalry that he became later. The historical Arthur lived sometime between 450—when the Romans finally left Britain, taking most of the people who could write with them—and the ninth century, when a monk named Nennius first mentions Arthur in his *History of the Britons*. But to Nennius, Arthur was ancient history, a king who had lived hundreds of years earlier. There are a few surviving historical records composed closer to Arthur's time, but he is not mentioned in a single one of them. This has led cautious scholars to conclude that there was no historical Arthur, that he is a completely mythical figure. However, since all the records from Arthur's time are so rare, fragmentary, and unreliable, most of those who have studied the subject feel that the fact that his name is not mentioned is not proof that he did not exist; he just may not have been popular with those who wrote the surviving chronicles.

After Nennius, however, the references to Arthur become fairly frequent, and by the twelfth century the Arthurian legend had developed to its full glory. Arthur became one of the great heroes of the Middle Ages and (with the possible exception of Robin Hood) the only one who remains a well-known and popular figure today.

From the scanty historical evidence that survives, we can draw at least a tentative picture of the figure who inspired the Arthurian legend. He was born near the end of the fifth century and was either of direct Roman descent or came from an aristocratic Celtic family that was closely identified with the Romans. A good deal of fuss has been made about his name because it is a bit unusual. Those who think he is a mythical figure say the name is a corruption of Artur, a pre-Christian god. Others who wish to link Arthur more closely with Rome believe the name was really Artorius. Still others say that Arthur is merely a confused reference to Ambrosius Aurelianus, a known late-fifth-century ruler. None of this confusion is really necessary, for Arthur is a name that does appear occasionally in the Celtic records.

The late fifth century was a time when the Christian and Romanized Celts were being overrun by the barbarian Saxton invaders. Arthur was probably appointed war leader by Ambrosius, to whom he may have been related. He managed to rouse the sagging spirits of his badly defeated countrymen and win a series of impressive victories against the Saxtons and their allies. One theory is that his success was due to his knowledge of the Roman arts of war, particularly the employment of armored horsemen. But the popular picture of Arthur and his knights going into battle looking like a group of tanks, completely encased in metal armor, is false; this cumbersome method warfare did not develop until the Middle Ages. When medieval writers took up the Arthur stories, they merely dressed the hero in the fighting garb of their own time. At best, Arthur would have worn an iron cap and a mail shirt, and his horse might have been lightly armored. Still, the barbaric Saxons would have nothing comparable. A well-coordinated armored cavalry charge by a small group of horsemen could easily spread panic among the numerous but poorly disciplined barbarian troops.

Arthur was killed in battle around 540, not by the Saxons but in a dispute with members of his own family. His body may have been buried in secret.

We do know that after the middle of the sixth century the Saxon conquest picked up in tempo until they controlled virtually all of present-day England. The native Celts fled in large numbers to Wales or Scotland, where the Arthurian traditions remained strongest. In fact, Arthur seems to have remained an underground hero even in Saxon-dominated regions. One of the reasons that there may be no contemporary or near-contemporary written references to Arthur is that the new rulers wished to wipe out all memories of a popular resistance hero. But as the centuries passed and the old antagonisms died, the Arthur stories came out in the open again. A dead hero, whose cause is irrevocably lost, rarely lacks for supporters.

The historical reality of Arthur has been given the imprimatur of *Debrett's Peerage*, the *Who's Who* of British aristocracy. Debrett's editor has tried to link Arthur with Queen Elizabeth II. However, the family tree that he has constructed is more hopeful than historical.

If we accept the reality of Arthur, we can start looking for places associated with his life. They are not hard to find. Visitors to the wildly romantic ruins of Tintagel Castle in Cornwall are often told that it is the birthplace of Arthur. It's good for the tourist trade and the casual visitor may leave Tintagel thinking that he has seen the remains of the castle at Camelot itself. That's nonsense, for the castle was built in the thirteenth century, a full seven hundred years after Arthur lived. There was an earlier castle on the site, but even that does not go back to Arthurian times. Besides, Cornwall is the wrong place. Tintagel is out.

Sir Thomas Malory, the fifteenth-century gentleman who wrote the most influential of the Arthurian romances, *Le Morte d'Arthur*, while languishing in prison for numerous crimes, placed Camelot at Winchester. There is a fine castle at Winchester, and if you go there you can see the famous Round Table, or at least *a* famous Round Table, hanging in the great hall.

The table at Winchester is made of worn oak planks and is eighteen feet in diameter. At the top of the table, there is a picture of a medieval Arthur seated upon his throne, scepter in hand. The rest of the table is painted in a spoke pattern in twenty-four alternating bands of white and green. At the end of the spokes are the names of Arthur's most celebrated knights. The table is just too perfect not to be a fake.

The tabletop itself may go back as far as the twelfth century, but the painting was commissioned by Henry VII in the sixteenth century. Henry was extremely anxious to identify his line with the great hero. (The Arthur legend was very strong at that time, and Henry's older brother, who died before attaining the throne, had been named Arthur. England narrowly missed having a real, identifiable King Arthur.) Henry had the table painted green and white, his family colors.

During the fourteenth century, Edward III of England and Philip VI of France both tried to build round tables, but they abandoned their projects as impractical. Henry VIII had to settle for a mere twenty-four at table. But according to the stories, Arthur had at least 150 knights. To have seated all of them comfortably, the Round Table would have had to have been at least 125 feet in diameter. Such a monstrosity could never have been squeezed into a fourteenth-century castle; a special hall would have been needed to contain it.

*Two views of
King Arthur and
his knights of the
Round Table*

47

Many archaeologists feel that the most probable site for Camelot is a place called variously Cadbury Hill, Cadbury Camp, or
Cadbury Castle. Three miles away are the villages of Queen's
Camel and West Camel, named from the stream once called
"Cam." Many Celtic streams were named Cam, which means
"crooked." The name Camelot—the origins of which are lost—
may have come from proximity to this stream.

Cadbury Hill appears to have been used as a fortress since the
Stone Age. Archaeologists have also found a line of trenches dug
by the British Army during World War I. In between those two
extremes, it seems that practically everyone who lived in the region fortified the hill. The discovery that sparked interest in the
Cadbury Hill/Camelot identification was the finding that the
walls of the fortress were heavily refortified in the sixth century—
Arthur's time. During that period, Cadbury Hill must have contained the most formidable military installation in southwest
England.

Folklore has long placed Arthur at Cadbury. The local people
have all sorts of legends about the ghost of King Arthur. There was
a place on the hill called King Arthur's well; the silver shoe from
Arthur's horse, they say, was dug up there. It is said that on the
night of the full moon, King Arthur and his knights ride around the
hill. In another story, Arthur and his men come riding down from
the hill on Christmas Eve to drink from a well by the village
church. Still another legend says that the hill is hollow and can be
entered by iron or golden gates. If you look through the gates on
St. John's Eve, according to a traditional poem, you can see the
king sitting in the middle of his court. But there was something
malevolent about this tradition, and no one had the courage to put
it to the test. When a group of antiquarians visited the hill around
the turn of the century, one old man asked them if they had come
to take the king away.

The Cadbury/Camelot identification has picked up a lot of influential supporters, and there are continuing excavations at the
site, but barring some really extraordinary find, the question will
probably remain open. Past excavations of early Celtic sites have

found them disappointingly bare of personal objects, so no one really expects to uncover a sword or helmet with Arthur's name on it.

The Cam and Camels near Cadbury conjure up another Arthurian association. This place has often been identified as Camlan or Camlaun, the site of Arthur's final and fatal battle with his evil kinsman Medraut or Mordred.

Cadbury is also quite near the ruins of Glastonbury Abbey, long rumored to be the burial place of Arthur. An ancient pathway runs between the two spots, and legend has it that people "sometimes, on rough winter nights, heard King Arthur and his hounds go by along that track."

A visitor to the ruins of Glastonbury will find this sign on the grounds: "SITE OF KING ARTHUR'S TOMB. In the year 1191, the bodies of King Arthur and his Queen were said to have been found on the south side of the Lady Chapel. On the 19th of April 1278 their remains were removed in the presence of King Edward and Queen Eleanor to a black marble tomb on this site. This tomb survived until the dissolution of the Abbey in 1539."

Since kings were always eager to associate themselves with Arthur, we can assume that Edward did not need the most rigorous evidence to declare that the tomb of the hero was found during his reign. The monks of Glastonbury may have actually faked the whole thing in order to raise money to restore the abbey after a disastrous fire. Still, the tradition of Arthur's burial at Glastonbury is strong and dramatically satisfying, because Glastonbury is so ancient.

Part of the Arthurian tradition holds that the king did not truly die but was wounded and carried off to the Isle of Avalon, where he "sleeps." Glastonbury was once a series of hills surrounded by a marshy lowland and connected to dry land by a narrow ridge. Thus, it could have been considered an island.

Why all the mystery surrounding Arthur's death and burial? Geoffrey Ashe, a British writer who has spent years exploring the historical basis for the Arthurian legends, says that the secrecy may have been deliberate: "In view of the circumstances of

Arthur's end—strife among his own people, while the Saxons were building up for a fresh advance—it may be that his lieutenants concealed their loss. Immediate publication would have dealt too heavy a blow to the native morale, and would have given too much encouragement to the enemy. A few loyal veterans . . . carried off the leader's body to some remote spot and buried it under cover of darkness hoping that the heathen might be restrained a little longer by the power of his name and fear of his return."

In case you think Arthur was just too good to be true, you should consider this old Celtic rhyme that begins:

> When King Arthur ruled this land,
> He ruled it like a swine. . . .

Recently Ashe has come to a new and rather startling conclusion as to the identity of the historical character who inspired the Arthur stories. In his book *The Discovery of King Arthur,* Ashe proposes that the legend was based on the fifth-century "high-king" of the Britons, Riothamus. In some of the Arthur stories the king is supposed to have fought against the barbarians in Gaul. Riothamus is believed to have led an unsuccsssful expedition agains the Goths in the region of Burgundy. The Arthur stories were always popular in France, though in Brittany rather than Burgundy.

What makes Ashe's theory startling is that this is the first time a possible historical Arthur has been identified because of his deeds outside of the British Isles. It had always been assumed that the "real" Arthur never left his native land. The proposition will doubtless be debated among scholars for years, but it has received a respectful first hearing.

See also: ROBIN HOOD; STONEHENGE

EL DORADO   When the Spanish conquered first Mexico and then Peru, a huge stock of gold came into their possession. Suddenly, men who had been poor soldiers became as wealthy as dukes. The dream of golden wealth fired the imagination of generations, and not only in Spain. Men dreamed that in addition to the Aztecs and the Incas there were other golden civilizations ripe for plunder. And there were always rumors that led them to believe that such a dream might indeed come true.

The most persistent and compelling of the stories was that of *el hombre dorado,* the gilded man. Basically, the story itself happens to be true. It had filtered down to the Spanish settlements in the New World from the high, almost inaccessible plateau of Cundinamarca, seventy-five hundred feet above sea level in what is now the nation of Colombia.

The story was that once a year the king of a land surrounded by mountains covered himself with a sticky substance and then rolled in gold dust. Completely covered, the gilded king walked to the shores of a lake called Guatavita, got into a canoe, paddled out into the center, and jumped into the water to wash off the gold dust. When he did this, the crowd that had gathered on the shore sent up a great cheer, and this became the signal for the start of a feast.

A nation that can afford to cover its king with gold must have had gold in abundance. Such a country would have to rival or surpass Mexico and Peru in wealth; so the thinking went. What no one had bothered to consider was that it does not take much gold dust to cover a man's body, and this showy spectacle might not even indicate great wealth. Many of the peoples of Central and South America had some gold but not enough to warrant mounting an expedition to find it. Only the Incas and the Aztecs, who had inherited gold collected over a wide area for centuries, had really fabulous quantities.

But the story of El Dorado, as both the king and the land itself came to be called, took so powerful a grip on the imaginations of generations of treasure-seekers that no amount of hardship or disappointment could break it. The search for El Dorado is not romantic adventure; it reads more like a horror story.

The first to set off on the mad search was Ambrosius Ehinger, a representative of the German banking family Welser, which had been given important concessions by the Spanish government. Ehinger had been sent to the New World to establish a commercial colony, but within weeks of landing in 1529 he heard the El Dorado rumors and began searching for the land of the golden king. Ehinger's expedition established the pattern for many that followed. He set off into the jungle with no firm idea of where he was going, following every rumor or story. Ehinger developed the theory that if he killed and terrorized enough Indians, they would reveal to him the location of the golden land. He cut a swath of devastation through the jungle that the Indians were to remember for generations—but he did not find El Dorado. After two terrible years, the expedition was destroyed by the jungle and by attacks from the Indians, who grew bolder as the expedition grew smaller, weaker, and more disorganizd. Ehinger himself was killed by an arrow, and a bare handful of survivors made it back to the coast to tell their story.

Dreadful as the tale of their sufferings was, it did not discourage other gold seekers, several of whom actually found the place where the El Dorado legend originated, but they refused to believe it because there wasn't enough gold to fulfill their fantasies. In February 1539, three separate expeditions met on the plateau of Cundinamarca near the spot where the El Dorado ceremony had been performed. The area was practically devoid of gold, and the ceremony had been abandoned about forty years earlier. The Chicbachas tribe, which had originated the ceremony, simply ran out of gold. There was no gold to be found on the plateau, and the Chicbachas got the small amount that they needed by trading with other tribes. But even that had strained their limited resources.

All of this became known to those who had scaled the plateau of Cundinamarca—they just refused to believe it. One of those who had actually found El Dorado in 1539, Gonzalo Jimenez, was still searching for it forty years later, and when he died he left his only

Sir Walter Raleigh, one of the last El Dorado seekers

living relative his royal grant to search for the golden kingdom. This man carried on the family El Dorado search for another fifteen years, perhaps setting a family record for unprofitable quests.

The possible location of El Dorado kept changing. As soon as one area was explored and found wanting, another area captured the attention of the searchers. Possible locations for the golden kingdom were scattered all over the map of the northern part of South America. By the mid-sixteenth century, it was generally assumed that El Dorado was in Guiana, which contained a considerable area of unexplored jungle.

One of the last El Dorado seekers was Sir Walter Raleigh. He set down the final and most spectacular versions of the El Dorado legend: "When the Emperor carouseth with his captains, tributories and governors, the manner is thus. All those pledged him are first stripped naked and their bodies anointed all over with a kind of white balsam. . . . When they are anointed all over, certain servants of the Emperor having prepared gold made into a fine powder blow it through hollow canes upon their naked bodies, until

53

they be all shining from the foot to the head, and in this sort they sit drinking by twenties and hundreds and continue in drunkenness sometimes six or seven days together." Raleigh, however, was no more successful in finding the golden kingdom than any of his predecessors had been.

While references to El Dorado continued to appear on maps well into the eighteenth century, the active hunt was really over. The man who finally put the lid on the whole El Dorado business was the great Prussian natural scientist and traveler Alexander von Humboldt. At the beginning of the nineteenth century, Humboldt conducted an extensive reconnaissance of South America. He retraced the routes of most of the El Dorado seekers and found what they found—nothing. Faced with so formidable and overwhelming a testimony, the land of El Dorado was finally banished from the world's maps.

THE GREAT PYRAMID   The Great Pyramid at Giza, just outside of Cairo, has been the object of more wonder and speculation than any other monument on earth. The reason for this is not hard to figure out; the statistics for the Great Pyramid are awesome. It was one of the seven wonders of the ancient world, and is the only one to survive until today. It was the largest monument ever built in the ancient world, and in some respects the largest stone monument ever built, at least until the construction of Hoover Dam in the early twentieth century.

Any way you wish to look at it, the Great Pyramid is huge. Its base covers thirteen acres, or seven blocks in midtown Manhattan. Originally, the pyramid was made up of more than two and a half million blocks of limestone and granite, weighing from two to seventy tons. The blocks rise in stepped tiers to the height of a forty-story building. In terms of solid masonry, the structure contains more stone than all the cathedrals, churches, and chapels built in England since the time of Christ.

The Great Pyramid

Though the pyramid certainly does stand today, it has suffered greatly over the centuries. Originally, it was covered with a smooth, closely fitted mantle of polished limestone, and it must have been dazzling in the bright Egyptian sunlight. The covering is long gone, and what remains looks like a gigantic set of brownish steps. But it is still an overwhelming sight.

The Great Pyramid isn't the only Egyptian pyramid; two others stand close by, and there are about one hundred pyramidal structures scattered along the western bank of the Nile. The Great Pyramid isn't even the first; that honor goes to the Step Pyramid at Sakkara. But the Great Pyramid is by all means the largest of the pyramids and the one upon which all the speculation has centered.

The Great Pyramid has been a tourist attraction since ancient times. The earliest written account we have of it comes from the Greek traveler and historian Herodotus, who lived in the fifth century B.C. and who, like any modern visitor to Egypt, was taken to see the Great Pyramid. Herodotus was told that the pyramid had been built as a tomb for an early king or pharaoh whom he called Cheops but who today is more correctly called Khufu.

Most modern scholars would agree that the Great Pyramid was indeed built as a tomb for Khufu, who ruled Egypt from about 2592 B.C. to 2569 B.C. This was during the Fourth Dynasty, an early period in Egypt's very long history, but a period of enormous power and energy. All the large pyramids were built at this time. Not only do the ancient authorities agree that the pyramid was built for Khufu, his name has been found painted in red on some of the inner stones.

No royal mummy was found inside the pyramid, which is hardly surprising since the pyramid, like practically all Egypt's ancient tombs, was thoroughly plundered in ancient times. There is a burial chamber located under the pyramid, and two chambers inside of it. These probably are the result of changes of plan during the construction of the monument.

There had been a great deal of speculation as to the significance of the pyramid shape; since we don't know what was in the builders' minds, we naturally cannot say for certain. There had been speculation about some sort of mystic power in the pyramid shape, but this seems unlikely. A better guess is that the pyramid shape was used because, if you want to build a very large monument, it is the easiest shape to use. The pyramid, with its broad base and very narrow top, is stable. Try to raise a large mound of sand on the beach, and it will inevitably assume a pyramid shape.

This is not to suggest that pyramid building is easy. Scattered along the Nile are several examples of pyramids that apparently failed. Building a pyramid, particularly with only the simple tools available to the Egyptians, was an enormous task. And the fact is that we are still not really sure how the Egyptians accomplished it.

The guide who took Herodotus to view the pyramid said that it had been built with the aid of some sort of wooden lifting device, and some students of ancient engineering believe that the builders employed a rather simple sort of wooden derrick that could have lifted heavy stones from one tier to the next.

There has been some speculation that the Egyptians made use
of a form of concrete, and that the blocks were actually poured
rather than cut and lifted, but this theory has never attracted
many supporters.

The most popular theory is that, as the pyramid rose, a ramp of
mud and rubble was either built up to it or corkscrewed around it.
The huge blocks were then dragged on rollers up the ramp and
levered into place.

Most of the building material was quarried close at hand. The
limestone for the facing could have been floated on rafts down the
Nile from the spot where it was quarried with relative ease, so that
getting the stone to the building site presented no insurmountable
difficulties. Finishing the stones so that they fitted together as
snugly as they did must have been one of the most laborious parts
of the entire construction. Ancient writers who saw the pyramid
while it still possessed some of its fine limestone outer sheath mar-
veled at how smooth the surface looked. They said that not even a
knife blade could be inserted between the blocks.

Aside from the sheer physical difficulties of building a monument of the magnitude of the Great Pyramid, it presents vexing
problems in planning as well. For example, to calculate the proper
angle at which a pyramid could be constructed without the blocks
all sliding off appears to require a fairly sophisticated knowledge
of geometry, knowledge that some observers suggest the ancient
Egyptians did not and could not have possessed.

One of the more astonishing things about the Great Pyramid is
that the sides of the base are oriented to within one-tenth of a degree of true north-south and east-west directions. The orientation
is so nearly perfect that it could hardly have been accidental. But
how could the Egyptians have determined true north, for, as far as
we know, they possessed no compass?

For the most part, scholars have been able to propose possible
explanations for all the construction problems raised by the Great
Pyramid. These orthodox explanations require no occult knowledge or magic on the part of the Egyptians, just the diligent and
painstaking application of some fairly simple principles. But the

builders have left no records, or if they did the records have long since been destroyed.

The Great Pyramid is such an enormous accomplishment, one that so completely outstrips anything that was done anywhere else for thousand of years, that many have rejected the simple, orthodox explanations. Others have raised objections based on racial or religious grounds, that is, a belief or prejudice that brown-skinned pagans could not possibly have had the brains or skills to build such a monument. The British occultist Basil Steward insisted in his book *The Mystery of the Great Pyramid* that it was designed and begun by a single individual "who belonged to the Adamic White civilization endowed with moral, scientific and cultural attainments far in advance of all other contemporary civilizations."

John Taylor, a nineteenth-century Englishman who became obsessed with the Great Pyramid, though he had never set eyes on it, decided that the builders were of "the chosen race in the line of, though preceding Abraham; so early indeed as to be closer to Noah than to Abraham." Some people misinterpreted Taylor and believed he said that Noah himself had directed the construction of the Great Pyramid. Well, why not, after overseeing the construction of the Ark, who would be better to direct the building of this other great project?

Those who hold grandiose theories about the origin of the Great Pyramid are not content with the notion that it was only a big tomb for an old Egyptian king, either; it must, they insist, be something more. What more? Perhaps a repository for all manner of ancient wisdom. These theorists do not regard the Great Pyramid literally as an ancient library; the "wisdom of the ages" was built into its very structure. By interpreting the various measurements of the Great Pyramid, some believed that one could do such things as calculate the distance from the earth to the sun, the circumference of the earth, the frequency of eclipses, and a huge quantity of other geographical and astronomical information. Out of such theories a whole science, or pseudoscience, called "pyramidology," sprang up.

And the pyramidologists went much further. They said that by proper interpretation of measurements, the earth's past could be revealed; they could find the date of the Flood, when the Hebrews were expelled from Egypt, the time of Christ's birth, and so forth. Many of these events occurred after the pyramid was built, and so it was assumed that the pyramid could be used to predict the future.

Most pyramidology was based on the calculations of a nineteenth-century Scottish astronomer, Charles Piazzi Smyth. Smyth was an excellent astronomer and mathematician, but he had another mission in life: to discredit ancient Egyptian "idolatry" by proving that the pyramid had been built under divine guidance and that it incorporated divine wisdom. He spent months making all sorts of complex measurements in the pyramid and then sent a paper on what he had learned to the celebrated scientific group, the Royal Society, of which he was a fellow. The other members thought his ideas were utterly bizarre and refused to allow him to read his paper at a meeting. Smyth promptly resigned from the Royal Society. Even before going to Egypt, Smyth had published his speculations in a massive volume, *Our Inheritance in the Great Pyramid* (1864), a book that remains the bible of pyramidology even today.

Smyth invented his own system of measurement, using such units as the "pyramid inch," in order to prove his theories. With so many possible measurements to work with and with an agreeably flexible standard of measurement, pyramidologists could be very impressive in relating various measurements to things that had already happened. But they ran into serious trouble when they tried to use the Great Pyramid to predict events beyond their own time. Pyramidologists predicted the Second Coming of Christ and the start of the Millennium so many times that pyramidology became something of a joke. Scholars referred to those who believed in it as "pyramidiots."

The popularity of what might be called classical pyramidology has declined a good deal in the last few decades, but there is still

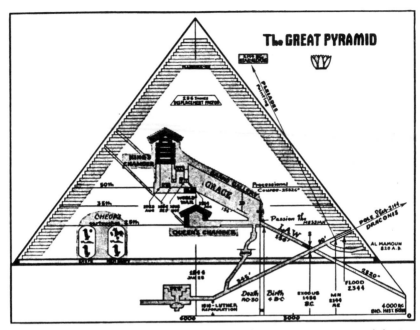

The interior of the Great Pyramid according to some pyramidologists

plenty of speculation about other "secrets of the pyramids." Most persistent is the contention that the builders of the Great Pyramid possessed all sorts of incredible astronomical, geographical, and mathematical knowledge, knowledge far beyond what should have been available to the ancient Egyptians. The "true builders" of the Great Pyramid are supposed to have been anyone from survivors of a theoretical pre–Ice Age supercivilization to visitors from outer space.

Some eighteenth- and nineteenth-century secret magical societies hinted that they held their initiation rites within the Great Pyramid, but such claims were pure fiction, for the "rooms" within the pyramid are tiny.

It has been popular in recent years to assume that all sorts of ancient monuments, from Stonehenge to the Mayan pyramids, were used for astronomical purposes. A good deal of effort has been lavished on proving that the Great Pyramid was basically an astronomical observatory rather than a tomb and that it contains a variety of significant astronomical alignments.

In a popular book called *Secrets of the Great Pyramid,* author Peter Tompkins concludes, "Whatever mystical, occult or science fiction tales may be associated with the Great Pyramid, it is still an extra-ordinary piece of masonry, and its designers must have been extra-ordinary beings. Who they were and when they built their Pyramid remains a mystery. So the quest continues. . . . But as more is discovered it may open the door to a whole new civilization of the past, and a much longer history of man than has heretofore been credited."

Professional Egyptologists who are quite sure they know the who, when, and why if not the how of the Great Pyramid cringe at such statements. Yet the sheer size and antiquity of the monument are so overwhelming that we can be certain that most people will continue to feel that there is indeed something extraordinary, mysterious, and unknown about it.

See also: STONEHENGE

THE KINGDOM OF PRESTER JOHN   One of the most eagerly sought-after lands was the one said to be ruled by a man who was both priest and king—the land of Prester John. Throughout the Middle Ages and well into the era that we have come to call the Age of Exploration, the belief persisted that out there, just beyond the border of absolute geographical knowledge, existed a vast and wonderful Christian kingdom.

At first, this kingdom was supposed to be in India, but when the Christians got to India and found no Prester John, they simply assumed that his kingdom existed farther to the east. When the entire continent of Asia was eliminated, the quest was then transferred to Africa.

The legend of the Kingdom of Prester John persisted, in spite of all the evidence to the contrary, because it served a function. During some of the darkest hours of European history, Christians could console themselves with the thought that at any moment the powerful priest-king and his hordes might come pouring out of the East to save them.

Pope Alexander III wrote to Prester John, Marco Polo looked for him, and so did Prince Henry the Navigator. Vasco da Gama even thought he had found Prester John's kingdom.

In 1221, a rumor swept Europe that a mysterious Christian monarch whom many identified as Prester John was slaughtering the Moslems of Central Asia and was going to march westward to relieve the beleaguered Crusaders, who were still clinging precariously to parts of the Holy Land. It was rumored that perhaps the monarch might even appear in Europe.

Only slowly and reluctantly did Europe recognize that this conqueror was not the mythical Prester John but rather the all-too-real Genghis Khan. Even then the fantasy did not die completely, for Europeans continued to insist that Genghis Khan and his Mongols were really Christians. This was not the first story of the coming of Prester John, and it would not be the last.

The origins of the Prester John myth are obscure, but there is some evidence that it started as a legend of the Nestorian Christians. The Nestorians were eastern Christians who had communities thinly spread from Syria to China. They were great merchants and travelers and were very accommodating to other cultures. Nestorians could be found in the camps of the Mongol Khans and in the sophisticated cities of China.

The Nestorians traced their origins back to the apostle Thomas, who, according to an apocryphal tract written in the third or fourth century, went to India and made many converts there but was martyred by Misdaeus, King of India. The king, then stricken with guilt, converted. The king's son Vizan—a name often mistranslated as John—was the successor not only to his father's royal title, but to St. Thomas's position as leader of the Indian Christians as well. Thus he became Prester John.

There is no authentic evidence that Thomas ever went to India. There were certainly no large Christian communities there, but once the legend began to circulate it seemed to attach itself to anyplace where there might be any kind of a Christian community. There was a Nestorian community at Samarkand in the steppes, a headquarters for the Mongol Khans; hence the frequent confusion of the Khans with the Christian monarch.

In 1145, a Syrian bishop arrived in Rome with a story that Prester John had just inflicted an enormous defeat upon the Turks. The man who had beaten the Turks was in fact Yeh-lu Ta-shish, ruler of a nomadic empire called Black Cathay. He was a Chinese-educated Buddhist, though he may have included some Nestorians among his followers. Like most central Asian nomads, Yeh-lu Ta-shish was fairly indifferent to religion.

In 1165, Byzantine emperor Manuel I got a long and very arrogant letter from someone who signed himself "Presbyter Johannes, by the power and virtue of God and of the Lord Jesus Christ, Lords of Lords." Page after page, Prester John told the emperor how wonderful and powerful he was; "if Thou canst count the stars of the sky and the sands of the sea, judge the vastness of Our realm and Our power."

As a note of modesty, his title "John the Priest King" was explained by saying that since he had kings and archbishops as his servants, "Our Eminence therefore prefers out of humility to be designated with a lesser name and office."

The Letter, as the document was called, came to the attention of Pope Alexander III, who seems to have written a reply to it. The Pope gave his reply to his personal physician, one Philip, who had "contacts with many persons in the East." But little is known of this Philip, and so there isn't a clue as to what happened to him or the Pope's reply.

The Prester John Letter is almost certainly a deliberate fabrication, a bit of medieval "romance of the mysterious east literature." Some of the elements in it seem to have been drawn from the Sinbad stories. Nevertheless, the Letter was widely circulated throughout Europe and remained popular reading for over a century.

Marco Polo was looking for Prester John but didn't find him. He did, however, pick up a rumor about a Wang Khan or King John who was a powerful Central Asian king and a Christian. Marco identified this ruler with Prester John. The rumor Marco heard was essentially correct. Wang Khan was a king of the Kereits, Turco-Mongol people who established an empire on the steppes and were finally defeated by Genghis Khan, whom Wang Khan had once befriended. The Kereits seem to have been converted to Nestorian Christianity about the year 1000. But as has already been noted, religion was a fairly indifferent matter to most nomads. Genghis Khan himself was always reasonably friendly toward the Nestorians.

Wang Khan was certainly not the Prester John of legend, for the legend had been around long before Wang Khan was born, and probably before the Kereits had been converted, too. The idea was in the air and had simply been attached to a convenient figure.

By about the fourteenth century, Asia had become well enough known in Europe for even the most hopeful to realize that there was no place left for a Kingdom of Prester John. So a Dominican friar named Jordanus de Severac had an inspiration. If Prester John did not live in Asia, then he must live elsewhere—in Central Africa. Some believed that Prester John had simply retired to the African side of his vast domains after being driven out of the Asian side by Genghis Khan.

Besides, there really was a genuinely mysterious Christian kingdom flourishing in the middle of Africa, the kingdom of Abyssinia or Ethiopia. The Ethiopian Church is very ancient; it had always been schismatic, but had been completely cut off from the rest of the Christian world by the rise of Moslem power in Africa. In the fourteenth century, Europeans knew less about Ethiopians than they did about the Mongols.

Portuguese explorers were convinced that the Kingdom of Prester John was in Africa. When Vasco da Gama's ships landed at

Medieval map of Africa showing the Kingdom of Prester John in the center of the continent

Mozambique, he wrote, "We were told that Prester John resided not far from this place; that he held many cities along the coast and the inhabitants of these cities were great merchants and owned big ships."

For decades, maps of Africa continued to refer to Ethiopia as the land of Prester John. The first European book ever written on Ethiopia, which appeared in the fifteenth century, referred to the king of that land as Prester John or simply "the Preste."

The Ethiopian monarchs, by the way, resented the identification; they traced their heritage all the way back to Solomon and Sheba's son Menelik and proudly pointed out that they possessed a

65

whole string of titles far more exalted than that of priest. (It is more probable that the Ethiopians were converted in about the fourth century.)

After the fifteenth century, the identification of Ethiopia with the Kingdom of Prester John became untenable, and with no further places left to locate the kingdom, the long-running legend finally expired.

LEMURIA AND MU   The legend of Lemuria got its start in the human longing for symmetry. The Greeks knew the world was round, and they were familiar with one-quarter of the globe, a quarter extraordinarily well filled with land. They assumed that the other three-quarters had equal amounts of land.

The voyages of Columbus and the other great seafarers of the fifteenth and sixteenth centuries changed a lot of ideas about the shape and size of the earth, but people still could not quite get over the idea that the distribution of land around the globe was not symmetrical—there should be at least as much land below the equator as there is above.

When Europeans first began to penetrate the waters of the South Pacific, they expected to find a large continent there somewhere beyond the west coast of South America. Mapmakers often put in an ill-defined land mass, which they labeled *Terra Australis Incognita,* or "the great unknown southern continent." A small island continent that we now call Australia was indeed discovered in the South Pacific, but that didn't really satisfy the desire for symmetry.

An idea once accepted so widely and enthusiastically as the great unknown southern continent never dies entirely. Over the centuries, it has bobbed up again and again under a variety of names and for a variety of reasons. Of course, it became clear the continent wasn't there any longer; it had somehow been "lost." It was an Atlantis of the Pacific.

Lemuria, the most enduring name for the lost Pacific continent, was first proposed by an English zoologist named Philip L. Schlater. He was trying to figure out how the same form of lemur could be found in Madagascar, Africa, India, and Indonesia. Lemurs can't fly or swim; they have to walk across land, so he suggested that all of these areas were once connected by a vast continent, for which he proposed the name Lemuria.

A German naturalist named Ernst Heinrich Haeckel was far more daring. He proposed that Lemuria was the "cradle of the human race." At the time Haeckel wrote, no known human fossils had been discovered, and placing man's emergence on a lost continent neatly got around the lack of evidence.

While biologists and naturalists were supporters of sunken continents and land bridges because they explained many difficult problems about the distribution of plant and animal life, geologists were much less charmed by such ideas. They could not easily conceive of forces that could raise and lower enormous land masses in such a relatively short time. However, over the past few decades, dramatic discoveries have indicated that all the southern continents were once connected but broke apart and drifted or were pushed away from one another by enormous forces under the earth's crust. Thus, the scientific need for Lemuria has vanished. But science has had very little to do with the popular search for lost Lemuria anyway.

In the years that followed the origin of the concept of Lemuria, the lost continent moved up in time. Supporters placed its submergence anywhere from the late Stone Age to the middle of the seventeenth century. Professor J. Macmillan Brown thought Lemuria sank between 1687 and 1722. The supporters moved the lost continent itself, too. Whereas Lemuria had once connected Africa and Asia so that the lemurs could walk from one to the other, later supporters put the continent in the middle of the South Pacific, the area where the waves are broken only by a scattering of small islands, but that is nonetheless the traditional location of the great unknown southern continent. Some saw the islands as the tops of the mountains of the drowned continent.

Lewis Spence, the Scottish mythologist, took this view in his book *The Problem of Lemuria:* "I have some difficulty in comprehending the kind of mentality which can view a map of Oceania [Australia and the island groups of the South Pacific] filled as it is with insular groups—without almost at once agreeing with the hypothesis of great land masses in an area so vast. Seriously are we to suppose that of all the earth's regions this alone, with the exception of the Atlantic, was destitute of continental land, especially when we behold the evidence of mountain peaks of that land still littering a space occupying so many thousands of miles?" Spence believed that physical evidence was not enough and that real progress could only be achieved from "inspiration and insight."

There is more than a tinge of racism in Spence's theories. His Lemuria was a land of many races, but the white race was the Lemurian aristocracy and "the conservators of all hidden knowledge and magic." Spence believed that white refugees from Lemuria brought civilization to the Indians of South America. He supported this belief by relating many supposed tales of white gods in South America. "The legends relating to a fair civilization cannot but apply to a white Lemurian aristocracy." Europeans were, of course, the truest descendants of the Lemurian aristocracy.

Madame Helena P. Blavatsky, founder of Theosophy, made Lemuria part of her cosmology. However, consistency was not Madame Blavatsky's strong suit, and at one time or another she put Lemuria in practically every part of the globe. Her Lemurians were equally confusing. They seemed to need no brain or "any physical vehicle to attain connection with the spirit." Despite this apparently insubstantial form, they were described as gigantic, apelike, egg-laying bisexuals, and their downfall was somehow connected with their discovery of sex.

James Churchward, whose books were popular in the 1920s and 1930s and who still enjoys a small following today, had another name for the great unknown southern continent: he called it Mu. The name was based on a mistranslation of some Mayan hieroglyphs. Churchward claimed that he had discovered the truth about Mu in documents that he had located in a monastery in

India: "The Garden of Eden was not in Asia but on a now sunken continent in the Pacific Ocean. The Biblical story of creation—the epic of the seven days and the seven nights—came first not from the peoples of the Nile or the Euphrates Valley but from the peoples of this now submerged continent—the Motherland of Man."

As is common in such theories, Churchward was eager to pick up the white man's burden. "The dominant race in the land of Mu was a white race, exceedingly handsome people, with clear white or olive skins, large soft, dark eyes and straight black hair. Besides this white race there were other races, people with yellow, brown and black skins. They, however, did not dominate."

Yet another name for the lost Pacific continent was Pan. This was the creation of John Ballou, a Newburgh, New York, dentist and spiritualist. Ballou said that he had been angelically inspired to write a new bible, which he called *Oahspe*. Like all books produced by automatic writing, *Oahspe* is very long and virtually unreadable. But through the murky prose, one can discern the familiar theme of the supremacy of the white race.

Lemuria popped up once again in the 1940s in the science fiction magazine *Amazing Stories*. The Lemuria stories were written by a Pennsylvania welder named Richard S. Shaver, but were heavily edited and rewritten by the magazine's editor, Raymond A. Palmer. They allegedly told the authentic story of the earth, beginning at a time when both Atlantis and Lemuria towered above the waves. The first story in the series was titled "I Remember Lemuria." It was claimed that Shaver could tap his "racial memory" to reconstruct earth's lost history.

Since Lemuria had so little grounding in fact or even in genuine ancient tradition, it slipped easily from the realm of reasonable speculation into murky occultism and downright fakery. But there it lives, and even prospers after a fashion. You can still buy editions of Churchward's books. Theosophy is not what it once was, but it is still around, and there are even a few lonely supporters of the Shaver stories.

See also: ANCIENT MAPS OF THE ANTARCTIC; ATLANTIS; MADAME BLAVATSKY; RAYMOND PALMER

Stonehenge There is no ancient monument, with the exception of the Great Pyramid itself, that has been the subject of more speculation, reasonable, unreasonable, and downright nutty, than that circle of enormous stones on Salisbury Plain in England known as Stonehenge.

By the time recorded history caught up with Stonehenge, people had already forgotten who built it or why. Certainly the Romans who conquered Britain didn't know who built it, and apparently didn't care. It isn't even mentioned in their records.

In the dark ages that followed the Roman withdrawal from Britain, few records of any kind were kept, so we don't know what people thought. But by the time Stonehenge entered recorded history, and that is the twelfth century, the monument had obviously already been the object of a great deal of popular speculation and had become an integral part of the complex legendary history that the people of the British Isles were fabricating for themselves.

Even the name is a puzzle. The first to mention it was the twelfth-century chronicler Henry of Huntingdon. He said that the word meant "hanging stones" and that it was a good name because the stones seem to "hang as it were in the air," probaby a reference to the lintels perched atop the great uprights. This is the feature of Stonehenge that first strikes the modern visitor, and there were more uprights and lintels in place in Henry's day than in ours.

Others have attempted to explain the name by saying that the stones of the monument were a place from which condemned criminals were hung. There is no evidence that this was ever done, but Stonehenge seems always to inspire morbid fantasies and bloody associations.

The great myth-collector and -compiler Geoffrey of Monmouth, upon whose work all the later stories of King Arthur are based, made Stonehenge part of the Arthur story. He said that Stonehenge was constructed by Arthur's uncle as a monument to Briton warriors treacherously slain on Salisbury Plain by the invading

Saxons. The magician Merlin planned the monument and moved the gigantic stones there from Ireland, to which they had once been brought by giants from "the farthest ends of Africa." The Merlin association with Stonehenge stuck for years.

In the seventeenth century, English architect Indigo Jones examined the ancient monument and declared that the Merlin story was "that ridiculous fable." He also rejected the idea that the ancient Britons, who were "savage and barbarous people, knowing no use at all of garment," could have built it. And he cast aside the theory that the Druids could have built Stonehenge, though that idea was to make a strong comeback later. The only people he thought capable of building Stonehenge were the Romans. The fact that the copious Roman records contained not one word about the construction of the monument, nor the fact that Stonehenge did not resemble in the least any known Roman monuments, did not bother the architect. That was his theory, take it or leave it.

Jones's opinion was an influential one, but certainly not the only one as to who built Stonehenge and for what purpose. The Danes, who had conquered Britain, and any one of a number of real or imaginary early British monarchs were also credited with the monument.

Round and round the controversy went, and all the time Stonehenge was becoming more famous and drawing to Salisbury Plain a flock of tourists, which has in recent times grown so large that it

Stonehenge

has threatened the very existence of the monument. The diarist Samuel Pepys visited the site in 1668 and wrote on June 11 of that year, "God knows what their [the stones'] use was!"

The first person to do any real systematic study of Stonehenge was the mid-seventeenth-century antiquarian John Aubrey. Aubrey was an intelligent and careful observer, but he was the first to admit he "wanted patience to go through Knotty Studies." Still, Aubrey made a more thorough study of Stonehenge than anyone had before. He also decided that Stonehenge had been constructed by the Druids, priests of the ancient Celts. Even Aubrey was unsure of his identification and confessed he was "gropeing in the Dark."

Dr. William Stukeley had no doubts whatever. About half a century after Aubrey reintroduced the Druid idea, Stukeley took it up with a passion. He wanted to reconcile Christianity with what he considered the "aboriginal patriarchal religion of the Druids." He was so vigorous in his defense of the Druids that he became known as "the ArchDruid."

The Druid identification with Stonehenge remains popular to this day, but it no longer commands any support among archaeologists or scholars. Stonehenge has been extensively studied since Stukeley's day, and the conclusion is that Stonehenge was built and rebuilt by a series of Neolithic peoples who inhabited the area over a period of some two thousand years.

Construction was started around 3000 B.C.; at that point Stonehenge was little more than a circular ditch and bank about six feet high with a broad entranceway called "the Avenue." What most of us think of as the "true" Stonehenge is the horseshoe formation of five trilithons (free-standing three-stone structures of two uprights capped by a lintel). Around this formation were thirty smaller, but still immense, uprights forming an outer circle, with thirty slightly smaller lintels making up a continuous level ring, its surface sixteen feet off the ground. This part of Stonehenge was put up about a thousand years after the first ditch was dug at Stonehenge. Later, still other stones were set in the circle or along the Avenue leading to the center of Stonehenge. The builders continued to make alterations for a thousand more years.

It is possible that Stonehenge remained a center of some sort even into Roman times, though it is doubtful that it was used by the Druids, who favored groves and streams for their worship. Besides, if it had been a center of Druidic resistance to the Romans, the Romans probably would have had it torn down. As it was, they simply ignored it. Gradually Stonehenge fell into disuse, and its original purpose was forgotten.

This rough chronological outline of the construction of Stonehenge is generally accepted today, but important questions about the monument remain: How was Stonehenge built? And why? However you look at it, the construction job would have been a formidable one. The large sarsen uprights weigh upward of fifty tons, the lintels that top them thirty tons. To many, construction feats of such magnitude seem beyond the capabilities of primitive people, and that is what led to stories about Merlin's magic. But in fact, Stonehenge is by no means unique. Primitive peoples all over the world have constructed massive monuments using only the simplest of methods and tools. What they did use, and use lavishly, was time and human energy.

With levers and ropes, two hundred men could have raised the uprights of the sarsen circle; perhaps an extra hundred would have been needed for the larger uprights of the trilithon horseshoe. Raising the thirty-ton lintels to the top of the uprights seems the most formidable task of all. We have no way of knowing exactly how it was done, but the best guess is that the lintels were raised a few feet at a time with levers. With each rise, a platform was built underneath the stone until finally, in slow stages, it was brought to the level of the top of the uprights on a series of wooden platforms. Another possibility is that earthen or wooden ramps were constructed alongside the uprights, so the lintels could be dragged up.

The sarsens were probably quarried in Marlborough Downs, about twenty miles from Stonehenge, and then dragged overland to the site. They would have been dressed or finished on site.

Carvings of dagger and axes in Stonehenge, which may indicate Mediterranean influence

Stonehenge also contains some smaller stones that are not found anywhere in the vicinity. These are the bluestones, and they weigh about five tons each. Originally, there must have been about eighty of them. They could only have come from one place, the Prescelly Mountains in Wales, 130 miles as the crow flies from Stonehenge. The easiest way to move these stones would have been by water, and the most direct route would have involved floating the stones on rafts over 215 miles of fairly safe waterways, then dragging or rolling them overland for another 25 miles. The transportation would have been a difficult and time-consuming task, but by no means an impossible or miraculous one.

The construction of Stonehenge would have demanded a great communal effort over a long period of time. Though there is a possibility that builders from more advanced Mediterranean cultures may have helped, Stonehenge is almost certainly a native project.

The final and most difficult question about Stonehenge is what was it used for. Why would a people, or in this case several different peoples, decide to put so much time and effort into building this monument? What did it mean to them? And for this question, we really have no satisfactory answers.

(BBC photograph)

Silbury Hill (top) and Avebury, two other ancient monuments in the Stonehenge area

Just about everyone who has theorized abut Stonehenge has declared that it was a temple. This is a negative judgment. It doesn't look like a castle or a fort; it has no obvious practical use at all—so therefore it must be some sort of place of worship. Druidophiles saw one of the stones as a table on which the initiates of the order eviscerated their human victims with the golden sickle. They named the stone the "Slaughter Stone." The name gives tourists a delightful chill, but it's nonsense. When Stonehenge was originally built, the so-called Slaughter Stone stood upright. It could only have served as a table since it has fallen over, sometime within the last few hundred years.

Since Stonehenge is roofless, most people have assumed that the worship that took place there had something to do with the sky, though it is possible that the monument once contained a structure roofed with wood that has long since rotted away. In the latter part of the eighteenth century, observers first noticed that if one stood in about the center of Stonehenge at sunrise on the summer solstice (June 21) and looked down the Avenue, he would see the sun rise above one of the oldest and most prominent stones in the monument, the Heel Stone. This observation was refined in 1901 by the astronomer Sir Norman Lockyer. And since that time, a huge number of other possible astronomical alignments have been theorized for Stonehenge. In 1963, astronomer Gerald Hawkins came to the conclusion that "each significant stone aligns with at least one other to point to some extreme position of the sun or moon." These alignments might have constituted an accurate way of determining the length of the year, an extremely important piece of knowledge for an agricultural society. Moreover, Hawkins said that some holes in the center of Stonehenge could have been used to calculate the cycle of eclipses. Foreknowledge of such an impressive yet apparently unpredictable event would have given the priests of Stonehenge tremendous power and authority.

Hawkins's theories got a tremendous amount of favorable publicity, and the majority of people today probably believe that Stonehenge was some sort of calendar or computer. The vast majority of professional archaeologists, however, think that Hawkins's theories are nonsense. "Tendentious, arrogant, slipshod and unconvincing" is what R.J.C. Atkinson, who spent years excavating Stonehenge, called them.

So with all the conflicting theories and lack of real solid evidence, we can only repeat what Samuel Pepys said over two hundred years ago: "God knows what their [the stones'] use was."

See also: CAMELOT; DRUIDS; THE LEY LINES

3

STRANGE

PEOPLE

$\mathbb{A}$KHNATON   Egypt under the pharaohs was the longest-lived and most stable civilization in history. From its beginnings around 3500 B.C. to its fall in 525 B.C., the civilization seems to have changed remarkably little. Even after Egypt was conquered by a series of foreigners, the new rulers were drawn to adopting the art, the customs, and even the gods of the pharaohs, right down to the time of Cleopatra.

There were individual differences, of course, there had to be, but from a distance the kings of Egypt seem to be portrayed as an endless line of stylized stone faces, all frozen in formal poses of royal and divine dignity. There is, however, one notable, even startling, exception; he is the Pharaoh Akhnaton, who ruled Egypt from 1375 to 1358 B.C.—part of the Eighteenth Dynasty, the period of Egypt's greatest glory and imperial expansion. But Akhnaton was no warrior; he was a religious reformer, or religious fanatic—the label depends on whether the labeler likes him or not. Most modern scholars like him very much indeed. He has been called the first monotheist, the first heretic, even the first individualist in history. But with equal justification he has been called an insane egoist whose religious obsession nearly ruined the nation he was supposed to rule.

He was the successor to Amenhotep III, often called "the Magnificent," a king who ruled a vast, prosperous, and generally peaceful empire. When he ascended the throne, it was under the name Amenhotep IV, but after a few years he changed his name to Akhnaton. Since the name an Egyptian king chose was often a sig-

Akhnaton (left) as imagined by Hollywood in the film The Egyptian

nificant statement of policy, a change in that name was doubly significant.

The Egyptians had a complex religion that included many gods, the chief of which was Amon, whose interests were supported by a large and powerful priesthood. The King changed his name from Amenhotep ("Amon rests") to Akhnaton ("Aton is satisfied") in honor of his new god. Unlike other Egyptian gods, which were represented in human or animal form or in some combination of the two, Aton, the new king's god, was represented as the disc of the sun, with rays, often ending in small hands, extending from it.

While Akhnaton has often been called a monotheist, this may be an exaggeration. The Aton religion certainly did not abandon the idea of the divinity of the king. But the change was nonetheless startling for a people who had been worshiping essentially the same way for some two thousand years. The king closed the temples of many of the other gods and was particularly harsh with

80

those of Amon. He tried to have Amon's name removed from all documents and temple walls. He moved his capital from Thebes, a city long identified with Amon, to a new city that he had built called Aketaton ("The City of the Horizon of Aton").

The artistic style changed radically. Probably the most famous single piece of Egyptian art, the bust of Akhnaton's wife, Queen Nefertiti, was done in the new style. But while Nefertiti is shown as a beauty, the representations of the king himself are grotesque, almost caricatures. He has a strangely elongated face, ridiculously narrow shoulders, wide hips, and a distended stomach. Instead of the stiff and ritualistic settings that kings of Egypt had been shown in for thousands of years, Akhnaton's artists often portrayed him in domestic scenes, receiving flowers from his queen or playing with his children.

It's not difficult to imagine that such radical changes deeply offended conservative and traditional Egyptian society. The changes certainly must have been vigorously opposed by the once-powerful priesthood of Amon. There is reason to believe that Aton worship never really extended beyond the royal family itself. The ordinary Egyptian probably knew little of what was happening. But Akhnaton seems to have devoted all of his energies to his new religion. Foreign affairs were neglected. Letters from ambassadors and client kings warning of deteriorating conditions on the frontier or complaining of promises unfulfilled have been found. These letters seem to have gone unanswered.

As time went on, Akhnaton seems to have increasingly lost control of, or interest in, his empire. He was isolated, even from his once-beloved Nefertiti, and may have been too ill to rule even if he had wished to.

Akhnaton's successors moved rapidly to modify or undo his religious revolution. The famous Tutankhamen, who came to the throne just a year or two after Akhnaton's death, had originally been named Tutankaton. The change from Aton back to Amon signified the triumph of the old gods over the new. However, many of the dazzling treasures of Tutankhamen's tomb were made

in the style that had grown up under Akhnaton. After Tutankhamen, Akhnaton was declared a "criminal," and his name was removed from all inscriptions. Yet a surprising, nearly amazing
amount of material from Akhnaton's period has been found. That
is due partly to the accidental survival of Tutankhamen's tomb,
but is primarily due to the fact that the city of Aketaton was
abandoned after Akhnaton's death. It was then covered with, and
largely preserved by, the sands of the desert. Thus, we know more
about Akhnaton than we do about those who tried to wipe out his
memory. But there is also a lot that we don't know; there are many
genuine mysteries of this period.

One of the most frequently discussed questions is, Did Akhnaton's religion have any effect on the development of monotheism
among the Jews? Hebrews were almost certainly present in Egypt
during Akhnaton's reign. The parallels between one of the hymns
to Aton, perhaps written by the king himself, and Psalm 104 of the
Old Testament, are startling.

The Aton Hymn

When thou settest in the western horizon of the sky,
The earth is in darkness like death
Every lion cometh forth from his den,
All serpents, they sting.
Darkness broods,
The world is in silence,
He that made them resteth in his horizon.

Bright is the earth when thou riseth in the horizon;
When thou shinest as Aton by day
Thou drivest away the darkness.
When thou sendest forth thy rays,
The Two Lands are in daily festivity.

The barques sail upstream and downstream alike.
Every highway is open because thou dawnest.
The fish in the river leap up before thee.
Thy rays are in the midst of the great green sea.

Psalm 104

Thou makest darkness, and it is night,
Wherein all the beasts of the forest creep forth.
The young lions roar after their prey,
And seek their food from God.

The sun ariseth, they get them away,
And lay them down in their dens.
Man goeth forth unto his work
And to his labor until the evening.

Yonder is the sea, great and wide,
Wherein are things creeping and innumberable,
Both small and great beasts.
There go the ships;
There is leviathan, whom thou has formed to play therein.

It is unlikely that Hebrew slaves would have been directly aware of the religious hymns of the Egyptian royal family. Egyptologist James Henry Breasted suggested that some emissary of Akhnaton may have taken the hymn to Palestine, where it became known by the later Hebrews. It seems more likely, however, that some of the lines of the hymn were taken over and applied to other gods and in that way became familiar to the Hebrews.

Still, the possible influence of Akhnaton's religion on the development of monotheism can provoke a lively argument among scholars. Where did Akhnaton's religous ideas come from? No one knows. There is some evidence of limited Aton worship during the final years of Amenhotep III, but this may have been due to the influence of the young man who was to become Akhnaton.

Did Akhnaton suffer from some sort of congenital illness that kept him from leading a physically active life and thus directed all his energies toward his religious activities? Certainly his pictures indicate that there was something wrong with him, but there is no agreement on what.

What happened to Akhnaton? The tomb that he had constructed for himself has been found open and empty. Indeed, it may never have been used. A hastily constructed tomb in the Valley of the Kings containing some relics of the period as well as a badly preserved mummy has long been the subject of controversy. Some experts who have examined the mummy believe that it shows some of the physical peculiarites that can be seen in the pictures of the king. Others insist that it is the mummy of a much younger man. Opinions remain divided.

There is one farfetched, but still intriguing, possibility. Upon the death of Akhnaton, some of his loyal followers took the mummy and hid it in a secret, as yet undiscovered tomb. From time to time, funerary objects that seem to have been destined for Akhnaton's tomb have turned up rather mysteriously in the shops of dealers in Egyptian antiquities. If tomb robbers had found an unknown royal tomb, they would probably only sell off a few items at a time to avoid arousing the suspicion of the authorities. So there is a hope—admittedly a faint one—that the final resting place of the most remarkable of all the pharaohs may still await discovery.

See also: KING TUT'S CURSE

ANASTASIA   On the night of July 16, 1918, Tsar Nicholas II and his family, along with a few of the Imperial family's loyal servants, were herded into a basement room in a house in the mining town of Ekaterinburg, where they had been held prisoner, and shot. The bodies were then taken to a disused mine, where they were burned; any bones remaining were dissolved with acid, and the ashes were thrown down the mineshaft.

The Tsar had been deposed and arrested by the Bolsheviks, but Russia was still in the grip of civil war, with the outcome very much in doubt. A living Tsar or any member of the Imperial family might serve as a focus for resistance to the revolution. Even identifiable remains might become inspiring relics to the White

Armies that were fighting to regain control of Russia. The Bolsheviks determined that all traces of the Imperial family be destroyed.

These facts were confirmed in an inquiry undertaken by the White Army. Yet without a body as physical proof of death, it was always possible for someone to turn up claiming that he or she was one of the members of the Imperial family, and had survived. Such things had happened before in history, particularly in Russian history, and inevitably it happened in the case of the Romanovs. Before long a series of self-proclaimed Romanovs came forward, each announcing that he or she had somehow escaped the mass slaughter at Ekaterinburg. Of all the Imperial family, the one whose identity was claimed more often than any other was the Tsar's youngest daughter, Anastasia. There were some fifteen claimants, but there is only one whose claim has ever really been taken seriously.

The story of the woman who claimed to be Anastasia began on the evening of February 27, 1920, in Berlin. A police sergeant rescued a young woman who had tried to drown herself in the Landwehr Canal. The woman, who was about twenty years of age, carried no identification papers and seemed profoundly depressed. She would not tell authorities who she was or give any reasons for her attempted suicide. She was placed in a mental institution and given the name Fräulein Unbekannt, "Miss Unknown." A physical examination showed that her body was covered with scars and that the bones of her upper jaw had once been broken. When she spoke at all, it was in German, but with a foreign accent.

Her condition improved slowly, and she impressed the staff at the institution with her courtesy and graciousness, but still she wouldn't tell anyone who she was. One of the other inmates had read an article about the Tsar and his family and was struck by the resemblance between the unknown woman and a picture of Anastasia. At first, the woman only became distressed when shown the photograph; months later, in the autumn of 1921, the woman declared that she was indeed Her Imperial Highness the Grand

Duchess Anastasia Nicholaievna. Thus began a long and inconclusive saga of claim and counterclaim.

The case of the young woman was taken up by the Russian émigré community. Some said they recognized her immediately as Anastasia; others insisted there wasn't the slightest resemblance and that the woman was an impostor.

The story of how she had allegedly escaped the slaughter of the Imperial family and ultimately wound up in the Landwehr Canal in Berlin came out slowly and in a disjointed, often contradictory, manner. It was later adapted into a coherent narrative by one of her émigré supporters.

She said that when she had been taken with her family to the cellar, she was not hit by the bullets but had fainted. The next thing that she remembered was waking up in a farm wagon and being smuggled out of Russia by a family called Tchaikovski. Alexander Tchaikovski, she said, had been one of the guards at Ekaterinburg but had secret Tsarist sympathies. When he found a member of the Imperial family still alive, he had her smuggled out of the house and to his family's farm.

Then, with the Tchaikovskis, she began a long odyssey across Eastern Europe. For a time, they lived off the sale of the jewels that had been sewn into her clothes. She bore Alexander Tchaikovski's child and married him, but then he was killed by Bolshevik agents. The last of the Tchaikovskis disappeared in Berlin, and then the young woman, utterly alone in the world and traumatized by her experiences of the past few years, tried to kill herself.

The woman was difficult even for her supporters. She was uncooperative, moody, often hysterical. One of the most telling arguments against her was her inability or unwillingness to speak Russian. Supporters, however, said that she spoke the language fluently in her sleep.

Then, in 1927, a private detective who had been investigating the case presented evidence that the woman who called herself Anastasia was in reality Franziska Senanokvsky, a Polish peasant girl who had been living in Berlin and who had disappeared three days before "Anastasia" was pulled from the canal. But even this could not be proved conclusively. We must remember that the events took place in a Europe that was just coming out of a terrible war that had displaced hundreds of thousands. Accurate records had often been destroyed or had never been made. Europe was full of people with no known identity.

"Anastasia's" response to the criticism was to flee to America to live with the émigré Princess Xenia, who she said was her cousin, and who believed in her genuineness. But the princess changed her attitude, and apparently money was at the core of the dispute. The woman who now called herself Anna Anderson began a legal battle to inherit the Tsar's property and thus cancel the ruling of a Berlin court that had passed the property to secondary heirs.

The case dragged on for years; indeed it was to become the longest lawsuit in history. It was not settled until 1970, when the West German Supreme Court dismissed Anna's final appeal.

After World War II, Anna had moved back to Europe and was living in a hut in the Black Forest when she again became world news as the result of a popular book, film, and many magazine articles. She returned to America to marry a professor of history and died in 1984 at the age of eighty-three, still insisting that she was the Tsar's daughter.

Anna Anderson's claim was almost certainly false, though there seems little doubt that the unstable woman had come to believe her own story. Still, there is at least a little room for speculation. Author Mollie Hardwick has pointed out: "Probably the strangest thing about the mystery of Anna's identity, a strange enough story in itself, is that there is no actual, concrete evidence that the Imperial family was ever slaughtered *en masse* . . . probably yes. . . . But reliable witnesses were never found."

The primary source for the story of the massacre was a prisoner captured by the White Army who signed a declaration, under torture, that he had seen the bodies of the Tsar and his family lying in pools of blood on the floor of the basement room. Hardwick notes that the story might have been politically motivated. "The White

Russians needed the assurance that the Romanovs had been butchered to blacken the reputation of the Bolsheviks."

Even before the woman calling herself Anastasia appeared, there were many rumors of the escape of Anastasia and possibly other members of the Imperial family. The Soviet secret police were alarmed enough by the rumors to institute searches of houses and trains. "With so much smoke," Hardwick notes, "there may very well have been fire."

CAGLIOSTRO   The man who called himself the Count Allendro de Cagliostro and who has been described by some as "one of the greatest occult figures of all time" was described by others as "the archquack of his age, the last of the great pretenders to the philosophers stone and the water of life."

Most people today believe that Cagliostro's real name was Joseph Balsamo and that he was born in Palermo, Sicily, in about 1743. His family was poor, and at the age of fifteen he was sent to a monastery for an education. There he proved to be an unruly pupil, implicated in many crimes, including the murder of an uncle who had befriended him.

During his disreputable youth, Balsamo picked up some knowledge of the forms of magic and alchemy. He used this knowledge to swindle a superstitious goldsmith named Marano out of sixty ounces of gold. When Marano found out that he had been duped, instead of going directly to the police he swore a vendetta against Balsamo. The threat was one to be taken seriously, and Balsamo left forthwith.

After that, his history becomes quite murky. He claims that he went to Arabia. By this time he was calling himself Count Cagliostro. He said he met with a mysterious Greek named Althotas and was taught the secrets of alchemy. He then went to Egypt, where he was received warmly by the priests of the various ancient temples. "The next three years of my progress were spent in

Cagliostro

the principal kingdoms of Africa and Asia. Accompanied by Althotas, and three attendants who continued in my service, I arrived in 1766 at the island of Rhodes, and there embarked on a French ship bound for Malta."

At Malta he says he was received warmly by Pinto, the Grand Master of the Knights of Malta and a famous alchemist in his own right. Then it was back to Italy, where, according to some accounts, he opened a gambling casino, while others assert that he supported himself as an alchemist and fortune teller.

During this time in Italy, he met and married Lorenza Feliciana, the intelligent and beautiful daughter of a bankrupt noble family. She also possessed "the least principal of any of the maidens in Rome," or so said Cagliostro's enemies.

The Count and Countess de Cagliostro, as the couple styled themselves, traveled throughout Europe, telling fortunes, selling alchemical secrets, raising spirits, and doing whatever itinerant magicians must do to get along. In London, Cagliostro claimed that he knew the secret of picking winning lottery tickets. But the people to whom he tried to sell this "secret" were swindlers, and everyone involved in the scheme nearly wound up in jail.

Lorenza was arrested in Paris, reputedly on Cagliostro's complaint, when she tried to run off with another man. After a few months in jail she was reconciled with her husband. Cagliostro then had the poor judgment to go to Palermo, where he was immediately arrested on a charge brought by his old enemy, goldsmith Marano, who had neither forgiven nor forgotten, but friends procured his release.

In England, Cagliostro became involved with Freemasonry, which was quite fashionable and noncontroversial. But that was in Protestant England. In Catholic France the attitude was very different, for the Freemasons had a strong anti-Catholic bias, and the Catholic clergy in turn hated the Freemasons with a passion. In Catholic lands, the order had to be genuinely secret. Under these circumstances it often assumed exotic forms; the most exotic was Egyptian Freemasonry, introduced or invented by Cagliostro.

Cagliostro was supposed to have come to know of this particular brand of Masonry after finding a "curious manuscript" in a London bookstall. The document dealt with the mysteries of Egyptian Masonry and abounded with magical and mystical references. Cagliostro also spoke of being initiated into Masonry by the mysterious Comte de Saint-Germain.

What was Egyptian Freemasonry? The question is impossible to answer because its rites were always secret and so many scandalous, though unsupported, stories were spread about it. Two things are known: first, men and women of all religions were admitted, whereas in other branches of Masonry only Protestant males could be members. The women's section was presided over by Lorenza. Second, the initiation fee was very high and probably helped to support Cagliostro and Lorenza in an opulent lifestyle. According to some stories, Cagliostro appeared at the final act of the initiation of a woman "naked as the unfallen Adam holding a serpent in his hand, and having a burning star upon his head."

According to Cagliostro, the secrets of Egyptian Freemasonry had first been revealed to the biblical prophets Enoch and Elias, but the system had been much debased until he rediscovered its original secrets. Cagliostro promised that those who became disciples of his society would be led to perfection by means of physical and moral regeneration. They would be returned to that state of perpetual youth, beauty, and innocence that mankind had been deprived of by original sin. His formula for eternal life was a curious mixture of magical theory and the medical practices of the eighteenth century.

While Cagliostro was riding high in public favor in Paris, he was implicated in a complex plot designed to steal a diamond necklace under the guise that it was being purchased by Queen Marie Antoinette. Cagliostro and his wife spent months in the Bastille before ever coming to trial.

He defended himself vigorously, giving a colorful account of his own life. The court probably didn't believe what he said, but there was no real evidence against him either. Both Cagliostro and his wife were acquitted, but they were also banished from France and forced to leave most of the wealth that they had accumulated. Fleeing to England, Cagliostro is supposed to have angrily predicted the French Revolution and the doom of all those who had persecuted him. He was urged by his friends to warn the king and queen of their fate, but Cagliostro said that they would not believe him, and besides there was no way to change what was predestined.

Cagliostro's reputation began to evaporate once he was publicly identified as Joseph Balsamo, the swindler of Palermo. He and his wife wandered from place to place, finally going to Rome in 1791—a fatal mistake, as it turned out.

When Cagliostro tried to start a lodge of his Egyptian Freemasons in Rome, he was arrested immediately. Masonry was anathema to the Roman Catholic Church, and to attempt to practice it in its most exotic form at the very heart of the Papal States was an act of rashness that bordered on the insane. He was charged with being a Freemason, a heretic, and a sorcerer, and was condemned to death. Lorenza was also arrested but was allowed to live on the condition that she "confess" and enter a convent. Ultimately, Cagliostro's death sentence was commuted by the Pope to a sentence of perpetual imprisonment in the Castle of St. Angelo. After an unsuccessful escape attempt, he was moved to the fortress of San Leo, where he was placed in a tiny rock-cut dungeon where he died in 1795.

Cagliostro remains a figure of interest to the occult-minded. There are those who claimed that he did not die in prison but escaped. Others said that as the possessor of the secret of eternal life, he could not die. In some occult philosophies, Cagliostro is one of the immortal, semidivine adepts or masters.

In 1910, a biographer of Cagliostro stated that the identification of the "Count" with Joseph Balsamo was false, based only on unsupported circumstantial evidence and Cagliostro's confession, which was extracted from him under threat of torture.

See also: SAINT-GERMAIN

JACK THE RIPPER   There have been a huge number of unsolved murders in history, some even more horrifying than those committed by Jack the Ripper. Yet the Ripper alone has attained a sort of mythic immortality. Even today, nearly a century after the events, the name, or rather title, given to the murderer is still instantly recognizable. There exists a small coterie of "Ripperologists," who constantly reexamine the evidence and every few years come up with yet another solution to the mystery. The Ripper murders have been the basis for numerous novels and films.

As in all matters of celebrity, it is not entirely possible to account for the Ripper's fame. But a good deal of it must certainly be due to the time and place of the crimes, late Victorian London, which was also the setting for the Sherlock Holmes stories.

The Ripper's murders were a shock to the Victorians, not only because violent crime of this sort was relatively rare in London, but also because they threw a spotlight on a part of life that comfortable Victorians either did not know about or pretended not to know about.

The crimes took place in the district known as Whitechapel, a rabbit warren of narrow streets, alleys, courtyards, and terraces. It was a district of warehouses, gin shops, opium dens, and brothels. Living, or rather existing, in this cesspool were the poorest of the London poor, Cockney, Jewish, and Irish. Whitechapel was a district of disease, starvation, and utter desperation.

The Ripper's crimes came as a shock in another way. The Victorians were famous for their near-denial that sex existed at all. Yet these crimes were undoubtedly sex crimes of the most vicious sort. The Ripper's crimes forced Victorians to acknowledge a whole side of life that they had worked hard and successfully to suppress.

Then, too, there was the sheer audacity of the crimes and the apparent mocking nature of the Ripper himself. He boldly dared the police to catch him, but they never did.

The Ripper's first known crime took place on the night of August 31, 1888. The victim was a forty-two-year-old prostitute named Mary Ann Nicholls. Not only had her throat been cut, but her abdomen had been slit open.

One week later, the Ripper struck again. This time the victim was forty-seven-year-old Annie Chapman, a pathetic prostitute dying of consumption. Her throat too had been cut, and as in Mary Ann's murder, she had been horribly mutilated.

This second murder made the public and police sit up and take notice. The two murders were linked with yet a third that had taken place early in August, before the murder of Mary Ann Nicholls. The victim had been another Whitechapel prostitute, but the woman had been stabbed rather than slashed, and the police doubted if she was a Ripper victim. The public, however, had no doubt that a mass murderer was loose in London. The Whitechapel district was now swarming with uniformed police looking for the killer. In addition, a group of businessmen formed the Whitechapel Vigilance Committee, and they lined up private detectives and civilian volunteers to patrol the area.

The Central News Agency in Fleet Street received a letter

written in red ink, boasting of the crimes. It was signed "Jack the Ripper." The letter may have been a demented hoax, but the nickname stuck.

On the night of September 29, the Ripper displayed not only his ferocity but his audacity. On that night, a man named Diemschutz discovered the body of a woman whose throat had just been cut. The blood was still pouring from the wound, so the murder could only have been committed moments before the discovery. Diemschutz heard footsteps, undoubtedly those of the murderer, in the darkness, but he never saw the figure. Jack the Ripper had very nearly been caught in the act. But the murderer had been interrupted and was not able to perform his usual mutilations; this apparently left some compulsion unsatisfied, for within an hour he struck again.

This "second event" was perhaps the most astonishing crime of all, for it was performed at a place called Mitre Square, which was flanked by tea warehouses guarded by a permanent watchman. In addition, the square was visited every fifteen minutes by a constable. The constable had been in the square at 1:30 A.M. and found it deserted. Fifteen minutes later, he found the hideously mutilated body of Catherine Eddowes. From the moment he had been interrupted, it had taken the Ripper a mere forty-five minutes to meet, kill, and butcher his second victim. He had done so with such skill, or luck, that a watchman sitting just a few yards away never heard a sound.

How had the murderer gotten away? It was an extremely bloody crime, and though there is some evidence that the Ripper wiped his knife on his victim's dress and washed his hands at a public fountain, he must have been covered with blood. Yet he made his escape through streets swarming with constables and members of the Vigilance Committee, as well as the usual late Saturday night crowds, apparently without ever being noticed.

The following Tuesday morning, George Lusk, chairman of the Whitechapel Vigilance Committee, received a package. It contained a letter, "from hell, Mr. Lusk," boasting of the crimes. The letter ended, "Catch me when you can, Mr. Lusk." This letter was no hoax, for the parcel also contained half a human kidney, Catherine Eddowes's kidney.

The newspapers, the police, and the Vigilance Committee received thousands of letters purporting to be from the killer—some sixteen of them may have been genuine, for they contained details of the crimes not known to the general public, and all were written in the same hand. Though the spelling and style differed considerably, they all contained the same element of ghoulish humor.

The double murder really aroused the public. The queen herself took an interest in the case. Whitechapel was so flooded with police and private investigators that they began arresting one another. But no clue to the Ripper was found. The commissioner of police admitted defeat and resigned.

It was six weeks before the Ripper committed his final, and in many respects most ghastly, crime. The victm was Mary Jeanette Kelly. Unlike the other Ripper murders, this one was not committed in the street but in Kelly's room in Miller's Court. In comparative privacy, the Ripper had several hours in which to completely butcher his victim. The scene that police found on the morning of November 10, 1888, was literally indescribable.

The Ripper's reign of terror was over, but it was only the beginning of the mystery. Within a month after the murder of Mary Kelly, the extra police were withdrawn from Whitechapel and the Vigilance Committee was told by the police to disband because its services were no longer required. Privately, members of the committee were informed that Jack the Ripper was dead; he had committed suicide by drowning himself in the Thames. The trouble was that the police never identified the murderer, and their evidence, if any, has never been made public.

The man the police apparently suspected was Montague John Druitt, a failed lawyer who drowned himself on December 3, 1883. Druitt left behind a suicide note, but if the note contained a confession we don't know about it because it has remained secret. Later investigators have built an impressive but far from conclusive case against Druitt.

There has been no lack of other suspects. Because the Ripper's mutilations were carried out with such surgical precision, many speculated that the killer was a mad physician. A prime suspect was a Russian immigrant named Michael Ostrog, a qualified physician and a raving maniac. He had been jailed several times for assault and was finally locked up for good late in November 1888. Some of Scotland Yard's investigators were sure that he was the Ripper, but there is no evidence linking him directly with the crimes.

A very popular theory is that the Ripper was a person of high rank whose identity was known, but the scandal was covered up. The most frequently mentioned candidate in this category was the Duke of Clarence, a grandson of Queen Victoria and a violently unstable character who was placed in permanent confinement sometime after the last Ripper murder. But again there is no direct evidence to link the duke to the murders.

Still another possibility is that the Ripper was a member of the police force. This would not only explain the reason the case was hushed up, but also the Ripper's extraordinary knowledge of Whitechapel geography and of the security measures taken by the police.

The daughter of Victorian psychic Robert James Lees said that her father had been able to identify the murderer in a dream. According to her father he was one of the royal physicians, who was then locked up, while her father was given a pension for his silence. The truth of this story is impossible to confirm.

Some have pointed out that the murders were committed at about the time of the full moon, or that the locations of the killing sites form a cross, indicating some sort of hideous religious ritual. Yet another theory is that Jack the Ripper was really a woman. According to British writer John Godwin, this would explain how the Ripper was able to escape so easily: "A female, even when stained with blood, wouldn't have rated a second glance during the East End panic. She could have walked anywhere at any time with the assurance that witnesses wouldn't register because all their observation faculties were focused on men! The woman con-

cerned might have been a midwife, which would account for
her knowledge of anatomy. She would be familiar—probably
friendly—with half the street girls in the district, nearly all of
whom had children. She could carry surgical knives as belonging
to her tools of trade. And she could approach any woman without
putting her on guard." Another intriguing but unprovable theory.

Unless the police files on Jack the Ripper do contain secret information, as some have charged, the case will remain the focus of
speculation forever.

KASPAR HAUSER   On May 26, 1828, a boy of about seventeen limped into the city of Nuremberg, Germany. His name, he
said, was Kaspar Hauser, but aside from that he seemed to know
only a few words and could not, or would not, tell anyone where
he came from. The boy carried no identification, but he did have
two unsigned letters.

The first, dated October 1812, was supposedly from his mother
to someone who was to take care of him. It said Kaspar's father
had been a soldier but had died. When the boy was seventeen he
was to be taken to Nuremberg to join the army, because that is
where his father had served. The second letter was from "a poor
laborer" who said that he and his wife had raised the boy in secret
and were now sending him to the army. The letter said the boy
knew nothing of his past. The letters, however, were almost certainly false, for both had been written by the same person and
were quite recent in origin.

At first, Kaspar Hauser was lodged in the Nuremberg jail; no
one knew quite what to do with him. This didn't appear to bother
the boy, who could sit for hours just staring at the wall. It was assumed that he was feebleminded, but he quickly learned to speak,
write, and eat with a knife and fork. Even after Kaspar learned to
speak, he did not shed any light on his past; indeed, his tale deep-
ened the mystery. He said that he had lived for as long as he could

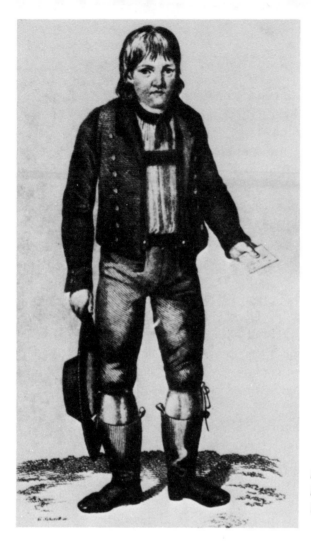

Kaspar Hauser as he first appeared in Nuremberg

remember in a dark room, so small that he had been unable even to stand up. He never saw who kept him there. Then one day he was drugged and woke up on the road to Nuremberg.

It was widely rumored that the boy was the illegitimate son of some important person. There was endless speculation as to who the "important person" might be. Kaspar received a great deal of attention, which he enjoyed, but people soon tired of him. Then one day Kaspar was found unconscious with a wound on his head. He claimed he had been attacked by a mysterious masked man.

98

The attacker was never found, and Kaspar's wound was not serious.

A wealthy Englishman who had befriended Kaspar had him moved to the small town of Ansback, where he again became the center of attention. But here too his fame was temporary. On December 14, 1833, Kaspar Hauser returned from a walk in the park dripping blood. He said he had been stabbed by a tall man in a black cloak, and he mumbled something about a purse.

In the park, the police found a silk purse with an enigmatic note inside, saying the attacker's name was "M.L.O." but not much else. It had snowed early that day, and on the scene of the alleged attack there was only one set of footprints—Kaspar's own.

Kaspar's wound proved to be far more serious than first believed, and he died within three days. His final words were "I didn't do it to myself."

Kaspar Hauser during the final years of his life

After his death, Kaspar Hauser became a folk hero. His gravestone reads, "Here lies Kaspar Hauser, Riddle of Our Time, His Birth was Unknown; his Death Mysterious." The case has been intensively investigated for well over a century, but no clue to Kaspar Hauser's true identity has ever been found.

LITTLE MISS 1565   One of the great fire disasters in American history took place on hot, muggy July 6, 1944. Thousands had gathered under the huge circus tent of the Ringling Brothers and Barnum & Bailey Circus that had been set up in a city-owned vacant lot in Hartford, Connecticut. The spectators were mostly women, children, and older men. In 1944, the young men were away at war.

At 2:40 P.M., the Flying Wallendas were in the middle of their celebrated highwire act when the band suddenly struck up the quick march "The Stars and Stripes Forever." That was a signal to the circus performers that something was wrong. Merle Evans, the bandmaster, had noticed flames creeping up the side of the tent near the main entrance.

It has been estimated that it took only about forty-five seconds for the fire to race from the entrance across the entire top of the tent. In ten minutes, only burning fragments remained on the ground, partially covering the injured and dead.

The exact cause of the fire was never determined, but the reason it had spread so quickly came out during an investigation. The main tent, 550 feet by 220 feet of twill cotton, had been waterproofed the previous winter with a very flammable mixture of white gasoline and paraffin. Under such conditions, a careless cigarette could easily have touched off the blaze. Water wagons that were supposed to be used in fighting fires turned out to be absolutely worthless.

The fire spelled the end of the "big top," that is, large circus performances held in tents in America. Six officials of the circus were charged and convicted of involuntary manslaughter, and all of them were sent to jail. The circus itself was nearly bankrupted by fines and lawsuits. Though the circus survived, shows today are usually held in auditoriums, not under tents.

The death toll from the fire was 168: 124 females, 43 males, and one whose body had been so mutilated that the sex could not be determined. A large percentage of the dead were children under nine years of age.

Seven of the victims remained unidentified after the fire. Six of these bodies were so badly burned that identification would have been difficult or impossible. The seventh, however, was different and has been the focus of wonder and speculation for decades.

The body was that of a girl about six years of age. Unlike the other victims, her features were nearly untouched by the blaze. The body was certainly easily recognizable. When after a few days the girl's body remained unclaimed and unidentified, a picture was circulated and ultimately printed by practically every newspaper and magazine in the country. The photo, while grim, should have been instantly recognizable by anyone who knew the girl. Despite this massive publicity effort, no one stepped forward.

Newspaper dubbed the unknown girl "Little Miss Nobody" or "Little Miss 1565," after her morgue number. An aura of mystery and tragedy surrounded her. After she was buried, a couple of Hartford police officers, one of whom had been assigned to crowd control at the circus on the day of the fire, began the practice of decorating her grave every Christmas, Memorial Day, and July 6, the anniversary of the fire. After the death of both the officers, the Connecticut Florists' Association continued the practice of decorating the grave. The July 6 ceremony is usually given press coverage and has become a form of memorial for all the fire victims. It also served to keep the story of Little Miss 1565 alive.

How this child could have remained unidentified after all the publicity has often been cited as one of the more puzzling incidents of modern times. Yet the mystery may have been solved, though the solution has not been revealed.

Judith Lowe, widow of one of the policemen who regularly visited the grave, wrote to *The Hartford Courant* in July 1981: "My husband, through much searching and persistence, was able to learn the identity of the child. The family asked not to be identified because of the heartache and agony they had already been through."

MADAME BLAVATSKY
There has probably never been a more colorful, more controversial character in all history than Helena Petrovna Blavatsky, or HPB, as she often signed herself. Fraud, adventuress, great spiritual teacher, she has been called all of this and much more.

She once wrote: "I am repeatedly reminded of the fact that as a public character, as a woman who, instead of pursuing her womanly duties, sleeping with her husband, breeding children, wiping their noses, minding her kitchen and consoling herself with matrimonial assistants on the sly and behind her husband's back, I have chosen a path that has led me to notoriety and fame; and that therefore I had to expect all that befell me."

Helena was born on August 12, 1831, at Ekaterinoslav in the Ukraine. Her father was a Russian army officer and the descendant of petty nobility. Her mother, an extraordinarily intelligent and independent woman, was a novelist and traced her family back to a ninth-century grand duke.

Helena was also strong-willed and independent, though of a somewhat hysterical character. At the age of sixteen she was jilted by the handsome Prince Alexander Galitsin. Her reaction was first to plunge her leg into boiling water in order to avoid attending a ball without him and then to marry a much older man, General Nikifor Blavatsky, on the rebound.

The marriage was a joke and lasted only three months. Helena fled from his house on a stolen horse and later fled Russia on a ship bound for Constantinople.

For the next twenty-five years of her life, she wandered the world, but where she went and how she lived are quite unknown. Later in life, she told many stories about these "lost" years, among them that she had visited the hidden masters in Tibet where she had been initiated into all manner of occult secrets. But there is not a single bit of hard evidence that she ever went to Tibet.

A young American traveler named Albert Leighton met HPB in about 1850 in Cairo, where she was taking lessons with a famous magician. He recalled that she could "fascinate the most indifferent man in a single interview."

At some point she began traveling with a Hungarian opera singer named Agardi Metrovitch, who remained her on-and-off companion for years. He often introduced himself as her husband, and perhaps he was, though she had never bothered to divorce General Blavatsky.

Every once in a while, HPB showed up back at her family's home in Russia, but the family was far from happy to see her and tried to keep her out of sight. However, suppressing Helena was an impossible task, and she quickly became a favorite among the younger people by holding seances and showing various tricks that she had learned in Cairo and elsewhere. Ultimately, Metrovitch turned up, which caused a great scandal.

HPB had a child, probably by Metrovitch, though she would not even admit that the child was hers. The child, who may have been ill from birth, died at the age of six. After that, Helena and Metrovitch started out for Egypt, but the ship on which they were traveling exploded, with terrible loss of life. Metrovitch was among the dead. It was said that he died saving Helena, though she never acknowledged this; indeed she later said he had been poisoned by agents of the pope.

In Cairo, Helena attempted without much success to earn a living as a spirit medium. She turned up again in Russia, then in Paris, but finally she decided to cut all ties with the past and start a new life in a new land. With virtually no funds at all, she embarked for New York in June 1873.

In the United States Helena moved quickly into spiritualist circles and while attending a series of seances in Vermont she met Colonel Henry S. Olcott, newspaperman, lawyer, and ardent spiritualist.

Olcott was an honest and upright, if rather dim, man with many important spiritualist contacts. Madame concentrated all her formidable powers of fascination on him. She flattered him and dazzled him with stories of her adventures, most of them probably untrue, for though she must have had many adventures, they may not have been the sort Olcott would have wished to hear about. She swore profusely, displayed a ferocious temper, smoked constantly (in an age when smoking was considered an infallible sign of an immoral woman), yet Olcott was charmed and ready to believe anything she said.

In 1875, for some unaccountable reason, HPB married a young Russian immigrant named Betanelly. She was accused of having been married seven times, and that figure may not be far off the

Madame Blavatsky

mark. He seems to have been a rather simple fellow, and after a few months Madame sent him away.

That same year, the faithful Olcott began getting mysterious letters from an organization calling itself The Brotherhood of Luxor. They were supposed to be a group of ancient Egyptian masters who were to lead others on the "path of wisdom." Their chief representative was HPB, and there seems little doubt that HPB herself was the author of the letters. Olcott was urged to form a study group. The circle that gathered about HPB and Olcott to discuss the various oriental mysteries adopted the name Theosophical Society.

In 1875, Madame also began writing her first book, an enormous and very confusing volume called *Isis Unveiled.* The book got no respect at all from regular reviewers, but it did pick up a following among the occult-minded section of the public.

HPB was always one for grand ceremonies, so when one of her followers, a shabby nobleman named Baron de Palm, died, she decided that his body should have a splendid public cremation. Services were held at the Masonic temple on Sixth Avenue, and members of the Theosophical Society, dressed in pseudo-Egyptian garb, attracted an enormous crowd and a lot of publicity.

Though HPB had attained a measure of celebrity in America, she was always restless. She had become interested in Indian philosophy, and one day, with Olcott in tow, she took off for India with the apparently lunatic idea of teaching Hinduism to the Hindus. For the first few months in India, poor Olcott was in a near panic; as he saw their limited financial resources melting away, he announced that they would surely starve. But he had underestimated HPB.

Her great strength had always been her audacity. She openly declared her distaste for Christianity and praised the superiority of the Hindu religion. As a result, Christian missionaries became her bitterest enemies, and the police began to suspect that she was a Russian spy out to disrupt the British rule in India. For her Theosophical Society in India, HPB proposed rules that absolutely forbade racial discrimination, a totally unique idea in the India of that day. The great mass of poverty-stricken Indians were not interested in HPB, nor was she interested in them. But she became popular among the small class of wealthy English-educated Indians. Here was a white woman who respected their religion.

Even the reserve of the British colonials began to crack under HPB's frontal assault. After a while, some of them decided to take a closer look at this odd woman and see what she could do. They were shocked by her slovenly appearance, outrageous manners, and vile language. But they were amazed by her "miracles," most of which seem to have been fairly simple parlor tricks, and attracted to the dynamism of her personality.

Once on the soil of India, the old Egyptian brotherhood seemed to be out of place. Gradually, it gave way to the Masters, or the Mahatmas. These were a group of adepts, mostly with Indian names, who were supposed to dwell in the mysterious and remote mountains of Tibet. With the Mahatma's ability to travel instantly from place to place, HPB told of many direct meetings with them. Even her followers reported occasionally seeing one or more of the Mahatmas in the flesh. Later, it was charged that the Mahatmas were really HPB's servants suitably garbed. In person, the Mahatmas rarely spoke. They were just glimpsed running across a lawn or ducking behind a bush.

When the Mahatmas wished to communicate, they usually did so by mail, and their output was prodigious. During the 1880s, Mahatma letters totaled hundreds of thousands of words every year. Even those devoted to HPB suspected that she had written the letters herself but that she had done so under the direction of the Mahatmas. Some even wondered out loud why the Mahatmas had chosen so strange and untrustworthy an individual as HPB as their associate.

Among the millions of words of the Mahatma letters are some genuinely spectacular flights of mystical fancy that rank among the best ever written. The speculations about archaic history and the cosmic future of mankind are mindboggling. Most of all, the

Mahatma letters convey a comforting message that there existed a powerful group that cared, really cared, about the most intimate and apparently trivial activities of the little group of Theosophists over whom they watched. Those who received letters were given the feeling that their training or period of testing was moving along satisfactorily and that very soon great secrets would be revealed to them.

The Theosophical Society prospered, and HPB's fame reached back to England and America, where she began picking up converts. After a lifetime of living at the edge of disaster, she had become a fairly wealthy woman, and she bought a large estate in Adyar, in the state of Madras. Here she planned to live in peace with her devoted followers and entertain visiting Theosophical notables from around the world.

In 1884, HPB was at the pinnacle of her international fame and glory, and she returned to Europe to make a triumphal tour. But back in India, she was betrayed by two of her disgruntled associates, who turned damaging evidence over to her enemies, the missionaries. The furor prompted the Society for Physical Research in London to send investigator Richard Hodgson to India to check on HPB's claims and the charges against her.

While Hodgson was inclined to be sympathetic to Theosophy, he was also a careful, patient, and resourceful investigator. He prowled around Adyar and the surrounding region for months, gently but thoroughly interrogating anyone connected with Theosophy. His report published in 1885 was overwhelming and devastating. He concluded: "For our part, we regard her [HPB] neither as the mouthpiece of hidden seers, nor as a mere vulgar adventuress; we think that she has achieved a title to permanent remembrance as one of the most accomplished, ingenious, and interesting impostors of history."

Even devout Theosophists began to regard HPB as an unstable and potentially dangerous woman; they wanted to have her shunted aside in order that the honest Olcott could become head of the Society. HPB, worn out by the attacks on her, agreed. She was hustled out of the country under an assumed name and apparently in a state of total collapse.

In Europe, she began to recover some of her old energy, and after threatening to expose everything and everybody in a lurid confession, she began what would be her masterwork, a huge volume called *The Secret Doctrine.*

When the book was finally published, critics snickered, Oriental scholars were outraged, and other scholars pointed out that the work was largely stolen from books by other occultists and crank scholars like Ignatius Donnelly's book on Atlantis. Nonetheless, *The Secret Doctrine* proved to be very popular.

In London, HPB began setting up her own branch of the Theosophical Society, which actually competed with the branch run from India by Olcott.

HPB made her greatest convert near the end of her life. That was the brilliant and energetic Annie Besant, a successful public figure who was widely respected among the intellectuals. Mrs. Besant knew all the criticisms of HPB and had rejected them. "Was the writer of *The Secret Doctrine* this miserable impostor, this accomplice of tricksters, this foul and loathsome deceiver, this conjurer with trap-doors and sliding panels? I laughed aloud at the absurdity and flung the [Hodgson] report aside with the righteous scorn of an honest nature that knows its own kind when it met them and shrank from the foulness and baseness of a lie."

HPB turned her power in the Theosophical Society over to Annie Besant, and on May 8, 1891, died quietly in Mrs. Besant's house. The anniversary of her death is called White Lotus Day and is still observed by Theosophists throughout the world.

See also: ATLANTIS; LEMURIA AND MU

THE MAN IN THE IRON MASK   In 1698, a mysterious prisoner was brought to Paris by Benigne de Saint-Mars, who had just been named superintendent of the Bastille. The prisoner was kept incommunicado and isolated in the Bastille, and whenever he was seen he wore a velvet, not an iron, mask. The mysterious prisoner died in 1703 and was buried in the cemetery of St. Paul under the name Marchioli. Before the prisoner had been brought to the Bastille, he had apparently served time in the Pignerol prison in Italy and on the island of St. Marguerita, near Cannes.

That is all that is authentically known about the mysterious prisoner. About fifty years after his death, Voltaire popularized the story in his book about the period of Louis XIV. It was Voltaire who appears to have originated or at least spread the erroneous idea that the prisoner wore an iron, rather than a cloth, mask.

The story of the Man in the Iron Mask reached its fullest flowering in about 1800. It was then that the legend arose that the mysterious prisoner was really the legitimate Louis XIV. According to the story, the throne had been occupied by a usurper, an illegitimate son of Louis's mother and the powerful adviser Cardinal Mazarin. A further elaboration of this legend held that the man in the mask married and fathered a child while in prison. This child was spirited off to Corsica and later became the grandfather of Napoleon Bonaparte.

Probably most people have heard of the Man in the Iron Mask through the novel by Alexander Dumas, *père.* In 1848, the prolific and popular Dumas published an historical romance entitled *Le Vicomte de Bragelonne;* though the book and the films adapted from it are sometimes called *The Man in the Iron Mask.* Dumas contended that the prisoner was really the twin brother of Louis, and that he had been imprisoned in order to save France from a struggle for succession. Like most of Dumas's historical novels, this one mixes fact and fancy freely.

A more mundane, but far more probable, explanation is that the prisoner was really Count Ercole Antonio Mattoli, a confidential secretary of the Duke of Mantua and a spy. He had been arrested for selling the details of secret and delicate negotiations between Mantua and France to another country. Count Mattoli was known to have been imprisoned at Pignerol and moved several times. He is believed to have died in 1703, the same year as the masked prisoner. And the prisoner, you remember, was buried under the name Marchioli, close enough to Mattoli.

But reasonable as this explanation seems, there are objections. The most telling is that the arrest and imprisonment of Count Mattoli was well known, and there seems to be no reason to have hidden his face behind a mask.

A theory that has become rather popular in recent years is that the masked prisoner was a servant named Eustache Dauger de Cavoye. One version of the theory holds that Dauger had served as an intermediary between Louis XIV and Charles II of England, that he was in possession of information that would have severely embarrassed the French government, and that he was deemed untrustworthy by that government.

A more exotic, and thus attractive, theory is that Dauger was the real father of King Louis XIV. Though the prisoner was officially reported to have been only forty-five when he died and would have thus been too young to be the father of the king, the age at time of death, like the name, may have been falsified.

It was widely suspected that Louis XIII was impotent. According to this theory, the young servant was chosen by Cardinal Richelieu to impregnate the queen and thus insure a smooth succession. The servant was then paid a sum of money and sent off to a remote place, probably Canada, but later he returned and asked for more money. At this point, Louis XIV may have decided to have his potentially troublesome father put someplace where he could cause no further trouble. But of course the whole affair would have to be handled in the greatest secrecy; hence the mask for the prisoner.

Though the theory seems farfetched, it would explain why the prisoner was treated in such an unusual manner. Generally, persons whom the king wished to be rid of were simply killed. But the man in the mask was treated well for a prisoner and allowed to die a natural death.

The true identity of the man in the mask will probably remain forever unknown.

NICOLAS FLAMEL   Of all the alchemists who are reported
to have succeeded in their quest to make gold, the most famous
and certainly the most well documented is Nicolas Flamel.

Flamel was a public scribe or notary who lived in Paris in the
fourteenth century. He had a good business, had married a
wealthy wife to whom he was devoted, and seemed to have had no
particular interest in alchemy. Then one night he had a strange
dream. An angel gave him a book and said, "Flamel, look at this
book. You will not in the least understand it, neither will anyone
else; but a day will come when you will see in it something that no
one else will see."

Flamel had almost forgotten the dream when in 1357 an unknown manuscript vendor offered him the very book of which he
had dreamed. It was a book filled with strange alchemical symbols
and words in an ancient language that he could not understand.
On the first leaf of the book there was a Latin inscription in gold
letters saying the book was written by Abraham the Jew and that
anyone who read it would be cursed "unless he were Sacrificer or
Scribe."

As a scribe, Flamel felt exempted from the curse. From the inscription, Flamel learned that it was an alchemical text that contained the formula used by the Jews to make gold to pay tribute to
the Roman Empire. Unfortunately, as the dream had foretold, he
did not in the least understand the rest of the book. And the more
he studied it, the less he understood.

He began making discreet inquiries among the alchemists of
Paris and began his own alchemical experiments. He labored for
twenty-one years without any success at all.

The patient Flamel was finally getting discouraged when he
suddenly hit on an idea. Since the book had been prepared by
Abraham the Jew, perhaps Jews would understand it. At that time
there were a large number of Jewish scholars in Spain. So Flamel
went to Spain and spent a year frequenting Spanish synagogues, to

Nicolas Flamel

no avail. However, on his return journey Flamel met a converted Jew named Maitre Canches, a scholar of the Cabala. Flamel had made copies of some of the drawings in his book, and Maitre Canches recognized them as coming from the *Asch Mezareph* of the Rabbi Abraham. This was a book that Cabalists thought had been lost. Though Maitre Canches died before he actually saw the book, he had given Flamel enough hints that he was able to work out the secret for himself.

Flamel recorded that on January 17, 1382, he was able to change half a pound of lead into pure silver. He then went ahead to prepare the Great Elixir, and on April 25 he transmuted a half-pound of lead into "pure gold, most certainly better than ordinary gold, being more soft and pliable."

Flamel wasn't greedy; he only accomplished this transmutation two times more in his life, and he continued to live in the same frugal, pious manner as before. His beloved wife died in 1397, and Flamel spent the rest of his life writing about alchemy and doing good works. When he died on March 22, 1417, he left behind a notable record of endowments to churches, hospitals, and other charitable institutions.

After his death, neighbors ransacked his property looking for "the secret"; they didn't find it, but two centuries later people were still searching, still without success.

Supporters of alchemy have pointed to the considerable fortune that Flamel amassed as proof that he could indeed make gold. However, his fortune is not beyond what might have been accumulated by a successful but frugal scribe with a rich wife.

That both Flamel and his wife actually died, there is no doubt. His tombstone has been found, as has his extremely detailed will. Yet there is also a tradition that in addition to transmuting gold, the alchemist also made the Elixir of Life, and that he and his wife attained immortality. They were reportedly seen alive and well in India in the seventeenth century. In the mid-eighteenth century, a number of people testified that the pair had attended the opera in Paris. However, they have not been heard from recently.

See also: ALCHEMISTS

POPE JOAN   It is inevitable that any institution as ancient, powerful, and shrouded in secrecy as the papacy would find itself the subject of fantastic rumors. One of the most persistent is that there once was a woman pope, called Pope Joan.

The speculation centers on the poorly documented reign of Pope John VIII (854–856). According to the most widely circulated version of this tale, the woman who was to become pope was the daughter of a British missionary to the Saxons who had become a nun. She fell in love with a monk, and in order to continue her clandestine affair she donned the robes of a monk herself. Being exceptionally clever, she soon rose in ecclesiastical ranks and found herself in Rome as a religious teacher, then as secretary to the reigning Pope Pius IV. On his death she was elected pope. But her passions could not be restrained, and she became pregnant, by either her bodyguard or a cardinal, according to different versions of the tale. Pope Joan hid her pregnancy beneath her robes, but she gave birth before an astonished crowd either while delivering a litany or when she was actually on the way to her coronation. She and the baby were immediately beaten to death by an enraged mob. Though some versions of the tale hold that the baby survived and will one day emerge as the Antichrist in the Final Days, there is not a shred of historical evidence to support this fantastic rumor. It seems to be entirely an invention of antipapists. The card called "the Female Pope" in the tarot deck doubtless derives from this legend. Many modern tarot decks call the card "the High Priestess."

There is another rumor that holds that the papacy is in its last days and that this was predicted by an obscure twelfth-century Irish saint who was regarded as a prophet by his contemporaries. Saint Malachy, named for the Old Testament prophet Malachi, was born in Ireland around 1094. He acquired the reputation of prophet during his own lifetime and went to Rome, where he was received with honor by Pope Innocent II. Malachy was also apparently a friend of the famous St. Bernard of Clairvaux, and it was for Bernard that he wrote the prophecies that describe each pope from 1143 up to what may be the end of the twentieth century, when the papacy itself is to come to an end.

As with most prophetic writings, those of Malachy are obscure and open to a wide variety of interpretations. Indeed, the authenticity of the prophecies themselves is open to question. According to one interpretation, only two more popes will sit on the Throne of St. Peter; the last one will assume the name carefully avoided by all popes to date: he will be called Peter of Rome. Peter will become Pope; "during the last persecution of the Holy Roman Church he shall feed the sheep amidst great tribulations and when these are passed, the City of the Seven Hills shall be utterly destroyed and the awful Judge will judge the people." This prophecy dovetails neatly with interpretations of other prophecies and the statements of individuals today who claim prophetic powers that the world will come to an end, or at least something very cataclysmic will happen, by the end of this century, the end of the second millennium.

Some of the more recent rumors that have surrounded the papacy are that Pope John Paul I, who died after a reign of only a few months, was murdered by enemies within the church—either right or left wing, depending on which version of the rumor you care to listen to. Another is that the present Pope, John Paul II, is really the Antichrist, appointed through Soviet influence, and his actions will lead to World War III and the end of the world.

See also: THE PROPHECIES OF FATIMA

R AYMOND PALMER   Raymond A. Palmer, or RAP as he usually signed his editorials, was the original UFO buff. Some people think he virtually created the whole UFO phenomenon. That's something of an exaggeration, but his influence on the early history of the subject was enormous, yet his name is almost forgotten, even by people deeply interested in UFOs. Many of them want to forget him.

The reason for this paradox may lie in Palmer's wild and unpredictable imagination and in his utter scorn for journalistic respectability. He was likely to say or do practically anything. Then there was his sense of humor. He even left his admirers with the uncomfortable feeling that he might be pulling their leg. Shortly before his death, he told an audience of UFO buffs in Chicago not to believe everything he said.

Childhood injuries had left Palmer hunchbacked and dwarfed. Isolated from other children, he turned to reading pulp fiction, particularly science fiction, and became one of the leading figures in the very active science fiction fandom of the 1920s. Soon he began grinding out his own pulp fiction and was paid at the going rate of a penny a word.

In 1929, Palmer was made editor of a struggling science fiction pulp magazine called *Amazing Stories*, which writer John Keel called "the very worst" of the dozen or so science fiction magazines then available on the newsstands. *Amazing Stories* was filled with stories and articles, often written by Palmer himself under a variety of pseudonyms. Palmer nursed the magazine to feeble financial health and won a band of devoted readers.

Early in the 1940s, Palmer received a long, rambling letter from a Pennsylvania welder named Richard S. Shaver purporting to reveal the "truth" about an evil subterranean race he called the Deros. Palmer rewrote the letter as a story entitled "I Remember Lemuria" and ran it. The results were fantastic and thoroughly unexpected. Mail from readers who said that they too remembered Lemuria poured in, and the circulation of *Amazing Stories* shot up. Shaver's rather paranoid recollections about the evil Deros and how they controlled life on earth struck a chord among that large number of Americans who have the paranoid feeling that they are being controlled by some evil force. They hear strange voices in their heads; so did Shaver. He seemed to be saying it for all of them, and they loved it.

Palmer bought a whole stack of Shaver's material, rewrote it, and began running it as "The Great Shaver Mystery"; detractors began calling it "The Great Shaver Hoax." Though written in fictional form and in Palmer's lurid pulp magazine prose, the stories were supposed to be true.

Among the many things discussed and illustrated in the long-running Shaver/Palmer series were round aerial craft, so that when the flying saucer era began, Ray Palmer and his readers were psychologically ready for it. That era began in 1947 with a reported flying saucer sighting by Kenneth Arnold. Others had reported seeing strange objects in the sky before, but Arnold's sighting somehow caught the attention of the press.

In 1948, in conjunction with Curtis Fuller, Palmer started *Fate* magazine, a publication devoted to the exploration of strange phenomena. The first issue contained a bylined article by Arnold defending his flying saucer sighting from criticism and ridicule.

Palmer's relationship with the publishers of *Amazing Stories* became strained at about that time, and he left to devote his time entirely to his own publishing ventures like *Fate*.

During this same period Palmer became involved in the most controversial incident in his career, the Maury Island hoax. Two men, Harold Dahl and Fred Crisman, claimed that they had seen a flock of flying saucers while boating off Maury Island, near Tacoma, Washington, in June 1947. They got in touch with Palmer, who sent none other than Kenneth Arnold himself out to investigate. Arnold decided that the story was too big for him, and he contacted the Air Force. Two intelligence officers were dispatched to interview Crisman and Dahl. On their return flight, their plane crashed and both were killed.

An investigation of the crash found nothing out of the ordinary and concluded that the entire Maury Island incident was a hoax. The investigation also concluded that Palmer had actually encouraged the hoax—he had known Crisman before the "incident" and thus was at least indirectly responsible for the death of the officers. Palmer put a different interpretation on the matter. He hinted darkly at some sort of "cover-up" and "conspiracy" and said he wanted "no more blood on his hands." This was the first, or one of the first, times that the "conspiracy of silence" theme was injected into ufological thinking.

In the early 1950s, Palmer moved to a small town in Wisconsin, sold his interest in *Fate,* and started his own publishing company. He continued to push UFO and hollow earth stories and published a bewildering variety of books and periodicals, many on occult or other "borderland" subjects. Most of Palmer's ventures were only marginally profitable. His most successful and longest-lived periodical was *Flying Saucers.* Although this magazine never had a circulation that exceeded a few thousand, it was for many years the largest-circulation American magazine dealing exclusively with the subject of UFOs. Palmer kept interest in the subject alive when no one else would.

Early on, Palmer himself had abandoned the mundane idea that UFOs came from outer space. He actively promoted the theory that they came from the Shaverian underground world and that they flew out of the hollow earth through holes in the North and South Poles. He also created the myth that Admiral Richard E. Byrd had explored the hollow earth during one of his polar expeditions.

Though the UFOs-from-the-hollow-earth idea never really

caught on, Palmer's influence on the popularity of UFOs in America and around the world was enormous. He was the subject's earliest and most consistent publicist. Says John Keel, he converted UFO reports "from a Silly Season phenomenon to a *subject.*"

What did Ray Palmer really believe about UFOs, the hollow earth, and all the rest? He once asked an admirer, "What if I told you it was all a joke?"

Palmer died on August 15, 1977. While some of those who had been his followers hinted there was something mysterious about his death, his family firmly asserted that it was from perfectly natural causes.

See also: THE HOLLOW EARTH; UFOs

R OBIN HOOD   The two great legendary figures of early England have received vastly different treatment in the modern world. King Arthur, if he existed at all, lived during the Dark Ages of the sixth century. Yet *Debrett's Peerage* not only accepts the reality of Arthur but tries to tie him directly to the present monarch. Robin Hood is a much later figure, probably thirteenth century, a time when records were much better. The tales of Robin are nowhere near as fantastic as those that have grown up around Arthur. Yet *The Dictionary of National Biography* in Britain ran an entire article on Robin Hood insisting that he never existed.

The difference in attitude toward these two figures may have as much to do with social class in Britain as with history. Arthur was a king, and Robin was a robber. He was a well-mannered, well-meaning robber, a man who mainly robbed greedy monks. While Robin Hood might poach a few of the king's deer, he was no rebel and remained steadfastly loyal to the monarchy. But when all was said and done, he was still a robber and a fairly lowborn one at that.

There have been attempts to identify Robin as Robert Earl of

Huntington, who had been done some sort of injustice and was forced to flee into the forest and take up the life of an outlaw. That idea first became popular in the seventeenth century. By the eighteenth century, Dr. William Stukeley, the eccentric parson and antiquary who did so much to place the Druids incorrectly at Stonehenge, had come up with a whole pedigree for the outlaw Earl. Unfortunately for Stukeley's theory, there never was a Robert Earl of Huntington, and the pedigree constructed for him was completely fictitious. Says historian J. C. Holt in his book *Robin Hood*, "The pedigree is false and the more general claim to nobility fictitious. In early ballads Robin was yeoman, nothing more, nothing less."

For candidates for the original Robin Hood, Professor Holt is confronted with an embarrassment of riches. He found that the earliest of the Robin Hood stories came from the area of York, well to the north of Sherwood Forest, Robin's legendary haunt, and of Nottingham, home of Robin's greatest adversary, the Sheriff of Nottingham.

There was, for example, Robert Hode, tenant of the archbishopric of York, who fled the jurisdiction of the king's justices at York in 1225. There was an entire family called Hood established in the area in the thirteenth century. They either brought forth the original Robin Hood or adopted the Robin Hood traditions into their family. There was even a family with the surname Robynhod. Holt concludes, "It is more likely than not that . . . the original of the story was a real person."

As the story developed, details from popular romances about other real-life outlaws and purely fictional elements were added.

See also: CAMELOT

SAINT-GERMAIN   The Comte de Saint-Germain never claimed that he possessed the Elixir of Life or that he had already

The Comte de Saint-Germain

lived several hundred years, but if others chose to believe such stories, he did not contradict them.

No one knows for certain who Saint-Germain was, though we can be fairly certain that his name was not Saint-Germain and that he was not a count. The best guess is that he was a Portuguese Jew and that he was born around the year 1710.

Nothing at all is known of his early life. Around the year 1740, he seems to have been arrested in London as a spy. Somewhat later he turned up in Germany selling his Elixir of Life. In around 1748, a French aristocrat visiting Germany met him, was intrigued, and induced him to settle in Paris.

Saint-Germain was a man of great charm and persuasiveness. He became a popular figure at the gatherings of the rich and well-born. Quite soon, the most incredible stories about him began to make the rounds of Parisian society. At one dinner party, so it was said, Saint-Germain was speaking with easy familiarity of King Richard the Lionhearted and of some of the conversations they had had while in Palestine together during the Crusades. When some of the other guests were openly skeptical, Saint-Germain turned to his valet, who was standing behind his chair, and asked him to confirm the truth of the story.

"I really cannot say, sir," the servant replied. "You forget, sir, I have only been five hundred years in your service!"

120

"Ah! True," said Saint-Germain. "I remember now—it was a little before your time."

On one occasion, the king's mistress, Madame de Pompadour, complained, "But you do not tell us your age, and yet you pretend you are very old. The Countess de Gergy, who was, I believe, ambassadress at Vienna some fifty years ago, says she saw you there exactly the same as you now appear."

"It is true, Madame," replied Saint-Germain. "I knew Madame de Gergy many years ago."

"But according to her account, you must be more than a hundred years old."

"That is not impossible, but it is much more possible that the good lady is in her dotage."

When Pompadour pressed Saint-Germain to give the king some of his celebrated elixir, he replied, "Oh, Madame, the physicians would have me broken on the wheel, were I to think of drugging his majesty."

Saint-Germain treated his reputation for great wealth the same way he treated his reputation for great age—he made no specific claims, but if people chose to believe that he possessed the alchemical secret of transmuting gold, or of making precious stones out of ordinary ones, he would not deny it.

Once he showed Pompadour and her ladies a great quantity of sparkling stones. Pompadour's practiced eye was quick to observe that almost all of the flashy stones were fakes. But amid this collection of paste jewels he displayed a superb genuine ruby. He also produced a small jeweled cross of good workmanship but moderate value. When one of Pompadour's ladies expressed admiration for the little cross, Saint-Germain presented it to her, professing to disdain all wealth. So it seems that by a clever mixture of real and false jewels, Saint-Germain managed to sustain his reputation for limitless wealth. How he really did make his money is something of a mystery. He may have made some by selling his Elixir of Life. Some may have come from his activities as a spy. Mostly, though, it appears he lived off the generosity of his many wealthy friends.

Around the year 1670, Saint-Germain left Paris, for political reasons some said. From that time onward, stories of his comings and goings are vague and unreliable. It was rumored that he was in London, in St. Petersburg, and in Germany. He seems to have spent his final days at the court of his friend the Prince of Hesse-Cassel, dying there in the year 1782.

What was the Comte de Saint-Germain? Many believe he was nothing more than an extremely charming and clever fraud. Even occultists who revere his memory admit that there was much of the actor about him. Yet his life was so shrouded in mystery that there is still room for doubt. His true identity remains unknown. The date and place of his birth are completely unknown, and the date of his death is uncertain. There were those who claimed, and still claim, that Saint-Germain never died. From time to time during the past two centuries, people have turned up saying that they have met Saint-Germain or that they actually were Saint-Germain. Most commonly, it is claimed that Saint-Germain has entered that vague world of semidivine and immortal masters or adepts.

Saint-Germain is reputed to have founded a secret society called the Temple of Mystery. (His less successful and younger contemporary, the Count of Cagliostro, claimed to have been initiated into this society.) After the long and difficult initiation period was completed, Saint-Germain passed on to his new followers the "great secret." The "secret" was that Saint-Germain and his Elixir of Life were fakes.

Lives of the Alchemical Philosophers states, "Several essential precepts were enjoined upon them, among others that they must detest, avoid and calumniate men of understanding but flatter, foster and blind fools; that they must spread abroad with much mystery and intelligence that the Comte de Saint-Germain was five hundred years old, and that they must make gold, but dupes before all."

It is highly doubtful that the very careful Saint-Germain, whatever his private thoughts, would ever have been so candid. But it makes a nice story.

See also: CAGLIOSTRO

4

WEIRD

TALENTS

DOWSING   Probably the most widely used magical or semi-magical practice in the world today is dowsing, also called divining or witching. Even today in many rural communities in America, the water dowser remains a familiar figure. Traditionally, the water dowser grips a forked stick in his hands and walks up and down over an area until he passes a spot where the stick, apparently of its own volition, moves suddenly—the movement may be up or down, depending on the dowser. This is the place where water is to be found closer to the surface and therefore is the best place in which to drill a well. Since the deeper the well, the more expensive it is, finding a spot where water is close to the surface can be a real economic boon.

Dowsing, though not only for water, goes back a long way in history. Some say that water dowsing goes back to the biblical story in which Moses strikes a rock with his rod and water pours forth. But this is almost certainly a later interpretation, and there is no solid indication that dowsing in any form was practiced in biblical times. Actually, the first real records of dowsing only go back to the sixteenth century, though it was clearly a well-established practice in Germany at that time. Dowsing spread from Germany throughout Europe and to the United States. Dowsing is also widely practiced in Asia and Africa, but whether these traditions developed independently of Europe, or are all derived from a single, more ancient tradition, is unknown.

In the sixteenth century, the forked sticks were used most frequently to locate metal ores. Some dowsers would begin the search

Dowsing for ore from Agricola's treatise on metallurgy

with these words: "In the name of the Father, Son and Holy Ghost, how many fathoms is it from here to the ore?" Dowsers may have felt compelled to use the religious formula to protect them from the wrath of the Church, which tended to look upon any magiclike activity as witchcraft. Indeed, during periods of witchcraft hysteria dowsers were in real peril.

Aside from the Church, dowsers had other opponents. Paracelsus, who held many highly unorthodox theories of his own, commented that if the dowser's stick is right once, it deceives ten or twenty times. George Agricola, who wrote a pioneering sixteenth-century treatise on metallurgy, said of dowsing: "Among

126

miners there are many great arguments about the forked twig, for some say it is of the greatest use to them in discovering veins while others deny this."

By the eighteenth century, the religious prohibitions against dowsing had disappeared, but the argument over its effectiveness has continued to the present day.

A survey of water dowsing in America found that it was most common in areas where water was hardest to find and where the farmer faced the most uncertainty. Science is often of little help in telling the farmer the best place to sink a well, so many farmers seem to feel that they have little to lose by calling in a dowser. One country farm official in Iowa commented, "Not too many have faith in witching [dowsing], but people use it in the absence of any other method of locating water."

Most of those who have studied rural dowsers feel that the vast majority of them are honest and sincere and believe deeply in what they are doing, though they have no explanation as to why the dowsing works. As practical-minded people, they say that all they care about is finding water. Some will offer a religious explanation—for example, that the power of dowsing has been passed down from Moses in some way. A few dowsers and their supporters have developed elaborate theories about electromagnetic waves affecting either the muscles of the dowser or the stick itself. Some use the scientific-sounding name *radiesthesia* to describe the technique.

The orthodox explanation for dowsing, assuming that the dowser is not a deliberate faker, is that the stick moves because of an unconscious and involuntary tightening or loosening of the muscles on the part of the dowser. The dowser is usually familiar with the area in which he is working. Underground water may betray its presence by clues on the earth's surface, such as certain rocks, the color of the soil, or the shape of the ground. After years of experience, the dowser may have become an expert at recognizing these subtle clues, even though he is not consciously aware of them.

When the dowser is seeking water, he walks around until the clues indicate a good place to drill. While walking, he grips the rod very tightly. All it takes is a slight change in the tension of his muscles to cause the rod to shake or point up and down. If the clues are right, the unconscious feeling "water is here" is signaled to the muscles of the dowser's hands, and "miraculously" the rod point to the spot.

The dowser may be as good as a geologist in finding water at a given location. There is also the fact, that no matter where you drill, you are likely to strike water eventually, so in a sense the dowser is rarely absolutely wrong. A variety of attempts to conduct controlled tests with dowsers has yielded ambiguous results, and the scientific community continues to seriously doubt that dowsers possess any unique powers.

Searching for water with a forked stick is only the most familiar form of dowsing or divining. Many other objects are used as divining or dowsing rods—everything from a wire coat hanger to a pendulum. Some diviners use no rod or pendulum at all but simply hold their hands out in front of them and wait for their muscles to experience a sudden involuntary downward pull. Nor is water the only thing searched for. Dowsers have looked for metal ores, oil, lost objects, buried treasure, and underground pipelines. During the Vietnam war there were widely published photos of U.S. soldiers trying to locate buried mines using a large pair of pliers as a divining rod.

There are also those who search for more esoteric things with the aid of a pendulum or divining rod. A popular party game is to hold a pendulum above the hand of a girl and a boy. It is supposed to make a circular motion over the girl's hand, and swing back and forth over the boy's (or vice versa). Some people take this quite seriously and have tried to determine the sex of an unborn baby by holding the pendulum over a pregnant woman's abdomen.

T. C. Lethbridge, an Englishman, was one of the most enthusiastic and sophisticated exponents of the use of a divining rod or pendulum to find all sorts of things. He believed that he could locate buried archaeological objects with a pendulum. And he used a divining rod to test for unknown forces that might exist within some of Britain's ancient megalithic monuments. At the Merry Maidens, a stone monument built about the same time as Stonehenge, his pendulum began to circle so wildly that it was practically horizontal to the ground.

Some researchers have even claimed to have successfully used the pendulum to detect the presence of ghosts or other unseen entities and supernatural forces.

See also: THE LEY LINES

DUNNE'S TIME THEORIES   In 1927, an interesting and influential book on prophetic dreams called *An Experiment with Time* was published in London. The author was J. W. Dunne, one of England's first pilots and aircraft builders. In his book, Dunne recorded soberly and without any attempt at sensationalizing some thirty years of experience that he believed he had had with prophetic dreams.

The first significant dream that Dunne recalled took place in 1899. He was staying at a hotel, and he dreamed of arguing with the waiter over the correct time. Dunne said that in the dream the time was half-past four in the morning, while the waiter insisted it was half-past four in the afternoon. Dunne woke up and looked at his watch. It had stopped at half-past four. He assumed that his watch had stopped at half-past four the previous afternoon and that he had subconsciously remembered this and had dreamed about it. So he wound his watch without resetting it, because there was no clock in his bedroom and he did not know the correct time. When he went downstairs the next morning, he made for the nearest clock so that he could set his watch correctly. To his complete surprise he found that his watch had lost only a few minutes—approximately the time between the dream itself and when he had wound his watch. Dunne then realized that his watch had stopped at four-thirty that morning, at the exact moment when he was dreaming about an argument over the time.

That was not a startling dream; it was hardly what one would call a prophetic dream at all, but it was only the beginning of J. W. Dunne's career as a prophetic dreamer.

From that point on, Dunne believed that he foresaw all manner of future events, large and small, in his dreams. Perhaps the most spectacular episode took place in 1902 when he was fighting with the British Army in South Africa. At his isolated outpost, mail and newspapers reached him only occasionally.

One night, Dunne said he had "an unusually vivid and rather unpleasant dream." He was standing on an island where the ground was beginning to crack beneath his feet. From the cracks, "jets of vapour were spurting upward." He realized that the island was in "imminent peril from a volcano."

In his dream Dunne gasped, "It's the island! Good Lord, the whole thing is going to blow up!" He felt that the island's four thousand inhabitants would be killed if they were not evacuated. The dream island was administered by the French, and at the moment of waking, Dunne dreamed he was entreating a certain Monsieur le Marie, "Listen! Four thousand people will be killed unless . . ."

When the next batch of papers arrived, the headlines on *The Daily Telegraph* read, VOLCANO DISASTER IN MARTINIQUE. This was the eruption of Mount Pelée, one of the worst natural disasters of the twentieth century. Martinique was a French-controlled island, but the total of those killed was forty thousand, not four thousand as Dunne had dreamed.

Of this he wrote: "The number of people supposed to be killed was not, as I had maintained throughout the dream, 4,000 but 40,-000. I was out by a nought [zero]. But, when I read the paper, I read in my haste that the number was 4,000; and, in telling the story subsequently, I always spoke of that printed figure as having been 4,000; and I did not know it was really 40,000 until I copied out the paragraph fifteen years later."

Dunne did not believe that he had actually foreseen the eruption of Mount Pelée, which had taken place before his dream. Rather, the dream seemed to be a premonition of reading a newspaper story about the disaster. He did not read of the disaster until several days after his dream.

The ability to dream of future or distant events was not regarded by Dunne as a special gift to him alone. He believed that everyone possessed the same ability if only they were aware of it. All one needed to do, according to Dunne, was to record one's dreams immediately upon waking; otherwise they would be forgotten or become garbled. After teaching his system to a small circle of relatives and friends, Dunne claimed that they too were able to see the future in their dreams.

Dunne's book was an immediate success. Although there was no proof that he actually had prophetic dreams as he claimed, people were inclined to take him at his word. He was a respected man with a solid technical background, and apparently a man who did not have a mystic or occult orientation. After Dunne's death in 1949, however, his widow published his private notes, which revealed that he was more of a mystic than he had publicly acknowledged. In his original watch dream, his notes indicate that it was an angelic choir that had awakened him and implored him to look at his watch. This was a fact left out of the original account. He had been convinced since childhood that he had a vital message for the world. A good part of Dunne's appeal was the public perception that he was a hardheaded nonmystical individual, and these revelations drove away many former admirers.

In 1922, the Society for Psychical Research decided to undertake a series of experiments based on Dunne's dreaming system. The tests were not successful. Dunne, who appears to have been utterly sincere in his belief, then volunteered to be tested himself. The results were discouraging, for of seventeen dreams that he recorded during the period, only one might be listed as being in any way prophetic, and this required stretching a point.

Interest in the possibility of prophetic dreaming continues, however, and in recent years highly sophisticated equipment has been used to try to more accurately record the contents of dreams. The results of these tests, however, remain ambiguous and open to a variety of interpretations.

In order to account for his prophetic dreams, Dunne developed a complex and sometimes nearly incomprehensible theory about "serial time." He concluded that we have different "selves" that live in different levels of time. Self No. 1 exists in "this world," stuck in the flow of Time No. 1. But Self No. 2 exists in another kind of time, a more flexible time that can rise above Self No. 1 and foresee the future.

In his book *Mysteries*, Colin Wilson explains some of Dunne's theory of multiple selves and time. "Self No. 1 is the 'me' who looks out through my eyes when I stare blankly out of a window; he is a mere observer, nothing more. Self No. 2 takes over when I sit up and pay attention, selecting what interests me and ignoring other things. This is undoubtedly a higher self than Self No. 1, as I realize if I try to write in a room full of children; it requires tremendous effort to focus on what interests me, and prevent Self No. 1 from taking over again. Then there is Self No. 3, the detached 'I,' who seems to be able to look down coldly on the 'observer' and the 'selector.' It is even more difficult to preserve this Olympian attitude for more than a split second at a time."

One of Dunne's more influential disciples was the writer J. B. Priestley. In his book *Man and Time*, Priestley argued that it was possible to alter the future if one had foreknowledge. Thus, Self No. 1 could dream about the future in Time No. 1. But by paying attention to dreams, one could rise to Self No. 2 and exist in Time No. 2, where free will is possible and where a change in the course of events is therefore also possible.

EINSTEIN'S BRAIN   When the great scientist Albert Einstein died on April 18, 1955, an autopsy was performed by Dr.

Thomas Harvey of Princeton, New Jersey, where Einstein spent his last years. Einstein's body was cremated, but his famous brain was removed and carefully preserved for study. Several sections of the brain were given to researchers around the country. However, for many years no findings on the brain study were published. Dr. Harvey moved on to a biological testing laboratory in Wichita, Kansas, and people began to wonder what had happened to Einstein's brain.

A reporter from *The New Jersey Monthly Magazine* tracked Dr. Harvey down in 1978, and the doctor offered to show the reporter the sections of the brain that remained in his possession. The doctor then reached into a cardboard cider box in the corner of his office and pulled out a Mason jar holding the specimen.

"I had risen to look into the jar, but now I was sunk in my chair, speechless. My eyes were fixed upon that jar as I tried to comprehend that these pieces of gunk bobbing up and down had caused a revolution in physics and quite possibly changed the course of civilization. *There it was!*"

Dr. Harvey, who has since moved to Weston, Missouri, said that on first examination the brain looked just like anyone else's. However, in 1984, there came the first published report of a detailed analysis of part of the great physicist's brain.

It was made by University of California neuroanatomist Marian Diamond and coworkers, who had obtained a sample from Harvey. They were looking for the ratio of two kinds of brain cells: neurons and glial cells. Neurons, which cannot divide, are the basic cells of the brain; glial cells, which can increase in number, provide support and nourishment to the neurons. Previous work had indicated that increased mental activity in animals produced more glial cells per neuron. The hypothesis was that Einstein's brain would contain more glial cells, and indeed it did. The difference was statistically significant.

"We don't know if Einstein was born with this or developed it later," said Diamond. "But it tells us that in one of the highest evolved areas of the brain there is evidence that he had greater intellectual processing."

FIREWALKING   The ability to walk barefoot across a bed of red-hot coals has been demonstrated repeatedly, most notably in places like the Fiji Islands and Sri Lanka. Recently, firewalking has become popular in the United States as proof of how the mind can control the body. The phenomenon has been investigated repeatedly, yet it remains controversial. Is it a demonstration of some unusual ability? Or is it really more of a trick?

As early as 1935, representatives of the British Medical Association went to Fiji to wach the firewalking ceremony. The doctors were impressed and puzzled. Rather than finding some sort of stage illusion as they expected, they found a real pit filled with red-hot volcanic stones. The Fiji firewalkers danced about on the stones without the aid of any sort of protection and without taking any opiates or other painkillers. Their feet were not in any way burned by the experience. But there was nothing abnormal about the firewalkers, either. When doctors tested them by putting burning cigarettes to the soles of their feet, the firewalkers reacted in a normal way, that is, they pulled their feet away and later the burned spot blistered. The doctors could offer no explanation as to why the feet of the firewalkers did not burn when they walked across the hot rocks.

Since 1935, firewalking has become something of a tourist attraction in a number of places. The firewalkers of Fiji have taken their act on the road. In the United States a man named Tony Robbins has been teaching firewalking as part of a self-mastery technique. His seminar is called "Fear into Power: The Firewalk Experience." Students "graduate" by walking unharmed across a pit filled with red-hot coals. They can do it, says Robbins, because they have mastered their fears.

Since firewalking is no longer a remote or exotic activity, it has also been studied far more closely, and a number of tentative natural explanations have been given for the phenomena. In fact it is probable that there is no single explanation for firewalking, because different groups of firewalkers have used different materials and techniques.

Omni magazine talked to Jearl Walker, a professor of physics at Cleveland State University, who used to give a firewalking demonstration and will still plunge his hand into a pot of molten lead. Walker believes that the secret to firewalking is what is known as the Leidenfrost effect. First the firewalker wets his feet (most do), and when the wet foot hits the heat, it instantly forms an insulating layer of steam. Vaporized perspiration from the foot might serve the same purpose. Of course, such insulation won't last long, but firewalkers move quickly. Professor Walker himself was burned during one of his demonstrations. That is why he gave it up.

A different view was expressed by plasma physicist Bernard Leikind, who believes that the secret is not in the feet but in the coals. The porous rocks, he says, do not convey enough heat to the foot of the firewalker to cause any damage if the firewalker is able to step lightly and move quickly. Most firewalking demonstrations use volcanic rocks, which are highly porous and poor conductors of heat.

Since the study of firewalking is not considered a high scientific priority, it is unlikely that the problem will be entirely solved in a satisfactory manner anytime soon.

I DIOT SAVANTS   The term *idiot savant* is used by psychologists to describe persons of low general intelligence who nevertheless possess an unusually high skill in some special task.

Take the case of Charles and George, identical twins with IQs in the 60s or 70s—very low indeed. Their skill was calendar calculation. Ask George what day of the week February 15, 2002, would fall on, and he would answer instantly—and correctly—Friday. He could also tell you August 28, 1591, was a Wednesday.

Charles was not quite as good: he was only totally accurate for this century, but George was completely accurate over a range of at least 6000 years. Over such a time period, Charles sometimes made mistakes—but not very often.

The twins could perform other amazing mental feats with the calendar. When asked in what years April 21 will fall on a Sunday they would answer correctly 1968, 1963, 1957, 1946, and so on. George could go all the way back to 1700. George could also tell you—correctly—in what months of the year 2002 the first will fall on a Friday. They are March, February, and November. They would also tell you things like the third Monday in May 1936 was the eighteenth.

Although Charles and George could not add, subtract, multiply, or divide, they could tell you how many weeks it would be to your next birthday, or how many weeks it had been since your last, and George could tell you how old Abraham Lincoln or practically any other historical figure would be if he were alive today. All George would need to know is the person's date of birth.

Tom Fuller was a slave who lived during the eighteenth century. He was known as "the Virginia Calculator." Though he never learned to read or write and certainly had never been taught any form of arithmetic, it took him about two minutes to figure out that there are 47,304,000 seconds in a year and a half. When asked how many seconds a man has lived who is seventy years, seventeen days, and twelve hours old, it took him about a minute and a half to answer correctly: 2,210,500,800.

Reuben Fields, who lived at the end of the nineteenth century, was also totally illiterate and unable to tell one written number from another. Yet he enjoyed solving problems like this: If the moon is a certain number of miles from the earth, and a grain of corn is so long, how many grains will it take to connect the earth and moon?

Johann Dase of Hamburg was universally regarded as extremely stupid, yet he could multiply two eight-figure numbers in fifty-four seconds, two twenty-figure numbers in six minutes, and two hundred-figure numbers in less than nine hours—all in his head. He could also find the square root of a sixty-figure number in seconds.

Not all those who possess these astonishing calculating abilities are idiot savants. Karl Gauss, one of the greatest mathematicians who ever lived, was doing amazing calculations at the age of three. American astronomer T. H. Stafford was able to multily two fifteen-figure numbers in his head at the age of ten. However, most people of normal or above-normal ability who possess such skills tend to lose them as they grow up. In the true idiot savant, the skill tends to increase with age.

This phenomenon has been investigated by psychologists for years, and still no one knows what particular mental abilities are involved. The psychologists speculate, however, that the skills may be due to the savant's obsessive ability to concentrate on a single area to the exclusion of everything else. The idiot savant thus develops the one-sided ability to do calculations or memorize dates. The highly intelligent person with this ability tends to lose it because his mind will go off in too many directions.

While the best-known abilities of the idiot savants usually involve mathematics of one form or another, some have been able to memorize and spell incredible numbers of words, or memorize the multitude of details on a map, or take apart and put together complicated machinery. The individual, however, does not necessarily know what the words or the map mean, or how the machine is supposed to work.

These are also musical savants who have perfect pitch and can easily transpose melodies on the piano from one key to another or memorize thousands of songs.

The ability of the savants appears to be inborn. But the idiot savant must not be so retarded that he cannot absorb at least some factual knowledge, for example, that there are seven days in a week and 365 days in a year.

Levitation Tales of holy men who could, at will, rise off the ground—levitate—or perhaps even fly around, are common in the East. Indeed, such an ability was sometimes regarded as almost commonplace and quite trivial. There is a story concerning the Buddha, who was sitting with a group of disciples discussing spiritual development when a stranger entered the room and asked if he could join the disciples. As proof of his worthiness, the stranger sat down in the lotus position, slowly rose a few feet off the ground, then proceeded to circle the room several times. The Buddha watched the performance without interest. When it was over, he told his disciples that they should not be distracted by such displays but should turn their attention to the more important matter of inner spiritual development.

Few in the West would be so blasé about such a demonstration; however, tales of levitating magicians and saints are certainly not unknown. Most of the stories are hopelessly vague and uncheckable. But such stories are so persistent that they are at least intriguing.

The feats of levitation attributed to St. Joseph of Copertino, a seventeenth-century Italian monk, are among the most amply documented and the most startling. Joseph, according to these accounts, was a rather simple ascetic who often fell into ecstatic raptures. Sometimes while in these mystic states his body rose from the ground.

One of the saint's more impressive feats was reported to have taken place during the visit of a Spanish nobleman and his wife to the monastery in which Joseph lived. The nobleman's wife and her retinue of women expressed a strong desire to see the famous friar. But Joseph did not like the idea, since he avoided all possible contact with women. However, his superior insisted that he visit the women in the church. Joseph said that he would do so, but that he did not know if he would be able to speak. So grudgingly the friar

St. Joseph of
Copertino

left his cell and entered the church full of women. The first object
that Joseph's eyes fell upon was a statue of the Immaculate Con-
ception. Upon seeing this, Joseph uttered a cry, rose into the air,
and flew over the statue. There he remained for some time in a
state of speechless adoration. Then he uttered another shriek, flew
back to the door, bowed to the Mother of God, kissed the ground,
and, with his head inclined and cowl lowered, hastened back to his
cell. Behind him, he left a group of ladies fainting with amazement
over what they had just witnessed.

In the nineteenth and early twentieth centuries, levitations became a fairly familiar part of many spiritualist seances. The logical
connection between levitation and spiritualism is rather tenuous,
but it was assumed that the medium was either directly picked up
by invisible spirits or that levitation was just another of his or her
extraordinary powers. Many mediums claimed powers well beyond merely communicating with the dead. The greatest of the
nineteenth-century mediums, the Scotsman D. D. Home, was re-

139

The nineteeth-century medium D.D. Home was said to levitate during seances
(New York Public Library)

ported to have floated out of one window and in through another in the presence of several witnesses. Unfortunately, the accounts of his levitations contain gaps and inconsistencies, and while they are often cited as the best evidence for levitation, they are flawed evidence.

There are several photographs of mediums allegedly levitating during seances, but they are not at all impressive. In most, the mediums seems quite clearly to be jumping rather than floating.

In June 1977, the transcendental meditation (TM) movement surprised just about everyone with the announcement that people

140

The British medium Colin Evans did public demonstrations of levitation during the 1930s. This is an infrared photograph taken in the dark. It is suspected that Evans simply jumped and was photographed in mid-leap.
(New York Public Library)

could be taught to levitate. The TM movement, founded by the Maharishi Mahesh Yogi, had gained a measure of scientific respectability with the claim that its system of meditation could promote deep and healthful relaxation.

Though there had always been a mystical and religious underpinning to TM, the levitation claim was so far out, so startling, that it threatened to shatter whatever scientific respectability TM still possessed. Orthodox science is not merely skeptical of the possibility; it is openly scornful, and TM leaders were extremely cagy about giving public demonstrations of this ability. Some who have

141

witnessed TM "levitation" say that it is really an athletic feat or a trick that involves learning to hop from the crosslegged lotus position. That is difficult to do, but it does not violate any known physical laws, and it's certainly not levitation.

In addition to levitating oneself, there is a large body of evidence, or lore, concerning the ability of certain individuals to levitate large objects. There are persistent tales that the stones of the pyramids of Egypt, of Stonehenge, and of some of the great Inca buildings were magically levitated. The logic behind such claims is that there is no other way in which such gigantic stones could have been moved by people who possessed only the most primitive technology.

Stories of the levitation of large objects are not common in today's world. However, there is supposed to be a large granite boulder in front of a Moslem mosque at Shivapur, India. The stone is said to become weightless when eleven people stand around it, touching it with their index fingers and chanting "Qamar Ali Dervish" loudly.

Parapsychologists have conducted extensive tests for what they call psychokinesis, or PK. That is the ability to move objects without touching them, or simply a scientific-sounding name for levitation, though subjects are rarely asked to levitate themselves or even large objects like a brick. Most PK tests concentrate on fairly small effects like influencing the fall of dice or moving a glass across a table. Today even more subtle effects are being tested: the possibility of affecting the flow of electrons over a cathode ray tube, for example. While parapsychologists have announced positive results on some of these tests, critics have been quick to point out shortcomings. Like so much else in parapsychology today, the existence of PK remains unproven as far as the bulk of the scientific community is concerned.

However, if some such ability does exist, it would certainly help to explain the vast body of anecdotal evidence of levitation.

See also: THE INDIAN ROPE TRICK

THE PROPHECIES OF NOSTRADAMUS   Nostradamus was
a sixteenth-century French almanac maker and prophet, far and
away the most famous nonbiblical prophet in his and our time.
Practically everyone today has at least heard his name, and any
new interpretation of his prophecies is likely to win a lot of believers.

Nostradamus was born Michel de Nostradame on December 14,
1503, at St. Remy, in Provence. He came from a family of prosperous Jewish merchants, but sometime either shortly before or
shortly after Nostradamus was born, the family converted (perhaps under pressure) to Catholicism. He was given a good education, and though he studied astrology as did most educated men of
his time, he did not seem to display any particular interest in the
subject while he was young.

In 1525, Nostradamus was licensed to practice medicine and
was quite successful in several towns in southern France. In the
town of Agen, he married a woman said to be "of high estate, very
beautiful and very amiable," though her name is lost. She bore him
a son and a daughter. Three years later, Nostradamus's wife and
children died in an outbreak of plague, and thus began a period of
trouble and sorrow for Nostradamus. His wife's family sued to
have her dowry returned. Patients became wary of a physician
who could not save his own family. Most ominous of all, Nostradamus came under the suspicious eye of the Inquisition, not for issuing prophecies, for he had done none of that yet, but for
allegedly making a slighting remark about a statue of the Virgin.
In 1538, he was ordered to appear before the Inquisitor at Toulouse, but rather than face what would certainly have been an unpleasant experience and quite possibly a dangerous one, he took to
the road, and from 1538 to 1544 Nostradamus again wandered

about, mostly in southern France. The first stories about his powers of prophecy come from this period of his life.

Nostradamus finally settled in the little town of Salon, where he married Anne Ponsarde Gemelle, a rich widow. At Salon, Nostradamus was engaged primarily in the business of making cosmetics, but even in this innocuous occupation he had a lot of enemies. The mid-sixteenth century was a time of fierce religious hatreds and paralyzing fear of witchcraft. Nostradamus, who had a Jewish background and was suspected of harboring Huguenot sympathies, was a natural target. Add to this his growing interest in astrological and magical studies, and it is not difficult to see why he was regarded with hostility and suspicion by his neighbors. In disgust, Nostradamus retired more and more from the practice of medicine among those he denounced as "barbarians" and plunged ever deeper into the study of magic and astrology.

By 1550, he appears to have been fully committed to the business of prophecy, and he issued his first almanac. Almanacs filled with prophecies were popular items in those days, and Nostradamus soon built a substantial reputation as a compiler of almanacs.

But it is not for his almanacs that Nostradamus is famous today. He undertook a much more ambitious project: he wrote prophetic verses, each containing four lines or quatrains. Nearly a thousand of these are arranged in ten books, called *Centuries.* The *Centuries* were to contain prophecies for the next two thousand years, or specifically until the year 3797. The first edition appeared in 1555, but complete editions apparently were not issued until 1557.

Nostradamus does not tell us how he arrived at his prophecies. Though they contain a measure of astrology, they are certainly not typical astrological predictions. The best guess is that he wrote primarily by inspiration—that is, he wrote down whatever verses came to him. As is typical of most inspired prophetic writing, Nostradamus's *Centuries* are couched in obscure, archaic, almost unfathomable language. Nostradamus has his admirers, but even the most devoted are unable to defend his merits as a poet.

The magic mirror in which Nostradamus was supposed to have shown
Queen Catherine the future monarchs of France

At the court of the reigning French king, Henry II, the *Centuries* were all the rage. They were particularly popular with Queen Catherine de Medici, a great patron of astrologers and magicians. There is an oft-repeated story that Catherine asked Nostradamus to forecast the future of her children. Nostradamus was said to have conjured up the angel Anael, who showed Catherine the future of her children in a mirror. Three of her sons were to become kings, but their reigns would be both brief and tragic. These sons paraded across the mirror once for every year of their reigns, but the parade did not take long. Then Catherine's hated son-in-law Henry, King of Navarre, who was later to succeed to the French throne as Henry IV, appeared in the mirror and took twenty-three turns, and when his descendants, who were to remain kings of France until the Revolution, began appearing, Catherine became so depressed that she called off the session.

The mirror scene is dramatic but unlikely, for Nostradamus is not known to have worked with the trappings of ceremonial magic. More probably, he simply cast horoscopes for the royal children. Even if the horoscopes had unambiguously predicted the gloomy end of Catherine's children, it is extremely doubtful if he would have given the queen such a bleak forecast. Monarchs were not fond of prophets who gave them bad news, and of this Nostradamus was well aware, for he was always careful to make his prophecies so ambiguous that they could not be turned against him. He may simply have predicted that Catherine's sons would be kings, which was quite true enough, as far as it went.

In the *Centuries*, Nostradamus's most famous prophecy apparently concerned King Henry II, though the king's name is never stated. We have no idea whether Nostradamus had Henry II in mind when he wrote the quatrain, or if the king's name was simply interpreted into the prophecy after events worked themselves out. The prophecy is contained in stanza 35 of *Century* 1 and reads:

> The young lion will overcome the old one
> On the field of battle in single combat:
> He will put out his eyes in a cage of gold:
> Two fleets one, then to die a cruel death.

On July 1, 1559, King Henry was riding in a tournament against Gabriel de Lorges, Comte de Montgomery, Captain of the Scottish Guard. The lances of the two riders met and splintered. Montgomery dropped his shaft a second too late and the jagged point pierced the king's visor and entered his left eye. Henry fell from the saddle and died in agony some ten days later.

According to a biography of the prophet written by his son Caesar, the common folk confused the prophecy with a curse and burned Nostradamus in effigy, while the Church considered burning the prophet himself. But Catherine remained his friend, and, so long as he had such a powerful friend, he was in no real danger.

Nostradamus returned to Salon an honored and wealthy man. While he was often denounced, he was also frequently consulted by leading figures in France, particularly Queen Catherine, and by nobles from other countries as well.

The prophet fell ill in mid-1566. On July 1, he was supposed to have told a friend at his bedside, "You will not find me alive at sunrise." True to form, he died that very night. In his will, Nostradamus expressed the curious wish to be buried standing upright, supposedly so that the boorish people of Salon would not step on his body.

Famous as he was in his own day, Nostradamus's fame has continued to grow after his death. The *Centuries* have been republished, translated, and interpreted unceasingly to this day. Unfortunately, the prophecies are by no means clear-cut. Nostradamus never says that a particular thing will happen to a particular person on a particular date. There are no specific names, few specific dates, and even locations are given only in the most general way. There is also no order to the predictions and no rules at all about how they are to be interpreted. The famed quatrain that is supposed to be about the blinding and death of Henry II is in *Century* 1. Another quatrain that is supposed to relate to events immediately following the king's accident appears in *Century* III. Most of the intervening quatrains have been interpreted as referring to events well in the future or far removed from France.

In the quatrain quoted earlier, you can see that Henry II is never mentioned. Later interpreters have simply assumed that he is "the old one." The king did not have his eyes put out in a "cage of gold," but the interpreters assume that the gold cage was a poetic symbol for the king's visored helmet, which does in some ways resemble a cage. But both of Henry's eyes were not put out in the accident, only one. And no one knows what the "two fleets" mentioned in the quatrain refer to. Some have suggested that this is a reference to the two wounds that the king received from the broken lance.

The second famous prophecy concerning Henry II comes in stanza 55 of the third *Century*. Here the prophet speaks of "a one-eyed man" ruling France. In the ten days between the king's accident and his death, Henry II was "a one-eyed man," the only one-eyed king ever to rule France.

One impressive quatrain is this one:

> Chief of Fossan will have throat cut
> By leader of the light and gray hound:
> The act gotten up by those of Tarpeian mount,
> Saturn in Leo thirteenth of February.

Even the skeptical writer L. Sprague de Camp admits that this quatrain "might support a belief in precognition." For "it is singular that on the thirteenth of February 1820, the Duke of Berry, who bore the title Lord of Fossano, was mortally stabbed by one Louvel, a man who had been a royal huntsman."

In the end, however, de Camp rejects the prophecy idea, for he does not think "that one good hit among a thousand questionable ones is very strong evidence."

If Nostradamus was a true prophet, why did he set his predictions down in such veiled language? Nostradamus said that he was deliberately vague because "rulers, sects, and religions would find them [the prophecies] so little to their liking that they could condemn them.

"My writings will be better understood by those who come after my death and by those who penetrate my meaning."

The interpreters of Nostradamus have been extremely clever at relating the quatrains to historical events—after the event has taken place. But when they have tried to use Nostradamus as a guide to events in advance of the time of the interpretation, they have often slipped badly. Typically, interpreters found in the quatrains predictions that suited their own purposes.

Those followers of Napoleon who were also devotees of Nostradamus found in the *Centuries* predictions that Napoleon would conquer England and have a long and peaceful reign. But they were wrong.

Followers of Nostradamus who had monarchist sympathies foresaw the restoration of the House of Bourbon after the fall of Napoleon, and they were correct, up to a point. But the Bourbon restoration was brief, and Nostradamians kept right on predicting the return of the Bourbons throughout the nineteenth century, and some may be looking for Bourbons still.

During World War I, French Nostradamians found that the master had predicted victory for France, while their German counterparts saw a German victory written plainly in the *Centuries.* During World War II, the same thing happened, and again the French were right. But they also saw the war taking some pretty strange turns. According to one, Nostradamus predicted that the victory would be led by a restored French monarch to be named Henry V, who would then annex Spain and Italy to France.

Nostradamus is widely credited with predicting World War II and its outcome. Erika Cheetham, one of the more popular of the current interpreters of Nostradamus, finds in his prophecies a clear prediction of the rule of the Ayatollah Khomeini in Iran:

> Rain, famine and will will not cease in Persia
> Too great a trust will betray its monarch.
> These actions started in France will end there,
> A secret sign for one to be sparing.

The Shah or monarch of Persia or Iran certainly did not fall because of excessive trust. But the Ayatollah had been in exile in

France, and from there he launched his successful revolution. Iranian exiles now plotting the overthrow of the Ayatollah now have refuge in France.

And what does Nostradamus have to say about the future? It doesn't look hopeful, according to Cheetham. "One cannot but feel that Nostradamus's vision of the twentieth century was one of war, brutality, famine and disaster."

5

NATURAL

MYSTERIES

Aɴɪᴍᴀʟs ᴀɴᴅ ᴇᴀʀᴛʜǫᴜᴀᴋᴇs   For centuries, folk wisdom has held that certain sorts of animals appear to sense an impending earthquake, long before humans or their sophisticated scientific apparatus become aware of it.

An 1888 report appearing in the British publication *Nature* lists some fairly typical examples: "The records of most great earthquakes refer to the consternation of dogs, horses, cattle, and other domestic animals. Fish also are frequently affected. In the London earthquake of 1749, roach and other fish in a canal showed evident signs of confusion and fright; and sometimes after an earthquake, fish rise of the surface dead and dying. During the Tokyo earthquake of 1880, cats inside a house ran about trying to escape, foxes barked, and horses tried to kick down the boards confining them to their stables. There can, therefore, be no doubt that animals know something unusual and terrifying is taking place. More interesting than these are the observations showing that animals are agitated just before an earthquake. Ponies have been known to prance about their stalls, pheasants to scream, and frogs to cease croaking suddenly a little time before a shock, as if aware of its coming. The Japanese say that moles show their agitation by burrowing. Geese, pigs and dogs appear more sensitive in this respect than other animals. After the great Calabrian earthquake, it is said that the neighing of a horse, the braying of an ass, or the cackle of a goose was sufficient to cause the inhabitants to fly from their houses in expectation of a shock. Many birds are said to show their uneasiness before an earthquake by hiding their heads under their wings

153

and behaving in an unusual manner. At the time of the Calabrian shock, little fishes like sand eels, which are usually buried in the sand, came to the top and were caught in multitudes. In South America certain quadrupeds, such as dogs, cats and jerboas, are believed by the people to give warning of coming danger by their restlessness; sometime immense flocks of seabirds fly inland before an earthquake, as if alarmed by the commencement of some sub-oceanic disturbance."

An article in a 1908 edition of *The American Review of Reviews* noted, "In connection with the fearful catastrophes of recent date in Italy, California and elsewhere, which like so many others of like nature, will long retain a hold on human memory, attention has again been called to the fact that many animals give intimations of such great disturbances in advance, by certain particular and often unusual conduct. It is particularly such animals as have

EARTHQUAKE "BELTS" OF THE WORLD

Map by U.S. GEOLOGICAL SURVEY

their abode underground that often indicate, days before the event, that something unusual in nature is about to occur, by coming out of their hiding places underground into the open."

While anecdotal evidence of this nature is never considered conclusive by scientists, by the 1930s it was considered interesting and suggestive enough for a couple of scientists in earthquake-prone Japan to begin performing experiments. They observed catfish in an aquarium. When there was no impending earthquake, the catfish were their usual lazy selves. But about six hours before an earthquake shock, they began jumping and swimming around in an agitated manner. According to an article in *Nature*, "Several months' testing showed that in a period when 178 earthquakes of all degrees of severity had been recorded, the fish had correctly predicted 80 percent of the shocks."

More recently, the Chinese, who have also suffered greatly from earthquakes, interviewed farmers about possible warning signs of earthquakes and came up with a large body of testimony about unusual animal behavior. According to *The Earthquake Information Bulletin*, "Through interviews and discussions with local people, the scientists collected information of 2,093 cases of unusual animal behavior in the time shortly before the earthquake. Nearly all the anecdotes were passed on to the scientists by survivors of the earthquake themselves; the majority of the reports involved domestic animals. Some examples included goats that refused to go into pens, cats and dogs that picked up their offspring and carried them outdoors, pigs that squealed strangely, startled chickens that dashed out of coops in the middle of the night, rats that left their nests, and fish that dashed about aimlessly."

The subject of animals as earthquake predictors is still a controversial one. It is certainly possible that survivors of an earthquake would display selective memories about what had happened just before the quake. Animal behavior that might have been observed a thousand times before could become "unusual" and "significant" in retrospect, after the catastrophe had taken place.

Yet the theory that animals do sense some sort of subtle changes before an earthquake is by no means an entirely implausible one. We do know that earthquakes are sometimes heralded by changes in the magnetic field or subaudible sounds. Many animals are more sensitive to magnetic fields and sounds than humans are. They might be sensitive to other more subtle changes as well.

See also: EARTHQUAKE WEATHER

THE BARISAL GUNS

THE BARISAL GUNS   Today we live in a far noisier world than ever before. What with everything from hard rock to sonic booms, we don't seem to find loud noises of unknown origin as mysterious, frightening, or interesting as we once did. But unexplained noises once ranked among the world's most speculated-upon mysteries, and even today some of these noises do from time to time catch public attention.

Of all the unknown noises, the most celebrated are undoubtedly what have been called the Barisal Guns. They were reported in the Sundarbans, a network of swamps at the mouth of the Ganges River in India. Barisal itself is a little village in the Sundarbans. An early account of the guns by G. B. Scott is typical of many: "I first heard the Barisal Guns in December 1871, on my way to Assam from Calcutta through the Sundarbans. The weather was clear and calm, no sign of any storms. All day the noises on board the steamer prevented other sounds from being heard; but when all was silent at night, and we were moored in one or other of the narrow channels in the neighborhood of Barisal, Morelgunge, and upwards far from any villages or other habitations, with miles and miles of long jungle grass on every side, the only sounds the lap of the water or the splash of earth falling into the water along the banks, then at intervals, irregularly, would be heard the dull muffled boom as of distant cannon. Sometimes a single report, at others two or three or more in succession; never near, always distant, but not always equally distant. Sometimes the reports would resemble cannon from two rather widely separated opposing forces, at others from different directions but apparently always from the southward, that is seaward. We were not very far from the sea when I first heard them."

Upon inquiring, Scott discovered that the phenomenon was quite well known in the area, but no one seemed to have a plausible explanation for the mysterious sounds.

Later, Scott himself encountered similar sounds in other parts of India. But they are certainly not limited to India. The *mist-pouffers* ("fog pistols") have often been reported off the Belgian coast. The Italians call similar sounds *marina* or *brontidi*; the Japanese, *uminari*. Lake Guns were well known in the region of Seneca Lake in New York State.

The journals of Lewis and Clark contain this entry for July 4, 1808, when the expedition was encamped at Great Falls, Montana: "Since our arrival at the Falls we have repeatedly heard a strange noise coming from the mountains in a direction a little north of west. It is heard at different periods of the day and night, sometimes when the air is perfectly still and without a cloud, and consists of one stroke only, or five or six discharges in quick succession. It is loud and resembles precisely the sound of a six-pound piece of ordnance at the distance of three miles."

And there are many, many more of these mysterious "guns" heard throughout the world. Some seem to have fired only briefly, while others still can be heard today. A lot of explanations have been offered for these sounds, none entirely satisfactory, and it is probable that there are several different origins for the sounds.

The most charming explanation was found by oddity-collector Rupert T. Gould in a story by W. P. Drury published in 1904. The hero of the story is lost in the Sundarbans in a small dinghy. Rounding a bend, he comes upon the wreck of a British ship, but the ship is still occupied by a few ancient men commanded by a senile midshipman. All suffer from two fixed ideas: that they must never abandon ship, and that they must fire guns at intervals to scare away wild beasts. Our hero realizes that these are the famous Barisal Guns.

Gould admits sadly that "it does not seem likely that the Barisal Guns are due to actual gunfire, or to human agency of any kind. They are probably a natural phenomenon, but whether this should be located in the air, the land, or sea remains at present an open question." It is still an open question.

Today, unexplained loud booms are often attributed to some sort of sonic boom. In late 1978 and early 1979, there was a whole series of loud booms heard along the East Coast of the United States. As reported in *The New Scientist*, "The affair started on 2 December, when two loud booms were heard and felt in the coastal town of Charleston [South Carolina]. Residents of the New Jersey coast heard their own boom later that afternoon. Thirteen days later Charleston was rocked by five more booms, and explosions were also heard off the coast of Nova Scotia. On 20 December, Charleston had two more explosions and New Jersey one. More followed in the different locations."

The phenomenon was investigated by a number of government agencies, and most investigators seemed to conclude that the booms were from planes, possibly supersonic military aircraft. But evidence for this theory is far from conclusive. It may be that the booms were the result of some sort of secret Air Force testing and that this is known, but those who know are keeping it a secret. However, the mysterious East Coast booms, like the Barisal Guns and many other mysterious sounds, remain officially unexplained.

CANALS OF MARS   Up until about a half-century ago, it was widely believed, even by many professional astronomers, that the planet Mars was crisscrossed by a network of "canals," quite possibly of artificial origin.

The idea of Martian canals first began in 1877 with the Italian astronomer G. V. Schiaparelli of Milan. While observing Mars through his telescope, he saw streaks on the face of the planet that had not been charted by any previous observer. This was not the

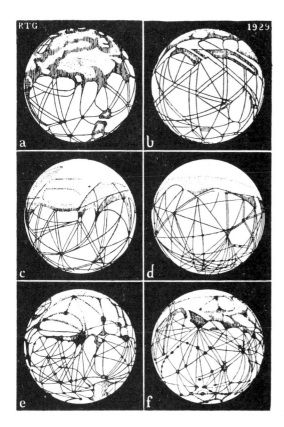

The canals of Mars as mapped by various observers

first time Mars had been observed through a telescope, far from it. How was it, then, that other observers, some with better equipment, had failed to notice the streaks? Schiaparelli was viewing the planet at an exceptionally favorable time. With the equipment available in the nineteenth century, astronomical observation was something less than an exact science and a great deal depended on luck. It was assumed that the Italian astronomer had been lucky.

Schiaparelli called the streaks *canali*, which really means "channels," a neutral word that does not imply artificial origin. However, when the word was translated into English it came out "canals," which certainly does imply artificial origin.

The Italian astronomer's observations were not accepted at once by his colleagues; indeed some never accepted them. But many astronomers of good repute also began reporting the canals of Mars. Sometimes it seemed as if they were actually vying with one another as to the extent of the network they observed.

Far and away the most influential figure in the entire Martian canal controversy was the American astronomer Percival Lowell. Lowell was the director of the observatory at Flagstaff, Arizona, at the time one of the finest in the world. Through his telescope, Lowell thought he saw a whole spider's web of rigidly geometrical canals. At the points where canals intersected one another, he saw a circular dark spot that he termed an *oasis*.

Lowell argued that the canals were of artificial origin and that they had been constructed by a Martian civilization in order to irrigate their largely dry planet with water that came from the melting of the Martian polar ice caps.

So radical a theory naturally aroused a good deal of opposition within the scientific community. But until his death in 1916, Lowell stuck to his guns, and his disciples and admirers carried on after him, mapping the canals of Mars. They even claimed to have

Percival Lowell
(The Library of Congress)

Mars as photographed by Mariner 9
(NASA)

been able to photograph the canals, though persons less convinced of the existence of canals could see no evidence of them in the photographs. In the end, earthbound photography could prove nothing, for the observer's eye was always more sensitive than the camera.

After Lowell's death, some of the heat went out of the Martian canal controversy, telescopes got better, and fewer and fewer observers reported seeing the canals. But the idea of canals on Mars certainly did not die out entirely, for a small but not insignificant number of observers continued to see them. The late Willie Ley, the dean of American science writers, said he had seen the canals while gazing through a telescope. He said he had been looking at

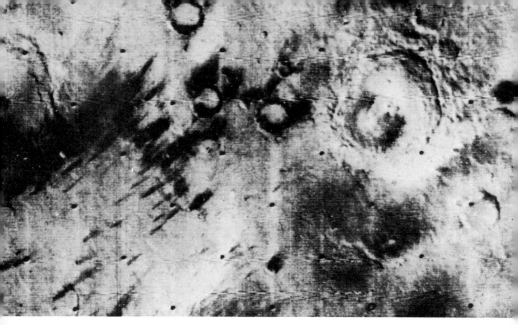

Close-up of the Martian surface shows craters and streaks but no canals
(NASA)

Mars through telescopes for many years but had never seen canals. Then one day, when the conditions were just right—there they were. He was convinced that those who had failed to see the canals just hadn't been observing under the proper conditions. He did not accept the idea that the canals were of artificial origin, but he was quite sure that Mars was marked by a network of more or less straight lines. Ley was not a professional astronomer, but he had a tough and skeptical mind and was well aware of the long controversy surrounding the canals of Mars and of the fallibility of human observation. He was a man whose testimony had to be taken seriously.

Yet when the first photos of the surface of Mars, taken by the Mariner space probes during the 1960s, were sent back, they showed the surface of the planet cratered like the surface of the moon. There were no oases, no canals, no signs of a high civilization present or past. However, the photographs did show what appeared to be irregular water-cut channels, like dry riverbeds. This

162

was an indication that at one time water may have been abundant on the Martian surface, though there may be other explanations for the existence of these channels. Some of the photographs have also shown faint straight lines. These are far too faint to account for the Martian canals, but no one knows what the lines might be. Astronomer Carl Sagan has termed them "a real Martian mystery."

The long-debated quesion of life on Mars is not fully settled either, and probably won't be until we actually put observers on the surface of the planet. The bulk of the evidence indicates that there is no life on the planet, but if life does exist it would probably be microscopic and of a very low order. There is virtually no active hope that the planet contains or ever contained intelligent life, much less a civilization capable of digging a planetary network of canals.

What, then, are the "canals" that so many people reported seeing for so long? No one really knows for sure, and there probably is no single answer. Basically, it is felt that the canals were the result of an optical illusion—the tendency of the eye to link up various disparate features. The eye is a far from perfect instrument for recording reality, as any collection of optical illusions will quickly demonstrate. Often the eye sees what it expects to see. Even the most passionate defenders of the canal idea admitted that the lines were extremely faint and hard to interpret. And perhaps, once the idea that there were canals was planted in an observer's head, by straining hard enough he was able to see them, even when they weren't there.

See also: MOONS OF MARS

D EATH OF THE DINOSAURS   The dinosaurs were the most spectacular land creatures ever to inhabit the earth. They ranged from chicken-size to truly gigantic and came in an amazing variety of shapes: two-legged, four-legged, horned, armored, fanged, clawed, crested, and what have you. Some were built like tanks, others like kangaroos. Yet there is not a single one of these creatures left on earth today. Rumors of some sort of dinosaurlike creature in the Congo remain vague and unsubstantiated. The dinosaurs as we know them all died off some sixty-five million years ago.

When the existence of dinosaurs was discovered in the early nineteenth century, people were fascinated by these exotic monsters—it's a fascination that continues to this day. Along with the fascination came a kind of scorn. The dinosaurs were big and powerful, but they're extinct. We humans are small, relatively weak, and yet we are still here. The term *dinosaur* has become synonymous with something that is big, slow, overspecialized, and generally out of date and useless.

The attitude is understandable; it makes us feel superior, yet it is totally unjustified. The dinosaurs ruled the earth—and that is no rhetorical excess—for some 140 million years. When we have been around that long, we may have some reason for looking down our noses at them, but not yet.

We should marvel not at the dinosaurs' failure but at their truly remarkable success. Yet they are gone, and that raises the question of what killed them, a question that has turned out to be very difficult to answer. The death of the dinosaurs is a genuine mystery.

At one time it was generally assumed that the dinosaurs just "got old" and died off. But only individuals get old; species and families of living things do not have a predetermined lifespan. The turtles and the crocodiles, who both evolved at about the same time as the dinosaurs, are still around. The limpets have been around virtually unchanged for a lot longer.

Another general assumption was that the dinosaurs somehow got too big and too overspecialized, and then failed to "adapt"—hence the view of the dinosaur as something obsolete. But questions arise: Too big for what? Too overspecialized for what? Failed to adapt to what?

There were many different species of dinosaurs. Some were large, others quite small. Some were grotesquely horned and ar-

Dinosaurs of the late Cretaceous
(American Museum of Natural History)

mored; others were sleek and streamlined in appearance. Some may have been very specialized, but others surely were not. The reasons of overspecialization and oversize do not apply to all dinosaurs.

Over the 140 million years of dinosaurian dominance, many species of dinosaurs died off and were replaced by others. Stegosaurus, with its strangely armored back and walnut-size brain, died out well before other dinosaurs. But the duckbilled dinosaurs, many of which sported fantastically elaborate crests, were flourishing till the last. Extinction of one species and its replacement by another is a common and constant occurrence in earth history. But what happened to the dinosaurs some sixty-five million years ago, at the end of the geologic period called the Cretaceous, is not at all common. At that time, *all* the dinosaurs died out, and they were not replaced. That is not an ordinary event in earth history.

Since fossils cannot be dated with great precision, there is no way of telling just how quickly the dinosaurs died off. Some scientists believe that the number of dinosaur species had become smaller toward the end of the Cretaceous. This would indicate that the dinosaurs were already in decline before the end finally came. Other scientists claim that this "decline" is really an illusion and that dinosaurs were as numerous and dominant as ever right up to the end. But everyone agrees that, whether the destruction of the dinosaurs took place over a day or over a million years, it still seems freakishly abrupt.

For a long time, there was the general impression that major climatic changes at the end of the Cretaceous were responsible for the death of the dinosaurs. The Cretaceous world was pictured as warm, flat, swampy, and overgrown with soft vegetation. The post-Cretaceous world was cooler; there were mountains and highlands, and many of the swamps had dried up. Vegetation was more modern, with an abundance of grasses and other hard-to-chew plants.

Certainly major changes did take place by the end of the Cretaceous, but major changes are always taking place on earth. In their 140-million-year history, the dinosaurs had already survived several radical changes in climate. Yet still they had adapted and flourished. As far as can be determined, the changes at the end of the Cretaceous were not greater than those that the dinosaurs had already survived.

At one time the most popular explanation was that the world had gotten gradually colder, and since dinosaurs were cold-blooded reptiles, they could not survive. There is now a considerable body of opinion that holds that the dinosaurs were not truly cold-blooded and were not really reptiles, and thus they would have been well able to adapt to cooler weather. Besides, if the cold-blooded crocodiles and turtles survived, why not the immensely successful dinosaurs?

Another popular theory is that the dinosaurs lost out in a "survival of the fittest" struggle with the mammals. This theory is appealing because it appears to imply evolutionary progress from the slow-moving, slow-witted, overbuilt dinosaurs to the smaller, faster, smarter mammals. It also reflects well on us, since we are mammals and it's our ancestors that "won." But such a theory has only mammalian chauvinism to recommend it.

Both mammals and dinosaurs appeared on the scene at about the same time, both with an equal chance to become the dominant group. The dinosaurs "won." The mammals remained small and insignificant until after the dinosaurs had disappeared. Mammals did not cause the death of the dinosaurs, but they certainly benefited from it.

This brings up another significant point about the extinctions at the end of the Cretaceous. Not only did the dinosaurs die out, so did the pterosaurs (the flying reptiles) and the great marine reptiles. No large animal of any kind survived the end of the Cretaceous. Small, primitive mammals lived on; so did the small ancestors of turtles, lizards, and birds, but all the big animals were gone. For the first few million years after the end of the Cretaceous, the earth was strangely devoid of large-size life. It was like an abandoned city inhabited only by rats and cockroaches. Slowly, larger animals began to evolve among the survivors, but the new land creatures never reached the size of the dinosaurs.

Even more unsettling is the fact that it wasn't just the large animals that died. The fossil record indicates that many species of plankton and marine mollusks also became extinct. The more scientists discovered, the deeper and more ominous the puzzle of the Cretaceous extinctions became. We were no longer dealing with the death of a group or species, or even with the death of an entire class of animals like the dinosaurs. This was mass death, involving hundreds of different species from all parts of the animal kingdom. The dinosaurs were only the most spectacular victims. There is also evidence of a major change in plant life, though the case here is not so clear. It seemed as if something extraordinary, overwhelming, and perhaps terrifying had happened on earth at the end of the Cretaceous. Theories of worldwide catastrophies had not been popular in science for over a century, but this period of mass death seemed unexplainable except by some sort of catastrophe; but what sort?

One theory that enjoyed considerable popularity in the late 1960s was that the extinctions were brought about by the explosion of a nearby star. Normally stars go through a relatively stable life cycle from their birth to their death. But sometimes, for reasons that we can only guess at, one will explode suddenly and violently into a supernova. If such an explosion took place within a few hundred light years of earth, the resulting radiation might account for the mass death. Even if the radiation dose did not kill the dinosaurs directly, it might have created a sudden cataclysmic climate change that would have.

Even though the explosion of this supernova would have taken place tens of millions of years ago, it would have been a catastrophe of such magnitude that some evidence of the exploded star should still be identifiable by astronomers. So far, they have found nothing, so this theory, which once got a lot of attention, has suffered from a lack of supporting evidence.

Another catastrophe-from-space theory holds that at the end of the Cretaceous the earth collided with a gigantic meteorite, or small asteroid, one that was about six miles in diameter. Asteroids of this size do roam the solar system, so a collision with earth is not impossible.

Such a collision would have thrown up huge clouds of dust that would have blocked the sunlight and resulted in a severe, if temporary, climate change. Theoretically, such a change could have caused the mass death. But where is the hole the asteroid made when it hit? Some say it is now covered by water and is thus unrecognizable, or that evidence of it has been obliterated by geological changes.

But the earth at the end of the Cretaceous would have been covered with a fine layer of dust from the collision, and evidence of that should still be traceable. Some scientists say that they have indeed found evidence of this dust layer, but others question such findings.

There is an exotic variation of the asteroid-impact theory. The mass extinctions at the end of the Cretaceous were apparently not the only ones; there may have been other similar periods. Indeed, some scientists estimate that there is a period of mass death on earth approximately every twenty-six million years. Scientists from the University of California in Berkeley have suggested that the mass extinctions occur when a small star they have named Nemesis passes close to the solar system and disrupts the orbits of comets that surround the solar system, sending millions of them plunging toward earth and other planets. The resulting impacts, the Berkeley scientists theorize, would account for the periods of extinction, including the death of the dinosaurs.

Scientists are now searching the skies for a faint red dwarf star where Nemesis should be at this time. However, Dr. Armand H. Delsemme, an astronomer at the University of Toledo, Ohio, says that the same effect on the comets could be produced by a giant planet twenty to sixty times more massive than Jupiter, the largest planet in the solar system. Such an object would be more difficult to locate than a small star, but not impossible.

An even more exotic theory holds that at the end of the Cretaceous the earth was struck by a rice-size fragment from a black hole. The fragment was so incredibly dense that it went in one side of the planet and came out the other, and in so doing thoroughly disrupted the weather patterns of the planet. Though this idea got a lot of publicity, it never had a great deal of support in the scientific community. Even the more modest Nemesis theory is highly controversial.

Finally, there is one theory that, while it does not explain the death of so many species of dinosaurs, does hold that the dinosaurs are not truly extinct. This theory holds that at least one line of the smaller dinosaurs evolved into creatures that still exist, indeed flourish, today—the birds.

Actually, the idea of a close relationship between dinosaurs and birds is not a new idea. The anatomical similarities have been repeatedly pointed out over the last century. But recent findings and theories have solidified the identification, and many scientists believe that modern birds are the direct descendants of the dinosaurs. Thus, in a sense, the dinosaurs never truly died out.

See also: METEORITE BOMBARDMENT

EARTHQUAKE WEATHER   People who live in earthquake-prone regions sometimes speak ominously of earthquake weather, a certain type of atmosphere that precedes a major quake.

A nineteenth-century English writer, Richard A. Proctor, provided this rather charming description: "You are sitting in the piazza, about afternoon teatime let us say, and you are talking about nothing in particular with the usual sticky, tropical languor, when gradually a sort of faintness comes over the air, the sky begins to assume a lurid look, the street dogs leave off howling hideously in concert for a minute, and even the grim vultures perched upon the housetops forget their obtrusive personal differences in a common sense of general uneasiness. There is an ominous hush in the air, with a corresponding lull in the conversation for a few seconds, and then somebody says with a yawn, 'It feels very much like earthquake weather.' Next minute you notice the piazza gently raised from its underpropping woodwork by some unseen force."

William R. Corliss, one of the most diligent and responsible collectors of accounts of anomalous events, notes in his *Handbook of Unusual Natural Phenomena:* "Beyond this appealing subjective account lies considerable testimony that the more cataclysmic quakes are presaged and accompanied by fogs, mists, darkness, and general obscurations of the atmosphere."

However, most of the evidence that he cites concerns conditions after a quake and thus could be directly due to the effects of the earthquake itself, primarily the release of gases and dust.

The most frequently mentioned "weather" preceding an earthquake is a sudden feeling of oppressive heaviness, the feeling one often gets before a severe thunderstorm. But there is no satisfactory evidence that any change in barometric pressure precedes a major earthquake.

"Earthquake weather" may simply be folklore, or it may be the result of some subtle but as yet unexplained change in the atmosphere that affects the perceptions of humans and quite possibly animals.

See also: ANIMALS AND EARTHQUAKES

THE FLAT EARTH   Legend has it that Christopher Columbus
was the first man to discover that the earth was a sphere. Actually
the Greeks, who had lived two thousand years before Columbus,
assumed that the world was spherical and had calculated its size
with astonishing accuracy.

During the Middle Ages, the spherical idea got lost in Europe,
along with a lot of other Greek scientific speculation, in the general decline of knowledge that followed the collapse of the classical world. There are certain passages in the Bible that, if taken
literally, suggest a flat earth. Medieval scholars wondered how the
Bible could speak of the "four corners" of the earth if the earth
were a sphere without corners?

By Columbus's time, however, such objections were no longer
considered valid, and the spherical earth had wide if not universal
acceptance among mariners. It wasn't so much that sailors were
afraid of sailing off the edge of the earth but that they feared any
long voyage into unknown seas. Columbus was the first man that
we know of with the courage, the opportunity, and the good fortune to undertake a voyage that he thought would take him
around the world to the Orient. He didn't make it because
America got in the way.

Still, the flat earth idea did not entirely die out with Columbus's
voyage or with the voyage of Ferdinand Magellan, whose ships set
out to circumnavigate the globe in 1519. As late as the 1940s,
there was a well-established and deadly serious group of flat-
earthers in the United States. They were centered in Zion, Illinois,
about forty miles north of Chicago. The town had been founded
by a sect called the Christian Apostolic Church of Zion and for
years was run, practically as a dictatorship, by sect leader Wilbur
Glenn Voliva. Zion was famous or notorious for having the bluest
of blue laws. A woman could be arrested just for wearing shorts on
the street, and anyone could be jailed for smoking or whistling in

public on Sunday. Chicago-area motorists soon learned to avoid Zion altogether.

Voliva proclaimed himself to be the only true fundamentalist and scorned "the so-called fundamentalists [who] strain out the gnat of evolution and swallow the camel of modern astronomy." To Voliva, the earth was shaped like a pancake, with the North Pole at the center and the South Pole distributed around the circumference. Ships were kept from falling off the edge by a wall of ice.

Voliva believed that the stars were small, flat bodies and not very far away. The moon, he said, was lighted from within, and as for the sun, "The idea of a sun millions of miles in diameter and 91,000,000 miles away is silly. The sun is only thirty-two miles across and not more than 3,000 miles from earth. It stands to reason it must be so. God made the sun to light the earth, and therefore must have placed it close to the task it was designed to do. What would you think of a man who built a house in Zion and put the lamp to light it in Kenosha, Wisconsin?"

A small, comfortable universe, familiarity, and what passed for common sense were the hallmarks of Voliva's appeal. The proofs of his theories were simple and local. A 1930 edition of a Voliva publication showed a photograph of Lake Winnebago, Wisconsin. The caption read, "ANYONE CAN GO TO OSHKOSH AND SEE THIS SIGHT FOR THEMSELVES ANY CLEAR DAY. With a good pair of binoculars one can see small objects on the opposite shore, proving beyond any doubt that the surface of the lake is a plane, or a horizontal line. . . . The scientific value of this picture is enormous." His own trips around the world did nothing to shake his belief, and he offered five thousand dollars to anyone who could prove the world was round. He never paid out a cent.

By the mid-1930s, Voliva's hold on his flock began to slip. He retired but announced that because of his special diet he would live to be 120. He died in 1942 at the age of 72.

Voliva was by no means the only flat-earth fanatic. The British natural scientist Alfred Russell Wallace took up the challenge of a man named John Hampden, who had offered five thousand pounds to anyone who could prove the world was round. Wallace easily won the challenge, but Hampden refused to give in and spent the rest of his life making Wallace's life miserable. There were threatening letters like this one sent to Mrs. Wallace:

> Madame—if your infernal thief of a husband is brought home some day on a stretcher with every bone in his head smashed to a pulp, you will know the reason. Do tell him from me he is a lying infernal thief, and as sure as his name is Wallace he never dies in his bed.
> You must be a miserable wretch to be obliged to live with a convicted felon. Do not think or let him think I have done with him.
>   John Hampden

First Wallace tried to ignore Hampden, thinking he would soon tire of the game, but he didn't. Then Wallace had Hampden hauled into court; each time he was found guilty and made to promise that he would stop harassing Wallace. Hampden always promised but he never stopped. Not even a jail sentence discouraged him. Meanwhile, all the court battles were draining Wallace's financial and emotional reserves. The harassment continued until Hampden died in 1891. The battle had raged for over twenty years.

Fortunately, there are no flat-earthers of the stripe of Wilbur Glenn Voliva and John Hampden today. There do, however, remain a few small societies devoted to spreading the flat-earth doctrine. Sometimes it is difficult to decide if such societies are really serious or not. For example, when the president of the British Flat Earth Society was shown one of the first satellite pictures of the entire earth taken from space, he looked at the picture for a moment and said calmly, "It is easy to see how such a picture could fool the untrained eye."

See also: THE HOLLOW EARTH

FREEZING THE DEAD   In the 1960s, the idea of freezing the
dead, or cryonics, was much discussed. The theory behind cryonics
is quite simple: the body of a person dying of a presently incurable
disease would be frozen and stored at a very low temperature and
thus would be preserved until sometime in the future when medical science had found a cure for the disease. The frozen body
would then be thawed out, the disease cured, and the individual
restored to full health.

The chief prophet of the cryonics movement was R. C. Ettinger,
who wrote several popular books on the subject. Cryonics has
been accurately described as being somewhere between a science
and a fad, for while there is some reasonable scientific basis for the
theory, there are also enormous and possibly insurmountable difficulties as well. The greatest is that the freezing itself may cause ir-
reparable harm to the body. Even when done under absolutely
optimal conditions (and no one is really sure what these are), most
scientists believe that the process would inevitably destroy some
delicate cells, particularly brain cells. Thus, even if the corpse
could be reanimated, there is no assurance that it would possess a
memory, self-identity, or all of those other mental qualities that go
into making up a human being. Even avid supporters of cryonics
agreed that it would probably be easier to find a cure for cancer
than it would be to find a "cure" for the damaging effects of freezing. But they expressed boundless faith in the ability of science to
overcome even this difficulty, somehow, someday. There was an
air of near-religious fervor about the cryonics movement.

Cryonics societies were formed throughout the United States,
and in January 1967 cryonics moved from theory to practice when
the body of Dr. James Bedford of Glendale, California, was placed
in a cold-storage capsule. Soon, many others were clamoring for
the chance to be frozen after death in the hope of living again
someday.

The newly formed cryonics societies faced a host of practical problems. It would be best for a person to be frozen before they actually died, so that the corpse could go into the frozen state with as little damage as possible. However, freezing a person before they were actually dead would technically be murder, even if the person to be frozen had agreed to the procedure in advance. This problem, however, remained a theoretical one, for there is no known case of a person being frozen before death.

A far more immediate problem was the cost. To properly prepare and freeze and store a body cost upward of fifty thousand dollars, plus a possible additional maintenance cost. This was far too expensive for the average person to consider, and even the well-to-do might blanch. It was also an open invitation for fraud, for there was really no adequate way of checking that the job had been done properly.

Proper maintenance presented an even stickier problem, for cryonics, like liberty, requires eternal vigilance. One of the first organizations to begin freezing bodies was the Cryonics Society of New York. But they went out of business in 1975, and the frozen bodies under their care were dispersed. The biggest shocker came in 1980, when an investigation of nine bodies under the care of the Cryonics Society of California revealed that the nitrogen coolant had run out and the corpses were badly decomposed. Though cryonics had never really become a mass movement, that blow just about finished it except for a small group of true believers who do maintain a small number of still-frozen corpses. If cryonics is not quite dead, it is at least in a state of suspended animation, and hopes for its future revival are clouded.

However, the idea of freezing the dead was used as the basis for a number of science fiction stories and television shows and has become part of popular mythology and rumor. The rumor usually contends that some wealthy person has had his body secretly frozen.

The most persistent subject of this rumor is Walt Disney. Why the creator of Mickey Mouse has been chosen for this dubious

honor is probably more a matter of historical accident than anything else. Walt Disney died on December 15, 1966. His body was
cremated, and the ashes were placed in Forest Lawn Memorial
Park, located in Glendale, California. A few weeks later came the
well-publicized freezing of the body of Dr. Bedford of Glendale,
California. It is this coincidence that apparently sparked the
rumor. The use of animated figures in Disney theme parks may
also have contributed to the psychological background in which
the rumor could flourish. In any case, the story was picked up by a
number of sensationalist tabloids both in the United States and Europe. The Disney family and the Disney organization have vigorously denied the rumor, and with the fading of interest in cryonics,
the rumor seems to have faded. It has also been rumored that
Howard Hughes, the members of the Ringling family of circus
fame, and all high Soviet officials are also frozen upon death.
There is no reason to believe that any of these rumors have a more
factual basis than the one about Disney.

THE GREAT SIBERIAN EXPLOSION   At 7:17 A.M. on June
30, 1908, something from space slammed into a remote area of Siberia and exploded. The blast created a "pillar of fire," visible for
hundreds of miles. The sound of the blast was heard five hundred
miles away. At a small village some forty miles from the site of the
impact, residents felt the heat of the blast and the shock waves. At
Kansk, a railroad stop 375 miles from the blast, windows and roofs
were rattled.

The impact was recorded on seismographs throughout the
world. A wide range of electrical and magnetic disturbances, as
well as unusual twilights and sunsets directly attributable to the
Siberian blast, were recorded throughout the world for months.

Obviously, this was an event of gigantic proportions. Yet it had
taken place in such a remote area that the world at large paid no
attention to it. In about 1921, a Soviet scientist named Leonard

**Trees devastated by
the 1908 Siberian
explosion**
(Sovfoto)

Kulik saw a copy of an old Siberian newspaper account of the 1908 explosion. The story fired Kulik with a desire to find out what really happened.

There were so many difficulties that a less determined man would surely have given up. Kulik's first expedition in 1921 got him only as far as Kansk. Though the impact itself had taken place hundreds of miles to the north, the event was still vividly remembered.

It wasn't until 1927 that Kulik was actually able to reach the blast area. It was in the taiga, a great pine forest that covers much of Siberia. During the long winter, deep snow makes the taiga impassable, and during the summer the taiga turns into a vast mosquito-infested bog—also impassable. Only during the brief spring is travel in the taiga relatively safe, and even then it is painfully slow.

On April 13, 1927, Kulik began to see the first signs of the catastrophe. What he saw was astonishing. For mile after mile, the ground was covered with burned and broken trees, all pointing in

177

the same direction, away from the center of the blast. All told, approximately one hundred square miles of pine forest had been devastated.

Kulik was convinced that a large meteorite had struck the earth, and he expected to find a meteorite crater at the center of the devastated region. It wasn't there. There had been an explosion in 1908, but no large solid object seems to have actually hit the ground. So the meteorite theory has lost favor.

A number of other theories have been offered: The explosion was caused by a meteorite made of antimatter and was totally destroyed by contact with the atmosphere. The culprit was a tiny piece of black hole that went right through the earth and came out the other side. The explosion was caused by a nuclear-powered extraterrestrial spaceship. There are others, equally farfetched.

However, the explanation that currently has the greatest scientific support is that Siberia was hit by a piece of a comet. Unlike a meteorite, which is solid, a comet is made up of frozen gases in which small particles of solid material may be embedded. The comet could have burned up in the atmosphere before reaching the surface. The passage of the comet through the atmosphere would have generated enough heat to create the "pillar of fire" that was reported. It would also have generated the shock waves necessary to fell all the trees and to be felt at such distant points.

We may never know the real cause of the great Siberian explosion, and that's probably a good thing, because in order to be quite sure what happened, the earth would have to experience a similar event for comparison. Next time, the impact might not take place in so remote and unpopulated an area.

See also: METEORITE BOMBARDMENT

THE HOLLOW EARTH   The British astronomer Edmund Halley, of comet fame, proposed that the earth might consist of several concentric spheres placed inside one another in the manner of a Chinese box puzzle. The two inner shells had diameters comparable to Mars and Venus, while the solid inner core was as big as the planet Mercury.

More startling was Halley's proposal that each of these inner spheres might support life. They were supposed to be bathed in perpetual light created by a luminous atmosphere. When there was an unusually bright display of *aurora borealis*, Halley postulated that it might have been caused by glowing gas escaping from the earth's interior into our atmosphere.

Halley proposed his theory in the seventeenth century, when scientific knowledge of the structure of the earth was still primitive. As time went on, the improbability of a hollow earth became apparent to scientists and scholars, but the idea was taken up by writers of imaginative fiction. Certainly the best known was Jules Verne, who wrote *Journey to the Center of the Earth* in 1864. Edgar Rice Burroughs wrote a whole cycle of novels set in the hollow earth.

Verne, Burroughs, and a lot of other writers of science fiction were inspired by the theories of an early nineteenth-century American eccentric named John Cleves Symmes. Like Halley, Symmes thought the earth was made up of five concentric spheres. But he added a new wrinkle. There was a huge opening, popularly called "Symmes Hole," at each of the poles. The ocean flowed in and out of these openings. The interior of the earth was also supposed to be inhabited.

Symmes, an army captain who had served with distinction in the War of 1821, was an enthusiastic evangelist for his theory. He traveled around the country trying to raise money to send an expedition to the north polar hole. He even petitioned Congress for money to finance the expedition, and the proposal garnered twenty-five votes. A rich doctor financed an 1824 expedition to the South Pole to find the Symmes Hole. The expedition was unsuccessful, but Symmes died with his idea intact, and a stone model of the hollow earth according to Symmes sits atop a memorial raised to him by his son at Hamilton, Ohio.

In 1906, William Reed published a book called *Phantom of the Poles* in which he stated, "I am able to prove my theory that the earth is not only hollow, but suitable in its interior to sustain human life with as little discomfort as on its exterior, and can be made accessible to mankind with one-fourth the outlay of money, time and life that it costs to build the subway in New York City. The number of people who can settle in this new world (if not already occupied) will be billions."

Reed's startling proposal received scant attention from a skeptical public. Somewhat more influential was Marshall B. Gardner, who wrote about Symmes's theory a few years later. Gardner rejected the "absurd" Symmes notion of five concentric spheres, but he enthusiastically adopted the idea of openings at the poles. According to Gardner, the interior of the earth was lighted by a small sun about six hundred miles in diameter. Unfortunately for Gardner, he published his book in 1920; in 1926, Admiral Richard E. Byrd made his first flight over the North Pole, and in 1929 he performed the same feat at the South Pole. As history records, Admiral Byrd did not find any gaping holes. Since the holes were supposed to be over one thousand miles in diameter, they would have been pretty hard to overlook.

Gardner did not abandon his hollow earth ideas, but he did stop lecturing and writing about them. However, others who have kept the faith have insisted that Byrd actually did discover the big hole at the pole and actually flew a good way into the interior of the earth, and that for some obscure reason the government is "covering up" this fact. Some hollow earthers insist that on later expeditions Byrd actually penetrated some four thousand miles into the interior of the hollow earth.

Satellite photograph has presented hollow earthers with another problem. None of the photographs of the earth taken from space show polar holes. But the hollow earthers are not about to be put down by such evidence. It's all part of the cover-up, they say. The satellite photos are all retouched to hide the hole. Actually, some of the early photos of the earth from space did show what appeared to be a gigantic hole at one pole. The pictures, however, were composites made up of many smaller photos. The "hole" was simply an area that had not been photographed. Nonsense, insist the hollow earthers; these were the real photos that slipped through the web of censorship by accident. As with the Byrd expedition, these "polar hole photos" have become pillars of the hollow earth faith.

An odd champion of the hollow earth was Richard S. Shaver, a

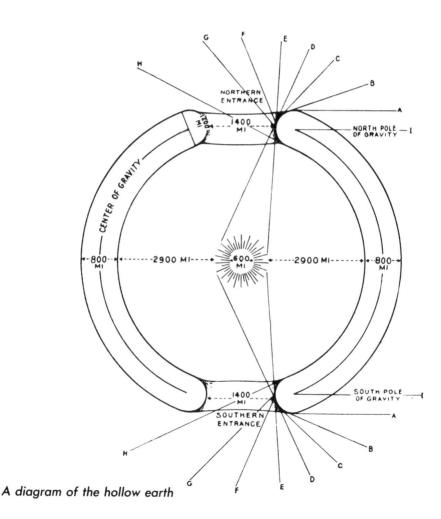

A diagram of the hollow earth

Pennsylvania welder who claimed that by "racial memory" he had reclaimed all of man's "forgotten" history. His tales included accounts of evil creatures called Deros who lived in huge subterranean caverns that honeycombed the earth.

There is also a vast body of occult speculation about a huge underground civilization known as Agartha. It is supposed to be the home of "hidden masters" whose powers range from the merely supernatural to the absolutely godlike.

More bizarre even than the theories of Symmes and Gardner was the one put forth by Cyrus Reed Teed, an herb doctor and alchemist from Utica, New York. Teed held that the scientists had gotten it all backward, and that the earth was hollow and we are living on the inside!

It's not quite as crazy as it sounds at first, for many of Teed's methods of accounting for observable phenomena in terms of the hollow earth were really quite ingenious. The sun was at the center of Teed's hollow earth and it was half light and half dark. It was the rotation of this two-sided central sun that caused the illusion that the sun rises and sets. The moon, planets, and stars were not distant objects but merely reflections of light. The reason that we couldn't see across to the other side of the earth was that the atmosphere was too dense. Some of Teed's other explanations, however, are utterly incomprehensible.

Scott Morris, the Games editor of *Omni* magazine, calls Teed's idea "one of the most absurd theories ever proposed." But he then points out that "what's most infuriating is that a little mathematical fiddling turns this crazy theory into a proposition that is virtually impossible to refute. The trick is done by inversion, a purely geometric transformation that lets the mathematician turn shapes inside-out. When a sphere is inverted every point outside is mapped to a corresponding point inside, and vice versa."

Teed did not arrive at his theories by mathematics but by mystical inspiration. He also decided that he was the new Messiah and adopted the name Koresh—Hebrew for Cyrus. He called his new religion Koreshanity, and the hollow earth was a basic article of faith. He wrote, "To know of the earth's concavity is to know God.

While to believe in the earth's convexity is to deny Him and all His works. All that is opposed to Koreshanity is antichrist."

Teed picked up several hundred followers, partly because he was a spellbinding orator and partly because his hollow earth had a certain appeal. It made the universe smaller, more manageable, more comfortable. The earth was no longer an insignificant bit of rock orbiting an obscure star; it was the whole universe!

Koresh moved his followers to a "New Jerusalem" in Florida, and before his death in 1908 he said that he would rise from the dead. Followers kept watch over the body for two days, but in the Florida heat it quickly showed signs of decay, and health officials ordered that the messiah of the hollow earth be buried. The cult lingered on and continued to make a few converts. In 1961, there were still thirty surviving members. The three-hundred-acre tract of land that it owned was turned over to the state of Florida for a Koreshan State Historic Park. The last Koreshanity adherent, who died in 1983, was a guide for the park.

Perhaps the most bizarre influence that Teed's ideas had was in Nazi Germany. Some of Teed's publications fell into the hands of Peter Bender, a German aviator who had been badly wounded. Bender was converted, and though he was to die in a Nazi concentration camp, the hollow earth ideas that he proclaimed sparked interest in the anti-intellectual climate of Nazi Germany.

In April 1942, the Nazis sent an expedition under Dr. Heinz Fisher, an expert on infrared rays, to the island of Rügen in the Baltic. One of the purposes of the expedition was to get a picture of the British fleet by turning their cameras upward and shooting across the center of the hollow earth!

Astronomer Gerald S. Kuiper observed: "High officials in the German Admiralty and Air Force thought this would be useful for locating the whereabouts of the British fleet because the concave curvature of the earth would facilitate long-distance observation by means of infrared rays which are less curved than visible rays." After the war Dr. Fisher complained, "The Nazis forced me to do crazy things."

Koreshanity is now well and truly dead. But there are still some hollow earthers out there. However, as Mary Martin Davis, editor of *The Hollow Hassle*, wrote in 1984, "When it comes to the hollow earth there's not a whole lot of us believers around."

See also: THE FLAT EARTH; RAYMOND PALMER

METEORITE BOMBARDMENT

The earth is under continuous bombardment from space. It has been estimated that a hundred billion meteorites hit the earth's atmosphere every twenty-four hours. Of these, only a tiny percentage are large enough to be seen burning up in the atmosphere. Estimated daily averages for meteorites actually striking the ground range from one to thirty.

Most of the meteorites that fall are still quite small and do little damage. Very occasionally a meteorite will plunge through a roof or break a window.

The largest known meteorite to fall in recent times struck the Ussuri Valley in eastern Siberia on February 12, 1947. It broke up before actually hitting the earth, creating a pattern of small craters rather than a single large one. The largest of the craters from the Ussuri fall was about twenty-eight yards across and six yards deep.

But the surface of the earth has been struck by much larger meteorites, though no one is quite sure how large, nor how often, really large meteorites hit.

The largest generally recognized meteorite crater is in the Arizona desert near Winslow. It has been called Canyon Diablo, Meteor Crater, Barringer Crater, and Arizona Crater. Whatever you want to call it, it's everybody's idea of what a meteorite crater should look like. It's almost a perfect circle, four-fifths of a mile across, with a circumference of nearly three miles. All around the rim of the crater, there is a sort of wall 130 to 160 feet high. This was formed by material forced up by the impact of the meteorite. From the edge of the wall to the bottom of the crater is 550 feet.

The meteor crater in Arizona
(American Museum of Natural History)

You could put the Washington Monument in the middle of the crater, and only six feet of it would stick up over the rim. What's more, the crater was once deeper, but the activities of weather and erosion have filled it in somewhat. The impact pulverized and blew out some three hundred million tons of rock.

There is no reason to believe that the meteorite that blasted out the crater in Arizona was the largest ever to hit the earth. It almost certainly was not. There are other scars on the earth's surface that may have been caused by the impact of even larger meteorites. One of the largest of these suspected craters is the Vredefort Ring in South Africa, which is some thirty miles wide. There has even been a suggestion that the Pacific Ocean is an impact crater, though this is extremely doubtful.

Wandering through the solar system are large chunks of debris called asteroids that could cause tremendous damage if they ever struck the earth. In 1963, the close approach of an asteroid called Icarus set off a real scare. Actually, Icarus only got within four million miles of earth, though that's close in astronomical terms. Icarus wasn't the largest asteroid to approach the earth, and it wasn't the closest.

The asteroid Apollo came within two million miles of earth in 1932. Adonis was within a million miles in 1936. There was some genuine concern among astronomers when Hermes skimmed

185

Model showing comparison of the asteroid Hermes and New York City
(American Museum of Natural History)

within a mere 485,000 miles of earth on October 30, 1937. That was still twice as far away as the moon, but it was the closest known approach of an asteroid to earth.

Apollo, Adonis, Hermes, and Icarus were each about a mile in diameter. Back in 1898, the asteroid Eros, which is fifteen miles in diameter, caused a stir by coming close to the earth. Eros is the largest known asteroid to have entered the vicinity of our planet.

Astronomers know a good deal less about the comings and goings of these wandering asteroids than you might suspect. In space, an object a mile or two in diameter and reflecting only a faint light is hard to find. We can track much smaller artificial satellites because they are beaming a signal, and because we know where they should be. By the time the asteroids come close enough to be seen, they are going so fast across the sky that it takes luck just to keep track of them. Astronomers were able to keep a watch on Icarus because they knew its orbit and thus knew where to look for it. But we don't know the exact orbits of Apollo, Adonis, and Hermes, so we don't know where they are now or when

186

they will again make a close pass at earth. Besides, it is very difficult to calculate exact orbits for bodies as small as the asteroids, because the orbits are so often perturbed by larger passing planets.

Astronomer Robert S. Richardson has said, "We are aware of these close-approaching asteroids only through the accident of discovery. No one knows how many objects ranging in size from a few miles in diameter downward may pass near earth each year without being noticed."

What would happen if an asteroid a mile or so in diameter slammed into the earth? It would be a disaster; everyone is agreed on that. But here is a great deal of uncertainty regarding how large and what kind of a disaster it would be. We simply have no experience with a cataclysm of that magnitude, so we have nothing to compare it with.

Dr. Harold Masursky theorized that an asteroid the size of Icarus would blast a crater as large as the crater Copernicus on the moon. Copernicus is sixty miles across and two miles deep. Cliffs a thousand feet high ring the rim of the crater.

What the other effects would be is anybody's guess. Every place in the world would be affected in some way. If the asteroid struck in the ocean, as it probably would since the majority of the surface of the earth is water, it would create a tidal wave that would swamp all the low-lying cities on the ocean's rim.

Some scientists have suggested that we make a greater effort to keep track of wandering asteroids, so that if one of them appears to be threatening the earth, rockets with nuclear warheads can be launched to blow the asteroid into relatively harmless fragments before it hits.

See also: DEATH OF THE DINOSAURS; THE GREAT SIBERIAN EXPLOSION

MOONS OF MARS   Phobos and Deimos were first discovered by the American astronomer Asaph Hall in 1877, but they had been "predicted" over a century earlier in 1726 by British satirist Jonathan Swift. In his celebrated book that we call *Gulliver's Travels,* Swift had an episode in which he described how the people of the island of Laputa had discovered the satellites, and he gave a reasonably good description of their size and rotational period. Swift could have had no possible way of knowing that the moons actually existed. His prediction has often been cited as one of the luckiest guesses in the history of science or literature. More daring souls have hinted that Jonathan Swift might have had some sort of "psychic" knowlege of the moons of Mars.

There may, however, be a more mundane explanation. In 1752, the French writer Voltaire also wrote about two moons for Mars. This was later than Swift, but still more than a century before the moons were actually seen. Voltaire had not used Swift, guesswork, or psychic powers; he had arrived at the figure by analogy. The inner planets Mercury and Venus had no satellites, Earth had one. The planets beyond Mars were known to have numerous satellites—therefore Mars should have at least two. Possibly Swift had reasoned the same way, but it was still a pretty lucky shot.

In 1862, conditions for viewing Mars were considered exceptionally favorable. By that time, astronomers suspected that the planet had satellites and were looking for them, but they didn't see anything. When Hall observed Phobos and Deimos fifteen years later, the conditions for viewing were less favorable, and he was using a smaller telescope than had been available in 1862. Why had the moons of Mars been missed? That question has led to some fascinating speculation.

There are certain peculiarities about the size and rotation of the two moons that make them look more like artificial satellites than natural ones. I. S. Shklovsky, a prominent Soviet astronomer, proposed the "fantastic idea" that they really were artificial satellites put up by some long-dead Martian civilization. Shklovsky has always been known as a fearless speculator.

Then an American scientist, Frank Salisbury, came up with an even more fantastic idea. In the journal *Science* he wrote, "Should we attribute the failure of 1862 to imperfections in the existing telescopes, or may we imagine that the satellites were launched into orbit between 1862 and 1877."

That is a far-out possibility indeed. But the nagging little question won't be solved conclusively until we get a much closer look at the moons of Mars than we have been able to manage so far.

See also: CANALS OF MARS

MYSTERIOUS LIGHTS   Throughout the world there are places where lights of unknown origin are frequently seen at night. Usually such phenomena quickly become encrusted in legend. The will-o'-the-wisp, for example, a flamelike light most often reported hovering or moving over swampy areas, is, according to legend, a lantern held by the soul of a sinner forced to wander the earth till Judgment Day in payment for some crime or blasphemy committed during his lifetime. As with most folklore, the story varies from place to place.

There are several locations where groups of spherical lights hovering just a few feet above the ground appear with great regularity. This phenomenon is best known in the United States, where the lights are generally referred to as "spook lights." Usually there is a local legend attached to the lights; in one mining area the lights are supposed to be the headlamps of miners killed in accidents.

Mysterious lights seen over the sea are usually attributed to some past disaster where a ship was burned at sea. Since the late 1940s, many mysterious lights have been attributed to UFOs.

Most if not all of these lights have a natural explanation. There has been surprisingly little scientific study, however, of the various phenomena. Spook lights like those in the Ozarks have been studied by scientifically oriented journalists. The usual conclusion is that they are the result of the refraction of distant automobile and train headlights.

The will-o'-the wisps are generally believed to originate in phosphorescent gases released from decaying matter in swamps, where they are most commonly seen. On March 20 and 21, 1966, what appeared to be a large glowing object was sighted rising from a swamp near the town of Dexter, Michigan. Those who reported seeing the thing quickly labeled it a UFO, and the incident got a great deal of publicity. The Air Force, which was still investigating UFOs at that time, sent its chief scientific consultant, Dr. J. Allen Hynek, to look into the case. Hynek told a press conference that he believed that the glowing object was not from outer space but rather was luminous "swamp gas"—the same sort of gas that is believed to produce the will-o'-the-wisp phenomenon. Almost no one believed that explanation, though it is a perfectly reasonable one. The explanation was denounced as part of an Air Force "whitewash," and it helped spark a new interest in UFOs during the late 1960s. Mysterious lights have rarely attracted so much attention in modern times.

See also: UFOS

THE SARGASSO SEA

A vast area of the Atlantic Ocean stretching from 30° to 70° west and 20° to 35° north has been named for the seaweed (*sargaco* in Portuguese) that floats there in great abundance. Since the time of Columbus, the Sargasso Sea has had an ominous and mysterious reputation.

The circulation of the ocean is such that seaweed as well as other debris from anywhere in the Atlantic may be carried by currents into the relatively calm center of the area. It is also an area where the wind can die for long stretches. Sailing ships were often becalmed there.

The first mariner that we know of to sail right through the Sargasso Sea was, of course, Christopher Columbus. Though he did have a couple of odd experiences while sailing through the Sargasso Sea, he took it pretty much in stride. Later sailors began to tell tales of terror about the region. It was said that the weed was so thick that ships would literally become stuck in it and that the weed would grow up the sides of the ships and hold them fast while the men on board perished from thirst under the broiling sun.

It was a ships' graveyard, according to some, a place where wrecks and derelict ships from all over the world were captured by the currents to drift aimlessly amid the weeds until they rot and sink. In legend, it was a place haunted by the ghosts of dead sailors and the home of all manner of strange and terrifying sea monsters.

The Sargasso Sea was used as a background by adventure novelists and later by filmmakers and cartoonists, but the legends about the Sargasso Sea are mostly just that. While there is a good deal of seaweed in the area, much of it from the Caribbean and the Gulf of Mexico, there is certainly not enough to stop a ship. Today, there is more oil and tar from oil spills than there is sargassum in the Sargasso Sea. A derelict ship, like any other piece of debris, would tend to be caught by the currents and drift into the Sargasso Sea. It would also tend to stay afloat longer than in stormier latitudes. But even in the Sargasso a derelict was a rarity. The most dangerous creatures of the region were not monsters but borer worms, which would attack a becalmed ship and eat into its wooden hull.

As Columbus passed through the Sargasso Sea, there were several times when his crew mistakenly sighted land, and once just a few hours before land actually was sighted, Columbus himself saw a mysterious and still-unexplained light on the horizon. But that may have been an illusion. He also seems to have observed the fall of a good-size meteor but was unconcerned.

That the compass needle on the *Pinta* no longer pointed directly at the North Star certainly was no illusion. In Columbus's day, it was believed that the needle of a compass points directly at the North Star. In fact, it points to the north magnetic pole, but this was the first time the variation had been noticed and recorded. Many of the men were alarmed, but Columbus took the variation in stride, assuming correctly that the needle did not point at the North Star but at something else. The variation in the heading of the compass helped to give rise to the belief that in the Sargasso Sea even the laws of nature were different.

Author Lawrence Kushce has noted that since the Sargasso Sea encompassed what later became known as the Bermuda Triangle, the Triangle seems to have inherited some of the older mystery, as well as the general feeling that this was a place where the ordinary laws of nature were suspended.

See also: THE BERMUDA TRIANGLE

SPONTANEOUS HUMAN COMBUSTION   The belief that people can suddenly and for no apparent reason burst into flames and be consumed was an exceedingly popular one in the nineteenth century. Though scientists generally consider such an idea absurd, there was and still is interest in the subject of spontaneous human combustion (SHC).

A number of authors have alluded to or described the phenomenon in their works. In *Life on the Mississippi*, Mark Twain wrote: "Jimmy Finn was not burned in the calaboose, but died a natural death in a tan vat of a combination of delirium tremens and spontaneous combustion. When I say natural death, it was a natural death for Jimmy Finn to die."

Herman Melville also made the popular link between a drunk and spontaneous combustion in his novel *Redburn*. Melville has a drunken sailor burst into flames. As the rest of the crew watch, they are horrified to see "two threads of greenish fire, like a forked tongue, darted out between the lips and in a moment, the cadaverous face was covered by a swarm of wormlike flames. . . . The uncovered body burned before us, precisely like a phosphorescent shark in a midnight sea."

In his 1834 novel *Jacob Faithful*, Frederick Marryat gave a description of human spontaneous combustion—the details of which he seems to have taken mainly from a report in the *Times* of 1832: "Nothing was burning—not even the curtains to my mother's bed appeared to be singed. . . . There appeared to be a black mass in the middle of the bed. I put my hand fearfully upon it—it was a sort of unctuous pitchy cinder. I screamed with horror. . . . I staggered from the cabin, and fell down on the deck in a state amounting to almost insanity. . . . As the reader may be in some doubt as to the occasion of my mother's death, I must inform him that she perished in that very peculiar and dreadful manner, which sometimes, though rarely, occurs to those who indulge in an immoderate use of spiritous liquors. Cases of this kind do indeed present themselves but once in a century, but the occurrence of them is too well authenticated. She perished from what is called spontaneous combustion, an inflammation of the gases generated from the spirits absorbed into the body system. It is to be presumed that the flames issuing from my mother's body completely frightened out of his senses my father, who had been drinking freely."

Unquestionably the most famous spontaneous combustion death in all fiction is Charles Dickens's description of the death of the drunken and miserly rag-and-bone man Krook in his novel *Bleak House:* "Here is a small burnt patch of flooring; here is the tinder from a little bundle of burnt paper, but not so light as usual, seeming to be steeped in something; and here is—is it the cinder of a small charred and broken log of wood sprinkled with white ashes, or is it coal, O Horror, he is here! and this, from which we run away, striking out the light and overturning one another into the street, is all that represents him."

Dickens insisted that such a manner of death was "inborn, inbred, engendered in the corrupted humours of the vicious body itself, and that only—Spontaneous Combustion, and none other of all the deaths that can be died."

Dickens was very serious about his belief in the phenomenon of spontaneous combustion and had read widely on the subject. In *Bleak House* he recognized that many would criticize his use of it,

Mr. Krook's flaming end. A drawing from Charles Dickens's novel Bleak House.
(New York Public Library)

as indeed they did. When the second edition of *Bleak House* was issued, Dickens put a lengthy defense of his belief in SHC in the preface: "I have no need to observe that I do not wilfully or negligently mislead my readers, and that, before I worte that description, I took pains to investigate the subject. There are about thirty cases on record of which the most famous, that of the Countess

194

Cornelia de Baudi Cesnate, was minutely investigated and described by Giuseppe Bianchini. . . ." and so on for considerable length.

The more Dickens was attacked, the more tightly he clung to the idea. Some critics were puzzled and amused by his persistence, and it was frequently commented on in the press.

Dickens was, however, far from the only Victorian fascinated by the idea of spontaneous human combustion. It was one of those subjects that held deep attraction for people of the era, probably because it was viewed as a sort of moral punishment for drunkenness. Sensational newspapers of the day often carried accounts of people who had suddenly gone up in flames in much the same way as sensational newspapers of today often carry accounts of people who have been kidnapped by UFOs. In recent years there has been a real revival of interest in the subject; it even became a running joke in a popular 1984 film satire on rock music.

One of the more recent cases that gained considerable attention was that of Dr. J. Irving Bentley of Coudersport, Pennsylvania. Dr. Bentley, who was ninety-two years old, was burned up almost entirely—but the rest of the house was relatively undamaged. The fire had been so intense that a hole was burned right through the floor, and most of Dr. Bentley's ashes were found in the basement. According to the local coroner, "All I found was a knee joint, which was atop a post in the basement, the lower leg with its foot on the bathroom floor, and the now-scattered ashes six feet below."

Another well-publicized case was that of a Mrs. Hardy Reeser of St. Petersburg, Florida. This sixty-seven-year-old widow was burned up under mysterious circumstances in July 1951. The armchair in which she had been sitting and an end table were also burned, but nearby papers and drapes and other highly flammable materials in the room were undamaged. All that was left of Mrs. Reeser were a few small pieces of charred backbone, her strangely shrunken skull, and an undamaged left foot. In life, Mrs. Reeser had weighed 175 pounds. Her charred remains weighed less than ten.

Devotees of the phenomenon of SHC can cite dozens of similar cases.

The conventional explanation in most of these cases is that the cause of the fire is smoking, and the victim is often old and disabled or drunk and therefore unable to respond quickly enough when the fire starts.

However, those who believe in SHC contend that conventional explanations ignore many important facts. The bodies are often reduced to a pile of ashes, obviously by an extremely hot flame, yet the surrounding area is virtually untouched. They also cite cases in which the victim was neither infirm, nor drunk, nor a smoker. The cases, they say, are too numerous and too strange to yield to the usual explanations.

Unconventional explanations today often center about a theoretical paranormal force that is somehow unconsciously released by the victim. In his study of the subject, *Fire From Heaven,* author Michael Harrison points to the similarity of SHC and some poltergeist cases that also involve fire. "SHC and poltergeist phenomena imply action and reaction between the 'force generator' and the 'victim'—the 'force' being the result of deliberate *intention,* even though the intention may not be consciously known to the human being generating the force."

A more bizarre explanation was put forth by Ronald J. Willis, a veteran collector of strange and unusual accounts. He has suggested that there might exist some sort of strange "fire beings which swoop down on certain individuals and incinerate them mysteriously. . . . What possible motivation these creatures could have is beyond our imagination, but then much of the Universe is still beyond our ken. It's not a pleasant thing to think about when going to bed late tonight."

THINGS FROM THE SKY   One of the subjects that most fascinated Charles Fort and that continues to fascinate his disciples

Falls of frogs were one of Charles Fort's abiding interests, as can be seen in this illustration for the cover of one of his books.

today is the numerous accounts of things that appear to fall mysteriously from the sky. Fort begins his *The Book of the Damned* (and by "damned" he meant excluded from orthodox science) in his typically roundabout fashion with an account of falling frogs: "Tremendous number of little toads, one or two months old, that were seen to fall from a great thick cloud that appeared suddenly in a sky that had been cloudless, August 1804, near Toulouse, France, according to a letter from Prof. Pontus to M. Arago.

"Many instances of frogs that were seen to fall from the sky. (*Notes and Queires* 8–6–104); accounts of such falls, signed by witnesses.

"*Scientific American,* July 12, 1873;

"A shower of frogs which darkened the air and covered the

ground for a long distance is reported as the result of a recent rainstorm in Kansas City, Mo."

Frog falls, however, are not nearly as numerous as fish falls. The sixteenth-century ecclesiastic and writer Olaus Magnus told of such events in his massive history of Scandinavia.

The March 1972 issue of *Australian Natural History* lists fifty-four separate falls of fish (and a few of frogs) recorded in Australia between 1879 and 1971. Australia is not particularly noted for its rains of fish; it is merely that someone bothered to collect the accounts and list them in chronological order. They make interesting reading. In February 1909, a man named T. Iredale reported that small fishes had rattled down on his tin roof during a storm. According to the *Australian Museum Magazine*, hundreds of little fish called gudgeons were found in the streets after a rain at Gulargambone, New South Wales. *The Sydney Morning Herald* reported that on July 17, 1959, hundreds of fishes about four inches long fell in Lismore, New South Wales.

And the fish are still falling, not only in Australia but all over the world. The autumn 1984 issue of the *Fortean Times*, a British-published journal that collects oddities, tells of a modest fall of small fish in East London in late May 1984.

Probably the best known of the fish falls was the one that occurred at Mountain Ash in the valley of Aberdare, Glamorganshire, Wales, on February 11, 1859. A man named John Lewis was standing out in the rain when fish began to pour down on him. One slipped down the neck of his shirt, and several got caught in his hat brim. The fall went on only for about two minutes, then it stopped, and ten minutes later started again for another two minutes. The fish fell over a very limited area, only about eighty yards by twelve yards. The fish were not only fresh, they were very lively. A few samples, allegedly still alive, were sent to the British Museum for examination. Authorities there determined that there were two types, minnows and sticklebacks. Later, the surviving fish were supposed to have been exhibited at the Zoological Garden in Regent's Park. They may have been the only famous min-

nows in history. That part of the story, however, sounds apocryphal, for it is difficult to imagine how the fish would have been
kept alive in 1859.

Scientists at the British Museum were inclined to dismiss the
Mountain Ash incident as some sort of joke. They suggested that
someone had thrown a bucketful of fish over Lewis.

Another explanation, and one that is most commonly raised to
explain falls of fish and frogs, is a whirlwind. This mass of rapidly
swirling air sucks up the creatures from lakes and ponds and de-

A nineteenth-century engraving showing a fall of fish.

posits them elsewhere, like the cyclone that transported Dorothy to Oz, except not as violent.

Forteans scoff at such explanations and raise a variety of objections. Often these falls have taken place too far from a body of water for a whirlwind to carry fishes or frogs; the falls took place on a perfectly clear day, with no evidence of any sort of a meteorological disturbance and so on. Much depends on the accuracy with which the events surrounding the fall were reported.

Fort had collected a few records of snake falls—not masses of snakes, just a snake or two at a time. Fort said that he had a letter from a Miss Margaret McDonald of Hathorne, Massachusetts, stating that a number of speckled snakes fell in the streets of Hathorne after a thunderstorm.

On May 26, 1920, what was identified as a poisonous snake from Egypt fell into a garden in central London. On the next three days, poisonous adders fell, or rather appeared, in various parts of London.

Commented Fort, "Common sense tells me that probably some especially vicious joker had been scattering venomous snakes around. But some more common sense tells me that I cannot depend upon common sense."

Not only animals fall from the sky. During July 1822, great quantities of seeds of unknown origin fell in various parts of Germany. The peasants, who were often short of food, tried to boil the seeds into an edible condition, but boiling did not seem to soften them.

Another vegetable substance that has occasionally been reported falling from the sky is straw or hay. A great quantity of it was reported to have fallen on London's Heathrow Airport on August 10, 1972.

Then there is the problem of "angel hair," a general term used to describe a variety of filamentous or stringy material that is supposed to fall from the sky or otherwise appear mysteriously on the ground.

According to Fortean naturalist the late Ivan Sanderson, "The published literature of so-called angel hair is massive. It crops up in heavy scientific journals, and from way back in the nineteenth century. Even modern meteorological publications mention it from time to time."

Generally angel hair seems to disintegrate when it has lain on the ground for a short time, so there have been few samples to examine.

Ice from the sky is another Fortean favorite, We all know that ice can fall from the sky in the form of hail. In violent thunderstorms, hailstones several inches in diameter have been known to fall. But what is one to say about what happened at a place called Ord, Scotland, on the estate of a Mr. Moffat in August 1847? There, a gigantic piece of ice, nearly twenty feet around, fell near the farmhouse. According to a contemporary account, "It had a beautiful crystalline appearance, being nearly all quite transparent. . . . It was principally composed of small squares, diamond-shaped, of from 1 to 3 inches in size, all firmly congealed together." The ice chunk melted before anyone could weigh it, but the writer observed that it was a good thing that it hadn't fallen on Moffat's house, because it would have crushed the inhabitants.

On October 16, 1960, in Melbourne, Australia, a couple of lumps of ice the size of footballs fell from a cloudless sky onto a golf course, narrowly missing some golfers, according to an AP story.

On March 23, 1984, a cubic foot of ice weighing about fifty pounds fell into the garden of the Powell home in Portsmouth, New Hampshire. The Powells had just come home from a trip when they noticed it. "There it was, sitting in the garden," says Mrs. Powell. "I couldn't believe it. It had spread flowers and stones all over the place where it had dug so deep."

In addition, there have been reported falls of stones, ashes, and undentifiable gooey stuff, and all sorts of other things lovingly collected and listed by Forteans. That same issue of *The Fortean*

Times that contained news of the 1984 East London fish fall also carries an item about a World War II artillery shell that crashed into the backyard of Fred Simmons in Lakewood, California, on January 1, 1984. The shell was nine inches long, weighed about twenty-two pounds, and was rusty. A bomb squad from the Los Angeles County Sheriff's Department found that there were no explosives in the shell. The shell, however, left a crater about four feet deep. One official suggested that some prankster may have dropped the shell from a plane, but no one reported seeing or hearing a plane at the time.

What does it all mean? The conventional answer to that question is that it does not mean a great deal, or more accurately, that it probably means a lot of different things. Different falls can be explained in different ways, and we are not dealing with a single phenomenon. Fish and frogs may be the result of a whirlwind; ice can come from freak hailstorms; and artillery shells are dropped by practical jokers.

But Charles Fort and his disciples think differently. They have a passion for finding an underlying unity in all these strange events. Fort hinted that all these "things from the sky" came from somewhere else, perhaps from another universe.

Ivan Sanderson said it more directly. "These things," he wrote, "don't really fall out of the sky (like rain or airplanes) but they 'come through' from one or more other 'universe.' They have been appearing since ever, *and they must come from somewhere.*"

6

MYSTERIES

OF MAGIC

$\mathbb{A}$LCHEMISTS   The word *alchemist* conjures up a picture of an ancient and bearded man bent over his crucibles and retorts in an endless quest to turn lead into gold. That picture, though accurate, is far from complete.

The transmutation of base metals into gold was only one small part of the alchemical quest, although it was always a popular and spectacular part. The true goal of the alchemist was "the Philosopher's Stone."

Alchemy was based on a philosophy that held that the universe was unified and harmonious and pervaded by a "universal spirit." This belief could be summed up in the statement "One is All and All is One." The alchemical problem was to somehow concentrate and purify matter to a substance that contained the "universal spirit" in its pristine form. This was the Philosopher's Stone.

The roots of alchemy stretch back to very ancient times. The idea that one material could be changed to another, that gold might be made from base metals, may have started among the goldsmiths of the pharaohs. The ancient Chinese also had their own forms of alchemy, apparently uninfluenced by practices in other parts of the world. But Western alchemical theory really became codified in the cosmopolitan city of Alexandria, Egypt, during the first centuries of the Christian era.

Much of alchemical theory is attributed to the writings of one Hermes Trismegistus. But these Hermetic books do not appear to have had a single author; rather, they are compilations, probably made by members of some of the heretical Christian sects that

205

found a home in Alexandria. The Hermetic books are a combination of magical lore, Greek natural philosophy, Christian doctrine, and occasionally some practical knowledge of metalworking.

Alchemy was lost to Europe during that period known as the Dark Ages, but it was rediscovered chiefly through Arabic sources in the years following the fifteenth century, often engaging the interest of some of the best minds in Europe. Though unorthodox practices like alchemy were often condemned by the Church, alchemy itself was treated with more indulgence than most. The occasional incautious alchemist might find himself persecuted as a sorcerer; others carried on their experiments openly often under the patronage of kings, clerics, and even popes.

Hopes, rumors, and shared assumptions kept the practice of alchemy alive for many centuries. Though there were stories of alchemists who had distilled the miraculous Philosopher's Stone, there was certainly no proof. Indeed, no one seems quite sure what the Stone was supposed to look like. It was often referred to as the Elixir or Tincture, indicating that it was a liquid. It was not only credited with the power of transmutation, it was also said to cure all diseases, prolong life indefinitely, and accomplish a whole host of other miraculous things.

The primary reason why it is so difficult to understand just exactly what the alchemist was after is that alchemy had a twofold nature: it was both practical and spiritual. The attempt to transmute base metals into gold was the practical side. In the Christian world, however, it was not possible to believe that the alchemist could succeed by human effort alone. The belief grew that the Stone could only be made with the aid of divine grace and favor. Thus, only the spiritually pure man could be a successful alchemist.

The result of such beliefs was the system called hidden or esoteric alchemy, which was concerned with the transformation of sinful man into perfect being. The analogy of the transformation of "base" metal into "pure" gold is obvious. The two kinds of alchemy were thoroughly intertwined, and often it is quite impossible to tell whether the alchemist is describing a physical experiment or a spiritual exercise. The stress on spiritual purity led to the paradoxical conclusion that in order to make gold, a man must be pure enough not to want gold. Such a belief excuses many failures.

By tapping the universal spirit, many alchemists came to the conclusion that they could create an artificial man, called the homunculus. There were numerous methods proposed for creating this being. Here is one of them: The alchemist assembles various "needful" substances. Just exactly what substances are "needful" unfortunately is not specified. These substances are enclosed in a glass phial and buried in horse dung for forty days. The rotting dung would heat the mixture.

"At the end of this time, there will be something which will begin to move and live in the bottle. This something is a man, but a man who has no body and is transparent. Nevertheless, he exists, and nothing remains but to bring him up—which is not more difficult to do than to make him. You may accomplish it by daily feeding him—during forty weeks, and without extracting him from his dung hill—with *arcanum* [secret spirit] of human blood. At the end of this time you shall have a veritable living child, having every member as well-proportioned as any infant born of a woman. He will only be much smaller than an ordinary child, and his physical education will require more care and attention."

The formula for creating the homunculus is obscure. Indeed, obscurity is the hallmark of all alchemical writings. Even in the comparatively simple matter of changing base metal into gold, the alchemists did not understand the transformations they were attempting to describe. The alchemist might say that Sol or the Sun was devoured by the green dragon, whereas the modern chemist would describe the same process by saying that gold dissolves in the acid *aqua rega*. The alchemist's description is a lot prettier but is less concise. To the alchemist "the black crow" meant lead, "the grey wolf" antimony and "celestial dew" signified mercury or "the mercury principle." But the words did not always mean the same

Alchemical art was beautiful and strange

thing to all alchemists, and the result was endless confusion. Often the alchemist abandoned words altogether and used signs or symbolic drawings. Medieval alchemical art is often beautiful and always strange.

The alchemist was also deliberately obscure. Many were simple fakers who promised to produce gold for a fee and never delivered. They covered imposture with a flow of fancy words meant to impress rather than inform. The alchemical confidence game worked time and again for centuries. It is said that Marie de Medici, wife of Henry IV of France, heard of an alchemist named Guy de Crusembourg, who was imprisoned in the Bastille. She gave him twenty thousand crowns for his alchemical experiments, assuming that as a prisoner, he could find no other way of spending the money. Guy found a way. He escaped from the Bastille, and the queen never saw him or her money again.

Even the honest alchemist felt the need to be obscure in order to protect his secrets, just in case he might discover any. The merest rumor that an alchemist had succeeded in his quest could be dangerous. One alchemist who also practiced medicine had effected some rather spectacular cures during an epidemic, and the rumor got around that he had the Elixir. A mob howling for the miraculous cure, which the alchemist did not possess, descended on his house, and the terrified man had to sneak away in disguise. The alchemist said that he knew of many of his fellow alchemists who had been murdered because they were thought to possess the Stone, when in fact they knew no more about it than their murderers.

The alchemical quest was one of the most compelling yet frustrating in history. Time after time, alchemists reported being just at the point of distilling the essence when the retort broke, or the crucible cracked, forcing them to start the laborious process all over again. In the late nineteenth century, the Reverend W. A. Ayton, an English clergyman and alchemist, claimed that he had actually prepared the Elixir and was just about to drink it when a long-winded visitor arrived. By the time the visitor finished talking, the volatile mixture had evaporated and could never be recreated again.

The Reverend Ayton was something of an anachronism. Serious belief in alchemy all but disappeared during the eighteenth century. By that time, the word *alchemy* had become almost synonymous with fraud or foolishness.

In defense of alchemy, it can be said that the knowledge gained working with various materials contributed directly to the development of modern chemistry. But it was the discoveries of chemistry that destroyed the theoretical foundation upon which the search for the Philosopher's Stone rested.

Some defenders of alchemy point out that while it is not possible to transmute lead into gold, it is possible through nuclear bombardment to transform one element into another, and thus the alchemical quest was not entirely wrong. The problem with such an argument is that while some of the goals of the alchemists might be attainable, the alchemical view of the structure of the physical world was completely wrong. Alchemists could have continued messing with their retorts and furnaces from now till Doomsday without coming one step closer to attaining their goals. It is a bit like trying to reach the moon by climbing trees.

Even today, alchemy is not totally dead. A British alchemist named Archibald Cockrin, who died in the 1960s, claimed that he had made a crystal of gold grow like a plant. There was still at least one frankly alchemical society operating in London a decade ago. Occult societies drop hints that they hold "the secret," and the symbolism of alchemy is still popular in the writings of today's occultists.

See also: THE EMERALD TABLET; NICOLAS FLAMEL

THE CABALA   *Cabala* is a Hebrew word meaning "that which is received, or tradition." The word appears under a number of English transliterations, including Cabbala, Qabbalah, and Kabbalah.

The sort of speculation found in the Cabala must have begun in ancient times, but what is properly called the Jewish Cabala is a system of mystical thought that was organized in southern France and Spain in the twelfth and thirteenth centuries. It continued to grow and develop for another three hundred years. The principal work of the Jewish Cabala is the *Zohar,* or *Book of Splendor.* It was written somewhere around the year 1280 by the scholar Moses de

Leon of Guadalajara, Spain. The *Zohar* is so esoteric and abstruse that it has been remarked that no man who has immersed himself in the study of it has ever emerged entirely sane. Judaism, like other religions, has always contained a mystical element, a belief that knowledge of God could be obtained directly through contemplation and revelation. Since the knowledge is supposed to be direct rather than something that is arrived at through reason or logic, it is extremely difficult, if not impossible, to explain in words. Thus, mystical writings are always obscure and difficult for the nonmystic.

Another feature that often appears in mysticism is secrecy. There is a fear that the ignorant and uninitiated will either be misled or somehow misuse the revealed knowledge. Among some mystical groups, there is a feeling that they will lose their power if their secret knowledge becomes generally known. Therefore, already obscure ideas are often made deliberately more difficult to comprehend. The "true meaning" or "inner meaning" of the mystical doctrines is kept entirely secret and is revealed only to those who have undergone a long period of initiation or testing.

It would be presumptuous to attempt to summarize centuries of cabalistic thought in a brief article. Cabalistic mysticism has never been in the mainstream of Judaism. Indeed, many Orthodox Jewish scholars have been deeply suspicious of it, for the Cabala contains some non-Jewish influences. But it is important to note that cabalistic theory places great emphasis on the power attached to certain words and numbers. Another element of cabalistic tradition is the belief that things are not what they seem and that a hidden meaning can be found in everything.

Among simpler folk, the scholarly cabalists, preoccupied with certain words and numbers, and secret and mysterious in their way of life, developed the reputation for being magicians. People began wearing amulets or charms inscribed with cabalistic names and symbols. The amulets were aimed at everything from protecting the wearer from the evil eye to producing invisibility.

Around the fifteenth century, Christians began to develop an in-

Cabalistic drawings

212

terest in the Cabala. At first, they attempted to prove that the truth of Christianity was the secret meaning behind the obscure Cabala. Later it was an interest in the magical possibilities of the Cabala that came to dominate the non-Jewish cabalists. Many early Christian students of the Cabala were either taught by Jews or were themselves converted Jews. They, at least, had some authentic knowledge of what they were dealing with.

By the seventeenth century, the original Cabala was almost lost entirely. The word *Cabala* increasingly became a blanket term used to describe any kind of secret and obscure magical lore. Many of the magic words were Hebrew words, which in the authentic Cabala have great power but not the sort of power attributed to them by the *grimoires,* or medieval books of magic.

Numbers or letters arranged in a square, according to certain rules, have been used as magic devices at least since the time of the ancient Romans. They have also been used extensively in China and India. But from medieval times onward, magic squares were attributed to the Cabala. The popular pack of fortune-telling cards called the tarot contains twenty-two major trump cards, or face cards. Each of these has a mysterious picture, like the Tower or the Magician, on it. There are also twenty-two letters in the Hebrew alphabet, a fact of considerable significance to Cabalists and to those occultists who use tarot cards. Some modern tarot decks even have Hebrew letters printed on them. There is no historical justification for the occultists' claim that the tarot is some sort of ancient Hebrew development, for there is no evidence that the cards were ever used before the fifteenth century.

The Cabala picked up another and more dangerous association. Because of its secrecy, the Cabala became synonymous with plot or intrigue. The word *cabal,* which means "a secret group gathered together for some sinister purpose," comes from the word *Cabala.* There has always existed a belief that some sort of secret group really controls the world and is responsible for all the awful things that happen in it. Throughout European history, the Jews were often accused of being that sinister, secret group. The fact that the "secret" Cabala was also originally Hebrew served to add to the deadly myth.

See also: THE GRIMOIRES

THE EMERALD TABLET   To the medieval alchemist, the founder of his art was Hermes Trismegistus, a king or sage who lived in ancient Egypt. A vast body of alchemical and magical writings were attributed to this Hermes, and they were enormously influential throughout Europe for several centuries. Alchemists often referred to their profession as the Hermetic Art.

Of all the Hermetic writings, the most important and most mysterious was the Emerald Tablet.

According to tradition, the Tablet was found in a cave. The words were etched in Phoenician characters on a slab of emerald clutched in the hands of the corpse of Hermes Trismegistus himself. The discoverer in one version of the story was Sara, the wife of Abraham, and the cave was located near Hebron. In other versions, the tablet was found by Alexander the Great in the hands of the celebrated ancient magician Apollonius of Tyana. Still another variation of the legend had Hermes giving the tablet to Miriam, the beautiful sister of Moses. The Arabs had Noah taking the Emerald Tablet with him on the Ark.

The Emerald Tablet was the work with which all good alchemists began their quest, and from it one can get the flavor of an important alchemical-magical tradition.

> True it is, without falsehood, certain and most true. That which is above is like to that which is below, and that which is below is like to that which is above, to accomplish the miracles of one thing.
>
> And as all things were by the contemplation of one, so all things arose from this one thing by a single act of adaption.
>
> The father thereof is the Sun, the mother is the Moon.
>
> The wind carried in its womb, the Earth is nurse thereof.
>
> It is the father of all works of wonder throughout the whole world.

The power thereof is perfect.

If it can be cast onto Earth, it will separate the element of Earth from that of Fire, the subtle from the gross.

With great sagacity it doth ascend gently from Earth to Heaven.

Again it doth descend to Earth, and untieth in itself the force from things superior and things inferior.

Thus thou wilt possess the glory of the brightness of the whole world, and all obscurity will fly far from thee.

This thing is the strong fortitude of all strength, for it overcometh every subtle thing and doth penetrate every solid substance.

Thus was the world created.

Hence there will be marvelous adaptations achieved, of which the manner is this.

For this reason I am called Hermes Trismegistus, because I hold three parts of the wisdom of the whole world.

That which I had to say about the operation of Sol is completed.

What does it all mean? No one can really say. The Emerald Tablet can be interpreted only in the most general way:

1. It is a statement of the basic magical belief of correspondence or interaction between heavenly and earthly events. ("That which is above is like to that which is below.")

2. Everything in heaven and earth has a single origin. ("So all things arose from this one thing.")

3. The original "thing" seems to be sort of a living universal soul, for the Tablet speaks of the "contemplation" and "adaptation" of the "one thing."

4. The possibility of changing base metals into gold is implied. The sun and moon mentioned in the Tablet may be gold and silver; they often were in alchemical writing.

Beyond these very general statements, the meaning of the Emerald Tablet is shrouded in mystery and controversy. Many have tried to explain the Tablet, but the explanations are usually as obscure as the original, and much longer.

Unfortunately, the wonderful legends about the Hermetic writings have fallen before the researches of historians. In the seventeenth century, the real origins of the Hermetic books, which were supposed to be incredibly ancient, were discovered, and the discovery helped to hasten the decline of interest in alchemy. The books seem mostly to have been composed in Alexandria, Egypt, during the first few centuries of the Christian era. They are largely the products of a variety of heretical Christian sects that flourished at that time. These sects incorporated ancient magical lore and Greek natural philosophy into their doctrines. One of the things that had most impressed medieval scholars about the Hermetic writings was that though they were supposed to be pre-Christian or even pre-Mosaic, there were numerous references to Christianity, which is perhaps why the Church itself looked with some kindness upon them, despite their clearly unorthodox nature.

The famed Emerald Tablet may actually be older than the other Hermetic writings, though we cannot be sure. The first known account of it appears in a book written in Arabic during the ninth century. Scholars believe that the true origin of the Emerald Tablet was Greece or Syria, rather than the traditional homeland of mysteries, Egypt. The real author is and doubtless always will remain unknown.

See also: ALCHEMISTS

THE GRIMOIRES   In the popular imagination, magicians always had books, or libraries of books, containing all their magical secrets. These books were jealously guarded, for if the knowledge they contained fell into the hands of the unwise or the unworthy, anything might happen.

A typical and often-repeated story concerning such books was told about the celebrated sixteenth-century German magician Cornelius Agrippa. Agrippa was living in the university city of Louvain in the Netherlands. One day he had to go on a trip, so he carefully locked his study in which he kept all his magic books. He gave the key to his wife with strict instructions that no one was allowed to enter the locked room.

Cornelius Agrippa

A student was renting a room in the magician's house, and he wanted very much to get a look at the inside of the great man's study. He managed to convince Agrippa's wife to give him the key. Upon entering the room, the student saw one of the magician's books lying open on the desk. He began to read aloud from the book. At the first words, he heard a knock at the door, which frightened him, but when he checked the door he found no one there, and he continued reading. There was another knock, which practically scared the student out of his wits. He tried to say "Come in" but was too terrified to speak. This time the door opened and a large, fierce-looking stranger entered.

"Why was I summoned?" demanded the stranger.

"I did not summon you," said the student haltingly.

"You did," said the stranger, advancing menacingly, "and the demons are not invoked in vain."

The student was now speechless with terror. The demon was enraged, thinking that he had been trifled with. He seized the unfortunate youth by the throat and choked the life out of him. The moral, clearly enough, is that if you use a magic spell to call up a demon, you had better know what to do with him.

When Agrippa returned home a few days later, he found his house overrun by demons. "Some of them were sitting on the

Summoning a demon with the aid of a magic book

chimney pots, kicking up their legs in the air; while others were playing at leapfrog on the very edge of the parapet. His study was so filled with them that he found it difficult to make his way to the desk." When Agrippa saw the open book on his desk and the dead student on the floor, he quickly guessed what had happened. The great magician dismissed the minor demons with little trouble; then he confronted the chief demon. Why, he asked, had the demon strangled the boy? The demon was unrepentant and insisted that the boy had deserved to die for calling him up without a good reason.

The story, though it seems to have been believed by many when it was told late in the sixteenth century, is clearly a macabre fable. But it illustrates the fact that magic books were extremely important and that many people believed the books contained exact and simple instructions for summoning up demons.

In the Middle Ages, these books of magic were generally called *grimoires,* a word that comes from the same root as "grammar," or

218

"gramarye," an old term for magic and enchantment. A fair number of these medieval grimoires, both complete and fragmentary, survive to the present day. Most magic books, however, were written in Europe between the sixteenth and eighteenth centuries, although they were based on much older material. The real authors of the grimoires are unknown, and the books are usually falsely attributed to some celebrated historical or legendary character.

The most influential of these books was *The Key of Solomon*, which was supposed to have been written by King Solomon of the Old Testament. In the Bible there is no mention of magic—a practice of which the Hebrews strongly disapproved—and King Solomon. But Solomon was praised for his wisdom and criticized for falling under foreign influences. Later, a whole body of legends about Solomon's magical practices grew up.

The Key of Solomon, which has survived in several different versions and languages, may have been composed anywhere from the thirteenth to the sixteenth century.

There is a good deal of variation in the rites described in the different versions, and occult scholars have argued over which version is more "genuine." But for the layperson, these arguments are

King Solomon

mere quibbles. One is first fascinated, then stunned, and ultimately bored by the agonizingly elaborate rituals described in the *Key.* Some brief excerpts from the book will give you the flavor of this grimoire.

The *Key,* and usually other grimoires as well, started with a solemn warning to those into whose hands the book might fall:

> This work of Solomon is composed of two books. In the first you can see how to avoid mistakes in operations with the Spirits.
>
> In the Second Book you are taught how to perform the Arts of Magic.
>
> You must take the greatest care that this Key of Secrets does not get into the hands of the foolish or ignorant.
>
> He who has it, and uses it, and uses it according to the instructions, will be able not only to perform magical ceremonies; he will be able in the case of errors to correct them.
>
> No operation will succeed unless the magician understands completely what he is about.
>
> I therefore most earnestly adjure the person who gains possession of the Key of Secrets not to pass it on, nor to share its knowledge with anyone, unless he is faithful, and can keep a secret and is proficient in the Magical Arts.
>
> I humbly pray the possessor of this, by the Name of God TETRAGRAMMATON, YOD HE VAU HE, and by the Name ADONAI, and by the other Names of God, the High and Holy, and he should treat this work as precious as his own soul, and share it with no foolish or ignorant person.

In the religion of the ancient Hebrews, and in the books of magic, the names of God were credited with enormous power. The Tetragrammaton, which literally means "having four letters," is the actual name of God. In most modern versions of the Bible, it appears as Jehovah. In ancient times the name was considered too sacred to use. The four Hebrew letters are *yod, he, vau,* and *he.* Transliterated into English they are YHVH and are usually written as *Yahweh.* The approximate meaning of the word is "he is." *Adonai* is Hebrew for "the Lord." Regardless of the meaning of the word to the Hebrews, to the compiler of *The Key of Solomon* they were powerful magic words.

Even for relatively simple magical operations, the preparations described in *The Key of Solomon* are elaborate to the point of impossibility. Before attempting any operation, the magician and his assistants must be in a state of "purity." This means that they are to abstain from all sensual activities for at least nine days and fast for three of those days. Then the magician must bathe in specially consecrated water and dry himself with a white linen towel. Only then can he put on the necessary "pure" magical garments. The garments were made of white silk or linen spun by a virgin girl. Sacred symbols were embroidered in red silk on the breast with a consecrated needle. The shoes were of white leather and were also covered with sacred signs. The crown of the magician was to be made from white paper. With a specially consecrated pen, YHVH was to be written on the front of the crown, *Adonai* on the back. Two other Hebrew sacred words were used: *El* was written on the right side, and *Elohim* on the left.

Each of these steps was to be accompanied by its own set of incantations, the burning of incense, and other rituals. It all had to be done at certain hours of certain days, for *The Key of Solomon* was heavily influenced by astrological theory.

The magician also had to be in the proper frame of mind and correct emotional state, for improper thoughts or feelings could destroy the entire operation. Only then could conjuring up the spirits, angels, demons, or whatever for the purpose of doing magic begin. Clearly, the legend of the unfortunate student who found Agrippa's open grimoire was kept alive by people who knew nothing of real grimoires. Those who seriously consulted such books and believed in their powers would never believe that a magical operation could be performed simply by mumbling a few words.

Not all grimoires were attributed to Solomon. Agrippa himself was supposed to have written a grimoire. Though he did write several weighty books on occult philosophy, he never wrote a book of spells, for he had little patience with that sort of magic. Some clever magician, or more likely some clever publisher, simply put together a magic handbook and attached the name of the celebrated Agrippa to it. Others who were erroneously supposed to have compiled grimoires include Albertus Magnus, a twelfth-century theologian and scholar, and Honorius the Great, an early pope. Abramelin the Mage, who is supposed to have written a celebrated book of magic, may or may not have been a real person. Other grimoires are attributed to totally unidentifiable figures with names like Little Albert.

See also: THE CABALA

T**HE ILLUMINATI**   What are the Illuminati? How powerful have they been? Do they still exist today?

You can get widely differing answers to these questions. To call the Illuminati mysterious or controversial would be a gross understatement. This much we do know. In the Moslem world, there was a small secretive cult called the *Roshaniya,* "the Illuminated Ones." They believed that they were inspired by special divine revelation, or illumination. The early history of this group is unclear, but in the sixteenth century a powerful branch of the society evolved in the mountains of Afghanistan. The Moslem Illuminati were a mystical warrior group, according to those who were sympathetic; they were bandits according to their enemies. From their mountain strongholds, they were able to control considerable territory. The Moguls, distant descendants of the Mongols who had finished off another celebrated secret society of killers, the Assassins, also brought down the Afghan Illuminati. By the mid-seventeenth century, the sect had been thoroughly defeated and dispersed. The few survivors had little power or influence.

About half a century after the power of the Moslem Illuminati was broken, a German society bearing the same name was formed. There is no solid evidence of a direct connection between the Moslem and the European Illuminati. Both groups had political as well as mystical aims, and both used an elaborate initiation ritual.

But the same can be said of many secret societies. The only interesting bit of evidence to support the theory of a connection between the two groups is that the German Illuminati claimed the Prophet Mohammed as one of their initiates, an unusual thing for a secret society in the West to do.

Mythologist and occultist Lewis Spence says that the term *Illuminati* first was used in the West in Spain during the fifteenth century. There was still a strong Moslem influence in Spain at that time. Spence, however, believed that the society in Spain "is probably a late Gnostic one hailing from Italy, and we find all sorts of people, many of them charlatans, claiming to belong to the brotherhood. In Spain such persons as laid claim to the title had to face the rigour of the Inquisition, and this is perhaps the reason we find numbers of them in France in the early seventeenth century as refugees."

Unfortunately, Spence cites no sources for this information, and there may be none. The first hard facts that we have about an Illuminati society in the West come from Bavaria, about the year 1776. The leader of this German group was Adam Weishaupt, a professor of canon law at Ingolstadt University. The group claimed to be mystically inspired to free humanity from "tyranny." A worthy aim, and a common one during that period.

Endless romantic and lurid stories were spread about the Illuminati, and modern books on secret societies delve lovingly into the supposed codes and symbols of the order. The Illuminati were even supposed to have had a safe that would explode if tampered with.

Weishaupt was dismissed from his position at the university after his society was discovered. He blamed his dismissal on the Jesuits, who hated him, and whom he hated in return. The order was quickly suppressed, but some believe that its influence was enormous. Says Spence, "Weishaupt fled, but the damage had been done, for the fire kindled by Illuminism was soon to burst forth in the French Revolution."

That is an outrageous accomplishment to attribute to a group

Adam Weishaupt

that apparently had a membership consisting of a young professor and a few of his friends. There are tales of the Illuminati in France being led by the mysterious Count Saint-Germain, though this enigmatic figure seems to have had no revolutionary goals. Certainly some of the aims of the French Revolution and those professed by Weishaupt and his associates were similar. But rather than attempting to understand the vast and complex interplay of historical and personal forces that bring about an event as momentous as the French Revolution, there are many who find it more convenient to lay it all at the door of a small secret group, in this case the Illuminati.

In one version of the lore of the Illuminati, they were supposed to be a secret inner group of the already-secret, and sometimes suspect, Freemasons. Weishaupt and his friends did join the Masons and attempted to take over some of its lodges, but the attempt was quickly exposed, and they were kicked out.

Enemies of the Illuminati said that the real "secret" of the group was that they were atheists and democrats, determined to kill priests and kings, and that this aim was not revealed to the initiate until he reached the very highest degree within the order.

224

There may have been some truth to this charge, at least in terms of what the Illuminati leaders believed, though there is no evidence at all that they ever killed any kings or priests. On the other hand, similar charges were often leveled against the Freemasons, and these were untrue. It was a charge that cut two ways: all those suspected of being atheists or democrats could also be accused of being members of a conspiratorial secret society.

Of the many stories told of the Illuminati, the most extravagant is that after Weishaupt was driven from Germany in 1776, he came to America, where he took the place of George Washington and changed the course of American history. The one existing picture of Weishaupt shows him looking vaguely (very vaguely) like Washington. To many in Europe, it seemed as if the ideals of the American Revolution were identical to those advocated by the Illuminati.

Tales of the Illuminati popped up again in the 1960s and 1970s. In occult circles, there was a rumor that a small, ancient, and highly secret brotherhood of Illuminati were now controlling world events. Just exactly what that meant, no one seemed to

The Illuminati were rumored to dispose of their enemies swiftly and permanently.

know. Nor was there any clear indication if the Illuminati were a force for good or evil. "Everyone was looking for Illuminati," commented one occult writer.

The Illuminati excitement may also have been something of a put-on. Counterculture author Robert Anton Wilson wrote a series of strange, presumably comic, novels based on the idea of the Illuminati.

See also: ROSICRUCIANS; SAINT-GERMAIN

INDIAN ROPE TRICK   Of all the magical feats of the "mysterious Orient," the most fabled is the Indian rope trick. There are many variations on the trick, but the most spectacular and best known is that given in a description by the fourteenth-century Arab traveler Sheikh Abu Abdullah Mohammed. The sheikh was visiting the court of an Indian prince and was made guest of honor at a great outdoor banquet. As was usual in such banquets, there was entertainment—jugglers and dancers. But the stellar attraction was the appearance of a celebrated magician. The magician, as the sheikh recalled, was a huge man with a fierce black beard, wearing a colorful, beautifully woven cloak.

As the climax of his performance neared, the magician took a wooden ball from which hung a piece of rope. He grasped the rope and whirled the ball about; then suddenly he released the ball, and it sailed high into the air. The ball went so high that it was lost from view. But what was truly amazing was that the ball didn't fall back to earth. The magician was still holding one end of the rope; the other end, which had been attached to the ball, also stretched up into the air, and it too seemed to disappear.

Assisting the magician throughout his performance was a young boy. The boy was now ordered to climb the rope, but he at first refused. The magician got angry, so slowly and reluctantly the boy began to climb. The higher the boy climbed the faster he went, and finally, like the ball and the end of the rope, the boy too disappeared, though the sheikh could not quite see where or how.

For a while there was silence. The crowd stared up at the rope waiting for something to happen. The magician too seemed to be waiting. As the crowd grew restless, the magician tugged at the rope a few times, but still nothing happened, and he appeared to grow furious.

After more time passed, the magician flew into a rage and, grabbing a scimitar, put it between his teeth and began to climb the rope. In a few seconds he too was lost from sight.

Suddenly the air was filled with what sounded like the screams of a boy fighting for his life. The sheikh was horrified and ran to the bottom of the rope and looked up, but all that he could see was the rope stretching up into nothingness. Still the screaming continued.

Then something dropped from the sky and landed near where the sheikh stood. It was a boy's hand. As the sheikh backed away in horror, he was nearly struck by another severed hand. Parts of the boy's body were raining down from the sky. The sheikh fell to his knees; he had never seen anything so terrible in his life.

Down the rope came the smiling magician. When he got to the ground, he threw his brightly colored cloak over the pile of bloody remains. He wiped his sword and put it back in his belt. He spun around and whipped his cloak from the pile, but now there stood the boy fully restored to life. The wooden ball fell from the sky and the magician caught it. Quite casually he wound up the rope, and to the applause of the crowd, he and the boy bowed and walked away.

The story continues that the sheikh was so overwhelmed by what he had seen that he fainted. When he revived, he asked how the trick was done. But people merely looked at him in a puzzled way and asked, "What trick?" He told the other guests what he had seen, but they assured him that nothing of the sort had happened and that all they had seen was a perfectly ordinary juggling and magic act performed by a man and a young boy.

Now this story has all the elements of a fable, but it was probably inspired by a fairly common Indian magician's marketplace trick, in which a magician appears to be supported in midair by a

A common marketplace illusion in India, as the magician is apparently supported by a piece of rope or other insubstantial substance.

piece of rope or some other insubstantial object. The trick may be the Indian counterpart of the common stage illusion in which the magician's assistant seems to be suspended rigidly about four feet above the ground. The magician then passes a metal hoop over the suspended figure to show that there are no supporting bars or wires. It is an impressive illusion, but an illusion nonetheless. Magicians are very secretive about their tricks, so it is not known how the illusion is accomplished. It is probable that there are several different ways.

Visitors to India in the nineteenth century, however, were not sure that what they saw in the marketplace was an illusion. Indeed, a well-known nineteenth century magician named Harry Kellar was astounded by the feats of an Indian magician that he saw during a visit of the Prince of Wales to India in the winter of 1875–76. The trick was part of a performance given in the Great Plaza of Calcutta before the Prince and fifty thousand other spectators. Kellar wrote: "After a salaam to the Prince the old fakir [a word originally meaning "poor man" and not "faker"] took three swords with straight crossbarred hilts, and buried them hilt downwards about six inches in the ground. The points of these swords were very sharp as I afterwards informed myself. A younger fakir stretched himself upon the ground a full length . . . and after a pass or two [by] the hands of the old man, appeared to become rigid and lifeless."

An assistant then came forward, and both taking hold of the head and feet of the young man "laid the stiffened body upon the points of the swords, which appeared to support it without penetrating the flesh. The point of one sword was immediately under the nape of the neck, that of the second rested midway between his shoulders, and that of the third [at] the legs. . . . The boy tipped neither to the right nor the left, but seemed to be balanced with mathematical accuracy."

A summary of the rest of Kellar's report was given by R.J.M. Rickard, editor of *The Fortean Times*.

"After the third man retired to the side, the master took out a dagger and dug away the soil from the hilt of the first sword, and removed it—the body remained motionless. The second and third swords were likewise taken from under the body, which, there in broad daylight and under the eyes of all the spectators, preserved its horizontal position without visible support about 2 feet from the ground. After a while the fakir summoned his assistant and holding each end of his stiff body gently lowered their companion to the ground, where after a few more passes he was animated once again. Kellar says that he could devise an illusion of this feat (given a closed room, devices, and an audience facing in one direction)—but not in broad daylight on unprepared ground and surrounded in the open by witnesses. Naturally this does not mean it definitely was not an illusion, but that it deserves study in itself as a remarkable phenomenon."

Rickard cites other accounts, including a 1936 levitation by one Subbayah Pullavar, which was minutely photographed and described by P. T. Plunkett: "Everything was now ready. Subbayah Pullavar marked out a circle close around the tent under which he was going to levitate, by pouring water onto the floor of the hot and dusty compound [and instructed] that nobody with leather-soled shoes was to go inside it. When Subbayah's assistant told us it was time for the tent to be removed we took up positions (on opposite sides) just outside the ring and photographed every position from every angle."

The photographs, which are exceptionally clear, show Subbayah Pullavar hovering horizontally in the air with no visible means of support except that of his hand, which is resting lightly on a stick, wrapped in a cloth that touches the ground at an angle. According to the written account, he maintained this position for about four minutes. It is of course possible, even probable, that the performer was balancing his body rigidly in the air by means of the stick. The trick looks supernatural, but then any good acrobatic feat does.

There have been several attempts to investigate the classic rope trick itself. In 1934, an English group offered a large cash prize to anyone who could successfully perform the rope trick.

A magician who called himself Karachi (real name Arthur Clause Derby, for he was an Englishman and not an Indian) took up the challenge, but not very impressively. He showed the audience an ordinary rope, then he stepped behind a screen. After that, something that looked like a rope rose up from behind the screen for about five feet and sank slowly back.

Karachi then took a second rope. He showed it to the audience and stepped behind the screen. This time the rope or whatever it was rose about eight feet. The magician, who was being assisted by his son, told the boy to climb the rope. The boy appeared to do so, then came right down again. That is about all there was to it.

The committee was disappointed. They said that the rope had really been lifted by a wire and that observers could actually see the wire. They weren't about to pay out anything for that sort of a performance. Karachi offered to do it again, but no one was interested anymore.

It is generally conceded today that the Indian rope trick and other feats of apparent levitation are really illusions produced by skilled magicians and that Western observers who went to India, their heads stuffed with tales of the "wonders of the East," were simply fooled.

See also: LEVITATION

ROSICRUCIANS   In 1614, an anonymous pamphlet describing the origins of a secret society called the Rosicrucians appeared in the town of Cassel, Germany. The pamphlet asserted that the society had been formed over a hundred years earlier by a wandering sage known only as CRS. According to later documents, the full name of this sage was Christian Rosae Crucis, or Christian Rosenkreutz; hence the name Rosicrucians. The members of the society were the heirs to all manner of ancient and secret occult knowledge. In fact, the early Rosicrucian documents are heavy with the language and symbolism of alchemy.

Over the next year, two other anonymously produced Rosicrucian documents appeared. One of them claimed that the brotherhood had decided to make their existence known because, as predicted, the tomb of their founder, Christian Rosenkreutz, had miraculously opened after 120 years. Inside was found the body of the sage himself, undecayed by the passing of time. In the dead man's hands was a document called *Book T*, which was described as "our greatest treasure next to the Bible."

The original Rosicrucian documents stated that membership in the society was open to all worthy men. If these men would make their interest known, they would be contacted. As far as can be determined, no one was ever contacted.

There is not a scrap of solid historical evidence for the existence of any individual named Christian Rosenkreutz, or indeed for the existence of any Rosicrucian Society at all prior to the appearance of the Rosicrucian pamphlets. The best guess, and it is only a guess, is that the Rosicrucian pamphlets were written and issued by a group of university students led by a man named Johann Andrea. Andrea was interested in mysticism, alchemy, and magic. A rose and a cross formed part of his family coat of arms. Andrea actually admitted to writing at least one of the mysterious documents. Whether Andrea and his friends were really serious about trying to form some sort of secret society is unknown. There has been speculation that the documents had political overtones or that the whole thing was an elaborate practical joke. There is also the possibility that Andrea was not really the author of the Rosicrucian documents after all.

In the succeeding centuries, a number of other mysterious Rosicrucian documents appeared, and a variety of Rosicrucian societies were formed. The term *Rosicrucian* ultimately proved so popular that it was debased and used as a description for practically any brand of hidden or occult knowledge.

Today the most familiar Rosicrucian society is the Ancient Mystical Order of Rosae Crucis (AMORC). Its mail-order ads have been seen by practically every literate person in the English-speaking world. While this society claims to be heir to an ancient tradition reaching all the way back to the time of the pharaohs, its history is fairly well known and a good deal less exotic. AMORC was formed in 1916 by H. Spencer Lewis, an American advertising man with an interest in the occult. AMORC's emphasis shifts with the tide of fashion in occultism. Today the organization stresses the development of psychic powers. The sixteenth century emphasis on alchemy is completely gone.

"Secret" Rosicrucian societies proliferated rapidly, and they exist in practically every country in the Western world. But the Rosicrucian "secrets" do not remain secret for long. Disenchanted members are forever revealing them. These secrets generally turn out to be disappointing. They may sound impressive, but they are nothing more than empty rituals or useless methods of card reading and crystal gazing. One hears that there are Rosicrucians and "real" Rosicrucians. In this view, the members of the known Rosicrucian groups are deluded individuals with no knowledge or power. The "real" Rosicrucians, however, are few in number, and only they are heirs to the traditions passed down from ancient times. The only trouble is there is no way of identifying the "real" Rosicrucians.

See also: ALCHEMY

THE WITCH CULT   Do real witches exist today? Did they ever? Those questions are not as easy to answer as it might seem, and the answers one gives depend to a large degree on one's definition of witchcraft.

Magic in one form or another has been practiced by all societies in all ages. A society's attitude toward magic varied; sometimes it was considered perfectly proper; other times it was forbidden, not because it didn't work, but because to deal in certain types of magic was supposed to be evil. For several hundred years in the West, the concept of evil or malevolent magic was synonymous with the word *witchcraft.*

In theory, ancient Hebrews shunned all magical practices as being contrary to God's law. The attitude is perhaps most clearly displayed in the episode of the witch of Endor in the Bible. King Saul had outlawed all magic in his kingdom. Yet when he felt that God would no longer reveal the future to him through dreams, Saul turned to magic. He found an old woman (usually translated "witch") from Endor and asked her to call up the spirit of the dead prophet Samuel. That Saul seems to have had no trouble finding this witch indicates that magical practices continued to thrive in the kingdom despite his ban. The witch did summon up the spirit, but the prophet was angry and delivered a terrible prophecy. Saul's defeat and death are regarded as God's punishment for engaging in forbidden practices.

Early Christians adopted the Jewish attitude toward magic, but in the vast and varied Christian world, all manner of magical practices flourished outside and even inside the official Church.

Witchcraft was not considered a major problem for the Church until about the fifteenth century, when a genuine antiwitchcraft hysteria swept much of the Christian world. The reasons for the change of attitude are complex and far from fully understood, but in addition to a fear of magic, there was also a fear and hatred of a variety of heretical or at least unorthodox groups that had sprung up. Some, but by no means all, of these groups were involved with magic. The concepts *witch* and *heretic* are so intermingled that it is often difficult to distinguish between the two. For the witch hunter, there was no need to make the distinction; both were parts of Satan's conspiracy to overthrow God and his Church.

Fear of witchcraft survived the Reformation; indeed, often the only thing that Protestants and Catholics agreed upon was that witches should be exterminated.

One of the last major witchcraft trials in the world took place in America in 1692. These were the notorious Salem witch trials. This violent outbreak of witch hunting among the Puritans was unexpected, for America had remained relatively free of witch-craft hysteria, while the flames of fanaticism had raged through Europe. In America, charges of witchcraft had been made fre-quently, but trials had been rare, convictions rarer still. Even a convicted witch might receive a light sentence and continue to live in the community. The practice of magic was not that serious a crime. But then, when the witchcraft hysteria had almost en-tirely died down in the Old World, it flared up briefly in the New World.

For all their notoriety, the Salem witchcraft trials were rela-tively mild affairs when compared with the hideous persecutions in Europe. Only nineteen people suffered the relatively merciful death of hanging. Although films sometimes show the witches of Salem being burned, no one was. There was little torture, and those whose trials dragged on for one reason or another were re-leased when public opinion turned decisively against the witch hunters.

A mere four years after the Salem witch hysteria began, many of the jurors who had helped to condemn the witches issued a public confession of their errors. The confession read in part: "We fear we have been instruments with others, though ignorantly and un-wittingly, to bring upon ourselves and this people of the Lord the guilt of innocent blood. . . . We also pray that we may be considered candidly and aright by the living sufferers as being then under the power of a strong and general delusion, utterly unacquainted with, and not experienced in matters of that nature."

As the tide turned, the general opinion grew that the whole witchcraft business had been a delusion. While a few ecclesiastics clung stubbornly to the notion of a satanic conspiracy, most people came to feel that there were no witches and never had been and that witchcraft was the invention of fanatic or greedy witch hunters. The term *witch hunting* became synonymous with looking for a crime that does not exist.

By the nineteenth century, witchcraft had acquired an almost romantic air. In his *Letters on Demonology and Witchcraft,* Sir Walter Scott explored the British belief in such things as witches and fairies. He identified both with ancient conquered races of Europe. Scott attributed no supernatural powers to either of these groups, but he had begun the process of making witchcraft not only real but attractive.

An important change in the modern attitude toward witchcraft came in 1921 with the publication of *The Witch Cult in Western Europe.* The author was Professor Margaret Murray, an anthropologist and Egyptologist.

Previous scholars had assumed that the many "confessions" made at the witch trials were either forced by torture or threat of torture, or were the delusions of minds that had been unhinged by fear. Professor Murray took the confessions seriously. She said that there had indeed been a large underground witch cult in Western Europe. But unlike the witch hunters, Murray did not believe that the witches were a pack of devil-worshiping evildoers. She said that they were pagans, followers of an ancient pre-Christian religion.

Professor Murray thought that the basic witch beliefs could be traced all the way back to man's theoretical primordial religion, the worship of the Great Earth Mother Goddess. Later, this goddess became identified with various fertility goddesses. Later still, the Mother Goddess was joined by a deity representing the male principle. This male fertility deity was a horned god, since horned animals, particularly the goat, had always been symbols of fertility.

In Professor Murray's view it was not hard to see how Christians who placed a high value on celibacy would be extremely upset by the orgiastic rites of a fertility religion. Add to this the identification of the horned god with their own devil, and Christians might indeed believe that they were faced with a satanic conspiracy. Also, Murray stated that since the witch religion was large and well organized, it really did represent a powerful alternative and a real threat to Christianity.

Professor Murray's arguments attracted a good deal of attention and sparked new scholarly and popular interest in the subject of witchcraft. But in her second book, *The God of the Witches,* published ten years after *The Witch Cult,* Murray went too far. She said that such historical figures as Joan of Arc, Thomas à Becket, and several kings of England had all been members of the witch cult. Both Joan and the martyred archbishop of Canterbury, who became Christian saints, had in reality been leaders in the cult. They had deliberately sacrificed their lives to fulfill the blood-sacrifice rite of the cult and to clear the way for a new leader. At that point most of Murray's scholarly sympathizers abandoned her. Today historians regard the Murray books as classic examples of crank scholarship. Even her admirers are made uneasy by some of the grandiose notions that she proposed.

According to Professor Murray, her theoretical witch cult finally died out in the eighteenth century, though some of its half-remembered rituals survived as folk customs in isolated parts of Europe and America. No thought was given to the idea that a flourishing witch cult still existed secretly in the twentieth century.

Then in 1949 an eccentric occultist named Gerald Brousseau Gardner announced that he was a witch, heir to the ancient witch cult that Professor Murray had described. Gardner said that in his researches he had discovered that some of his ancestors had been burned as witches. When this information got around, he had been contacted by some local witches and initiated into a coven, just before the outbreak of World War II.

Witchcraft was a secret underground religion, but Gardner said that he had decided to break the vow of silence because witchcraft was "a dying cult," and authentic information about it should be passed on to the general public before it was lost entirely.

According to Gardner, the witchcraft cult had many names; it is the Wicca religion ("religion of the wise"), the Old Religion, or the Craft. As described by Gardner, witchcraft is a remarkably gentle and benign cult, heavily influenced by the Celtic romanticism of Sir Walter Scott.

True, witchcraft rites were performed in the nude, but asked Gardner, "In these days of nudist clubs is that so very terrible?" And those words were written in 1955. The witchcraft rites in the Gardnerian tradition do not sound shocking; indeed, they sound downright dull. True, there were rumors that Gardner didn't "tell all" and that some of the rites involved ritual sexual intercourse and flagellation. But as rumors go, even these were fairly mild.

Gerald B. Gardner
(Courtesy of the Witches Almanac
1972 edition)

Gardner stirred up a lot of anger among those to whom the very word *witch* is a red flag. But in the end there was more interest than anger, and Gardner himself became so respectable that he was actually invited to Buckingham Palace. He died in 1964.

Before he died, however, Gardner was forced to eat his words about a "dying cult." Self-proclaimed witches began popping up all over the place, all claiming that they too were heirs to the ancient religion. Many offered alternatives to pure Gardnerian witchcraft. The Old Religion was split into competing sects.

One result of all this brouhaha was that it stimulated a new scholarly interest in the subject of witchcraft. The bulk of historical opinion now holds that witchcraft, that is, the practice of magic, was more common than previously believed, but that there was no organized witch cult. Murray is still dismissed as a crank, and Gardner as a fabulist who simply made up all the stories about being initiated into an ancient cult. Indeed, Gardner never offered any evidence that anyone else belonged to the witch cult before he started one.

Interest in modern witchcraft, or paganism as it is frequently called today, reached a high point in the late 1970s. As a religion dominated by a female god, it attracted some interest among radical feminists. Since then, publicity and probably membership in various witch groups has declined, but witch groups, either open or secret, still do exist.

Most of those serious about the subject of witchcraft today will grudgingly admit that the evidence that they are carrying on an unbroken ancient tradition is slight. They talk of being adherents of a "reconstructed religion," a religion "based on" ancient pagan practices.

Modern witchcraft represents a mixture of occultism, a sort of ecological nature worship, some feminism, and sex without guilt. Though there are places where a person calling him or herself a witch could face hostility, even persecution, in most areas witchcraft is regarded as little more than a harmless and even charming eccentricity.

7

CLASSIC

MYSTERIES

ANIMAL MUTILATIONS   From time to time there appears to be waves of unexplained killings and mutilations of animals, usually cattle. During the 1970s, stories of cattle mutilations throughout the Western states created a genuine climate of fear among many ranchers and farmers.

Such a wave gripped parts of Nebraska and South Dakota during the late summer and early fall of 1974. Cattle had been found dead for no obvious reason, and parts of their anatomy were missing. Both ranchers and local law-enforcement officials were stumped as to the cause of these seemingly bizarre deaths. Soon rumors began to spread that the mutilations were being carried out by members of a satanist cult that practiced animal sacrifice. A local psychiatrist warned that the mutilations might be the work of a madman who sooner or later was likely to switch to human victims.

Even stranger explanations were soon advanced. A few people reported seeing "the Thing," a hairy "man animal" in the region. Though no one actually said he saw "the Thing" killing cattle, the connection seemed obvious enough. Bigfoot was roaming the range, chewing up the livestock.

Then there was the UFO explanation. At about the time the mutilation scare was at its height, there were several reports of Unidentified Flying Objects in the region. Somehow the UFOs and the cattle mutilations became connected in the minds of many people. They seemed to suspect that alien creatures from UFOs were killing cattle and then taking off pieces as specimens.

Even in the world of strange beliefs this one seemed farfetched, yet the connection between animal mutilations and UFOs had been made before. Back in 1897, people all over America were reporting a "mysterious airship" at a time when there were no airships. On April 19, a Kansas farmer named Alexander Hamilton said that a mysterious airship "occupied by six of the strangest beings I ever saw" hovered over his cow lot. A rope was dropped from the ship around the neck of a calf in the lot. The struggling calf was lifted off the ground, and both airship and calf disappeared. The next day, pieces of the butchered animal were found scattered all over a neighboring field.

The astonishing story was told and retold in countless UFO books and articles, but an investigation by Jerome Clark of *Fate* magazine proved that the story was a hoax and that everyone who knew Hamilton's reputation as a joker got a good laugh out of it. They were astonished that anyone could have ever taken it seriously.

Charles Fort collected a number of animal mutilation accounts from England and noted that in most instances the mutilations were attributed to phantom black dogs, a traditional creature of the folklore of the British Isles.

In 1903 in Staffordshire, England, a large number of horses, cattle, and sheep were mutilated under mysterious circumstances. The blame was not placed on a phantom dog, however, but on a man named George Edaji, the son of an Indian father and an English mother. He was actually imprisoned for the crime in an atmosphere charged with hysteria and racism. Edaji was ultimately exonerated, largely through the efforts of Sir Arthur Conan Doyle, creator of Sherlock Holmes, who was convinced that the Edaji case was a gross miscarriage of justice. Though Doyle was already involved with spiritualism at that time, he thought that Edaji had been framed by a stableman who hated Indians, and not that the mutilations were the work of any other worldly agency.

Fort, however, took a darker view of animal mutilations. He wrote: "This is fringing upon an enormous subject that leads away

from the slaughtering of sheep to attacks, some of them mischie-
vous, some ordinarily deadly, and some of the Jack the Ripper kind
upon human beings. Though I have hundreds of notes upon mysterious attacks upon human beings, I cannot develop an occult crim-
inology now."

A celebrated animal mutilation case in the 1960s took place in
Colorado. In the fall of 1967, a horse named Snippy that was
owned by the Harry King Ranch was missing for several days. The
animal's badly mutilated carcass was found on September 9. The
cause of death was not immediately apparent, and the condition of
the carcass was so bad that members of the King family suspected
that something unusual and quite terrible had happened to it.

There had been a fair number of UFO sightings in the region
just prior to the disappearance of Snippy. At that time, the University of Colorado was engaged in a highly publicized and highly
controversial study of the UFO phenomenon, so UFOs were very
much on the minds of the people of Colorado. The mystery of
UFOs and the mystery of Snippy's fate were assumed to be connected somehow.

Several other strangely mutilated horses and cows were also reported in the same area. As the story gathered steam, there were
more UFO sightings and an unfounded rumor that the area in
which the dead horse had been found was radioactive. Members of
UFO groups descended upon the scene to investigate, and the
whole matter became very confused.

Veterinarians came to different conclusions about what had
killed Snippy. One suggested that since there had been a thunderstorm in the area around the time the horse died, Snippy might
have been struck by lightning. The lightning, according to this
theory, would have accounted for some of the damage done to the
horse. Another vet who examined the carcass found indications
that it had been shot in the back leg. While the shooting would not
have been an immediate cause of death, the wound could have
become infected and thus weakened the animal, leading to its
death. The veterinarians agreed, however, that most of the "muti-

lations" had actually been caused by small predatory animals that had attacked the carcass.

Snippy's bones were put on display in a local gift shop, but the interest that surrounded the animal's mysterious death and mutilation soon died down and the case was forgotten.

The animal mutilation excitement that began in the autumn of 1974 was much more widespread than that generated by the Snippy case. The original Nebraska–South Dakota episode had inspired enough fear in the region to require two meetings between veterinarians, local law-enforcement officials, and interested farmers. The reports of two state veterinary laboratories were presented. Both reports stated that every animal brought to the labs had died from natural causes and that the "mutilations" were caused by small predators tearing away at the soft parts of the animal's carcass. Not everyone was reassured by these lab reports, but they did serve to calm the fears of the majority.

During the height of the scare, night patrols had been organized throughout the afflicted region in order to catch redhanded the satanic cultists, alien invaders, or whatever, at their deadly and dirty business. The patrols never came across anything that was out of the ordinary.

The South Dakota Crime Bureau, which had looked into the mutilations, issued a statement that said that in the view of the bureau, the cattle deaths were natural and that nothing unusual had in fact happened. The bureau concluded that there was neither cause for alarm nor reason to continue any investigation. After that, local newspapers, which had been having a field day with the story, reported no more mutilations. Whether that was because there were no new mutilations to report, or because people were embarrassed to report them, or because the newspapers themselves felt such stories were no longer worthy of attention, is unclear.

But there were further waves of cattle mutilation accounts in other areas in the West, and these prompted further investigations, all of which concluded that nothing unusual was going on.

Dead and partially eaten animals are a common feature of ranch life. The stories, however, inspired several sensational novels and at least one film. Ultimately, the public seemed to lose interest and by the late 1970s the cattle mutilations were rarely mentioned anymore.

How had it all begun? James R. Stewart, an assistant professor of sociology at the University of South Dakota, who had followed the original outbreak wrote: "There are two possible answers to this question. First, perhaps given the conditions of strain and anxiety, farmers with firsthand experience and knowledge were simply caught up in the delusionary spiral. Second, there exists the possibility that some farmers reported mutilations because their insurance policies would reimburse them for acts of vandalism but not for deaths resulting from natural causes. I have no evidence that claims were paid for mutilations, but this possibility might motivate some to report mutilated, and not simply dead, cattle."

Since stories of mysterious animal mutilations have a long history, there is no reason to believe that new waves will not be reported in the future.

See also: JACK THE RIPPER; THE MYSTERIOUS AIRSHIP; UFOS

THE BERMUDA TRIANGLE   Unexplained disappearances, particularly unexplained nautical disappearances, have long fascinated people. And for centuries there have been rumors and fears that there are places in the sea where mysterious and terrible things do happen frequently. The most recent manifestation of this ancient belief is the Bermuda Triangle.

The term itself is not ancient. It was coined in 1964 by writer Vincent Gaddes in an article in *Argosy* magazine to denote a triangular area, with the east coast of Florida as one point of the triangle, Puerto Rico another, and the island of Bermuda the third. Within this region, Gaddes told the readers of *Argosy*, an exceptionally large number of mysterious disappearances took place.

Other writers have called the area the Hoodoo Sea or the Devil's Triangle, but the Bermuda Triangle is the name most frequently used. However, the outlines of the area have been generously stretched and bent by other writers until the term Bermuda Triangle has been used to denote a rather large nebulous area of the South Atlantic.

By the mid-1970s, the Bermuda Triangle had really displaced UFOs as the number-one popular mystery, and it was the subject of several enormously popular books, innumerable magazine articles and had formed the background for several novels, films, and TV shows.

While hundreds of mysterious disappearances have been attributed to the Triangle, the key case on which the fame of the Bermuda Triangle rests is the disappearance of Flight 19. Briefly what happened is this: On December 5, 1945, five TBF Avengers took off from the Fort Lauderdale Naval Air Station on what was supposed to be a routine training flight. The route was to be a triangular one that was to take them over Grand Bahama Island and back to their home base in about two hours. The weather was good, and there was nothing to indicate that this flight would not be exactly like hundreds of others that had taken off from the Fort Lauderdale base.

But about two hours after the start of the flight, at about the time it was scheduled to be returning home, the Fort Lauderdale base began picking up radio messages indicating that all was not well with Flight 19. According to the messages, the men of the flight were lost and confused. The plane's compasses didn't seem to be functioning properly. There was more rather confused and garbled conversation between the planes, and after four P.M., when the leader of the flight was heard turning over command to another pilot, all communication with Flight 19 ended.

Search operations were begun immediately, and during the search one of the planes, a Martin Mariner, also disappeared. No trace of the five TBF Avengers or their fourteen crew members was ever found.

TBF Avengers, the type of plane that disappeared in Flight 19
(Official U.S. Navy Photograph)

Afterward, many stories spread about one of the airmen being found in a rubber raft, babbling about "weird airships" that had abducted the others. Or about transcripts of the final communications from the flight containing an hysterical description of a gigantic flying saucer. All of this, the rumors went, had been covered up by the Navy.

Wild rumors aside, however, there never was an official explanation for the disappearance of the flight or the search plane. It seemed a most mysterious disappearance, and even before the Bermuda Triangle was invented people were talking about it.

Gaddes may have been prompted to write his article by the disappearance of the *Marine Sulphur Queen* early in 1963. This large

A Martin Mariner

tanker was carrying a load of molten sulphur from Beaumont, Texas, to Norfolk, Virginia. In the early morning hours of February 4, 1963, she sent a routine radio call from a position approximately 270 miles west of Key West. That was the last that was ever heard of her. A vast search recovered a few life jackets and a bit of debris but nothing more. No official explanation of the loss was ever given.

An older mystery, a genuine one, was dragged into the larger Bermuda Triangle mystery. It concerned the disappearance of the crew of the five-masted schooner *Carroll A. Deering* in January 1921. The ship was found beached and abandoned on Diamond Shoals, near the Cape Hatteras Coast Guard station, on the morning of January 30. The sails had been set, indicating that there had been no attempt to avoid the shoals, and there was not a trace of the crew or the slightest indication of what had happened to them. Though Cape Hatteras is not in the Bermuda Triangle, the ship had passed through the area, and it was assumed that the crew disappeared there.

Actually, the *Deering* had been sighted by the Lookout Shoals Lightship off Hatteras a few days before it was found abandoned. The crew was sighted on board, but they were behaving oddly:

they were, for example, gathered on the foredeck, which normally would have been forbidden. One of the men, described as having bright red hair, shouted that they had lost their anchors in a storm and wished to have that reported ashore. None of the crew were known to have red hair.

A short time later, a steamship passed by, heading in the same direction as the *Deering*. The lightship tried to hail the vessel, but the latter would not acknowledge the signals. The steamship was too far away for the lightship to determine the identity of the mystery ship. Some speculated that the steamship was the *Hewett*, a steamer that had disappeared in that area at about that same time.

There was no explanation for the disappearance of the crew of the *Deering* (or of the *Hewett*, for that matter), but there were plenty of theories. The most popular one was that both ships had been overrun by Bolsheviks. In those days, whenever something mysterious happened a lot of people assumed that the Reds were somehow responsible, just as in a later era many assumed that extraterrestrials were the culprits. No evidence of a Bolshevik plot was ever found.

These cases and many others were strung together and dramatized until by the mid-1970s the Bermuda Triangle was a subject that everyone had heard of, and practically everyone had his or her own theory about what had happened. There were endless speculations, not only about UFOs but also about mysterious magnetic forces, or the area being a gateway to another dimension.

Then in 1975 the great triangle bubble was punctured by a librarian named Lawrence David Kusche. Kusche, who also happened to be an experienced pilot, did what few others who had written about the subject had done: he went back to the original records to find out what had actually happened, rather than merely repeating the legends as they had been built up over the years.

In the case of Flight 19, for example, Kusche determined that a series of small but ultimately disastrous misjudgments on the part of the flight commander and the ground stations had led to the tragedy. Instead of the flight having disappeared in the middle of a bright sunny day, the pilots were forced to ditch their planes in the darkness in a stormy sea because they had run out of fuel. The weather, which had only been fair when the flight took off, had deteriorated rapidly. That no wreckage had been found under the circumstances was hardly surprising.

The Martin Mariner search plane had exploded in the sky, and that explosion had been witnessed. The planes, sometimes nick-named "flying gas tanks," were notorious for exploding.

The *Marine Sulphur Queen* was a poorly designed, badly loaded vessel that probably broke up in heavy seas and sank so quickly that the radio operator never got a chance to send a final message. Since some wreckage from the ship was found, it clearly did not "disappear."

The disappearance of the *Deering* crew remains a mystery, but according to Kusche the most likely explanation is that there was some sort of mutiny by a notoriously unruly crew against an over-age and possibly ill captain. The weather would not have helped, for the coast was being battered by the worst storms in memory. In any case, whatever happened certainly didn't happen inside the Bermuda Triangle.

Kusche went down the list case by case, either knocking down or casting severe doubts on the many legends of the Bermuda Triangle.

Not all the disappearances could be easily or conclusively ex-plained, but as Kusche and others have pointed out, there is an enormous amount of air and sea traffic through the Bermuda Triangle area, and the number of disappearances, mysterious or otherwise, in that area is not at all excessive.

Kusche put the results of his research into a book, *The Bermuda Triangle Mystery Solved,* published in 1975. A second book, *The Disappearance of Flight 19,* in 1980, was a more detailed examina-tion of that most famous case. Kusche's work got more attention than the usual debunking books, and even those who were very much predisposed to believe in the mystery of the Bermuda Triangle found their faith shaken.

Hardcore proponents of the Bermuda Triangle, like Charles Berlitz, who had written two enormous bestsellers on the subject, refused to debate the debunker publicly. Kusche's work, plus the public's general fickleness in regard to popular mysteries, caused interest in the Bermuda Triangle to drop sharply.

Today a few still cling to the notion that there is "something" mysterious about the Bermuda Triangle—but no one is quite sure what. There is some talk of electromagnetic effects that create hallucinations, but that is a far cry from the Bermuda Triangle of the 1960s and 1970s.

See also: THE SARGASSO SEA

CRASHED SAUCERS   One of the most persistent rumors to come out of the UFO era is that a flying saucer (as they were called in those days) crashed somewhere in the West in the late 1940s and that both the alien craft and the bodies of the little men who had been aboard were secretly spirited away by government investigators and hidden at Wright Patterson Air Force Base in Ohio. The rumor continues that ever since, the government has been engaged in an elaborate cover-up to hide this startling incident.

The first major public airing of this rumor came in 1950 when Frank Scully, a former writer for the show business paper *Variety*, put out a book called *Behind the Flying Saucers*. Scully's book built the story up with accounts of tiny Venusians in what looked like flying suits, two crashes, and a disgruntled scientist named Dr. Gee who was supposed to be the source of all this sensational information. It turned out that Scully's real informants were a couple of notorious con men who were later jailed for trying to sell fraudulent oil-locating devices. *Behind the Flying Saucers* was the first best-selling UFO book, but the revelations about its sources killed any serious interest in the story. Yet the rumor of the crashed saucer refused to die. It appeared and reappeared in ever more exotic forms. According to one rumor, President Dwight Eisenhower himself visited the secret hangar in which the remains of the spaceship were stored in 1954. An even more bizarre variation of this rumor was that spaceships had landed at Edwards Air Force Base in California in 1954 and that Eisenhower went there for a meeting with the aliens. The rumors were the basis for at least one motion picture.

Various groups have attempted to pressure the government into revealing what they believe to be secret information about the crash or crashes of the alien spaceships by invoking the Freedom of Information Act. So far, nothing sensational has been disclosed, which has led to charges that the cover-up continues.

To date the most ambitious attempt to prove that there is "something" behind the crashed saucer rumors is the book *The Roswell Incident* by Charles Berlitz (of Bermuda Triangle fame) and William L. Moore. The book, published in 1980, focuses on the incident that may indeed have been the basis for all the later rumors.

On July 2, 1947, something landed or crashed on a ranch near Roswell, New Mexico. Investigators from a local Air Force base visited the ranch to view the debris. The initial press release issued by the Roswell base was sensational: "The many rumors regarding the flying disc [later flying saucers, and later still UFOs] became a reality yesterday when the intelligence office of the 509th Bomb Group of the Eighth Air Force, Roswell Army Air Field, was fortunate enough to gain possession of a disc through the cooperation of one of the local ranchers and the sheriff's office of Chaves County.

"The flying object landed on a ranch near Roswell sometime last week. Not having phone facilities, the rancher stored the disc until such time as he was able to contact the sheriff's office, who in turn notified Major Jesse A. Marcel of the 509th Bomb Group Intelligence Office.

"Action was immediately taken and the disc was picked up at the rancher's home. It was inspected at the Roswell Army Air Field and subsequently loaned by Major Marcel to higher headquarters."

That press release was picked up by newspapers all over the world. Though the release doesn't say anything about the flying disc actually being an alien spacecraft, that was certainly the impression that most people got.

Immediately afterward, revisions of the original release were issued by the Air Force. The flying disc, said Air Force spokesmen, was nothing more than a downed weather balloon. The Air Force even allowed photographers to take pictures of Air Force officers holding pieces of what they said had been the balloon. Until Berlitz and Moore dug up this incident again, it had pretty well been forgotten. It could easily have been the incident that sparked the original rumors and inspired the Frank Scully book, though he had placed the flying saucer crash elsewhere.

Berlitz and Moore interviewed many who had been connected with the original incident, though most of the important witnesses—the rancher who had actually located the crash and the men who allegedly carried away the debris—had either died or were unavailable for other reasons.

There are a large number of sensational rumors reported in the Roswell Incident and a fair indication that the Air Force was quite touchy about secrecy in 1947. But most of the testimony indicates that the "wreckage" consisted primarily of pieces of a thin, flexible, metallic-looking substance that could indeed have been the remains of a weather balloon. The military could be secretive and evasive even about weather balloons in those Cold War days. The book presents no compelling evidence that an alien craft crashed near Roswell, New Mexico, or anywhere else in 1947.

This is, of course, not the conclusion favored by Berlitz and Moore, and interest in the Roswell incident and the whole spectrum of crashed UFO rumors will continue.

See also: UFOS

CURSE OF THE HOPE DIAMOND   Tales of romance and menace have been attached to many of the world's large gemstones, but none has a more romantic and sinister aura than the great Hope Diamond. It is said that everyone who has ever possessed the diamond has been cursed with extreme bad luck. That is something of an exaggeration, but the story is still an extraordinary one.

What was to become the Hope Diamond first appears in history in the seventeenth century when a French trader named John Baptiste Tavernier brought a large, blue, 112.50-carat diamond from India. Tavernier would not say where he got the diamond, but according to rumor it was stolen from the eye of an idol in the temple of Rama-Sita near Mandalay. There was also a rumor that the god would revenge himself on anyone who possessed the stolen diamond.

Tavernier sold the diamond to the only man in France who could truly afford it, King Louis XIV. The merchant himself ultimately seems to have suffered severe financial reverses, and he died unexpectedly during a trip to Russia.

The king had the diamond cut into a heart shape, and at that time it was called the French Blue. If there was a curse on the diamond, it didn't trouble Louis XIV, for he was France's most powerful and longest-lived monarch. The diamond passed down through the royal family to King Louis XVI, who gave it to his wife, Queen Marie Antoinette. Both the king and queen lost their thrones and their heads during the French Revolution. A close friend of the queen's, Princess de Lamballe, who often borrowed the diamond, was said to have been torn to pieces by an angry mob.

The diamond was apparently stolen during the Revolution and recut. Part of it reappeared rather mysteriously in London, now reduced to a mere 44.50 carats. It was purchased by banker Henry

The Hope Diamond
(The Smithsonian Institution)

Thomas Hope, who gave the gem the name by which it is now known.

Hope himself never seems to have been afflicted by any particular ill fortune. After Hope's death, the diamond passed to other members of the family, but only one ever complained about it. She was May Yohe, a singer who married Lord Francis Hope. The couple was divorced, and the ex-singer died in poverty in 1938. She always blamed the diamond for her ill luck.

But by that time the diamond had long passed out of the Hope family. It was sold in 1901 to a jeweler who went bankrupt, and then to another jeweler who shot himself. The diamond's next owner was a dissolute Russian nobleman who shot his showgirl lover while she was onstage and later was reportedly stabbed to death by a group of Russian revolutionaries.

The next owner was a Greek jeweler who fell off a cliff. The diamond was then sold to Sultan Abdul Hamid of Turkey. The Turkish empire was crumbling, and the sultan himself was going mad; for these reasons he got the nickname "Abdul the Damned." Ultimately the sultan was deposed, and the diamond passed through the hands of several dealers until it was acquired by the famous French jeweler Pierre Cartier, who in turn sold it to Edward B. McLean, heir to an American newspaper fortune, and his independently wealthy wife Evalyn.

It was with the McLean family that the idea of a curse on the Hope diamond was really solidified. Shortly after purchasing the diamond, McLean's mother died; so did two of the servants in the McLean household. Edward McLean himself seems to have been rather wary of the gem, but Evalyn McLean loved it and haughtily dismissed all notion of a curse. She often wore the diamond, now set in a necklace.

By far the most tragic and extraordinary death in the McLean family was that of ten-year-old Vinson. The boy had been called the hundred-million-dollar baby because of the huge sum of money he was due to inherit. Vinson was usually very carefully watched, but one day he slipped away from the servants, ran out in front of the family home in Washington, D.C., and was instantly struck and killed by a car. Since the boy was usually so thoroughly protected, this seemed to be a case of extraordinarily bad luck, or worse.

The McLean marriage was never a happy one and ended in divorce. McLean himself had always been a heavy drinker, and the divorce shattered his fragile mental stability. He was committed to a mental institution, where he died.

Still, Evalyn McLean refused to part with the diamond. When Charles Lindbergh's son was kidnapped, she tried to use the Hope Diamond to help raise ransom money. The attempt was unsuccessful.

In 1946, the McLean's only daughter died as the result of an overdose of sleeping pills. The newspapers recalled that at her wedding five years earlier, she had worn the Hope Diamond.

Evalyn McLean herself died a year later, but she was quite old and there was nothing unusual or untimely about her death. To the end she firmly rejected any notion of a curse.

The McLean gems, including the Hope Diamond, were purchased by the famous New York jeweler Harry Winston for about one million dollars. Winston put the famous diamond on display in New York and elsewhere for several years and then decided to donate it to the nation.

Winston took the unusual step of sending the diamond to the Smithsonian Institution by ordinary parcel post. He paid about $150 for insurance on the package, but otherwise took no extra precautions. Winston said he had no second thoughts about sending one of the world's most valuable diamonds through the mail.

The package arrived safely, and the great blue diamond is now one of the most popular exhibits in the Smithsonian. Exhibited along with the diamond is the package in which it was sent. Some have suggested, probably not seriously, that the diamond must have put a curse on the postal service from which it has never been released.

While many of those who did own the diamond do seem to have been unlucky, many others such as Louis XIV, Evalyn McLean, Harry Winston, and Henry Hope himself do not seem to have experienced any extraordinary bad luck. In addition, some of the stories told about the diamond, particularly about its early history,

Evalyn McLean wearing the Hope Diamond
(UPI)

simply may not be true. The diamond changed hands many times, and often buyers and sellers wished to keep their identities secret, so it is impossible to be sure who actually owned the diamond. Of course, once the Hope Diamond got the reputation of being cursed, anything bad that happened to anyone who was even remotely connected with it was blamed on the curse.

The story of the curse of the Hope Diamond is so dramatically satisfying that it will probably be circulated forever.

THE *JOYITA* MYSTERY   On October 3, 1955, the sixty-nine-foot motorship *Joyita* left Apia, Western Samoa, for the port of Fakafo in the Tokelau Islands, 270 miles to the north. Under normal conditions the voyage would have taken about forty hours.

When the ship failed to arrive as expected, an extensive air and sea search was launched, but no trace of the *Joyita* was found. It was assumed that she had become another one of those ships that had sunk without a trace.

It wasn't until November 10, some thirty-eight days after the *Joyita* had disappeared, that the British colony ship *Tuvalu* sighted a derelict drifting helplessly some 450 miles west-southwest of the port from which the *Joyita* had departed. As the *Tuvalu* came closer to the badly damaged hulk, it became clear that the *Joyita* had finally been located. But that was only the beginning of the mystery.

The search was resumed, this time for possible survivors, but none were ever found. The *Joyita* was towed to port, and an investigation surrounding the disappearance of the twenty-five passengers and crew of the ship was begun.

There was no shortage of theories as to what had happened. One that popped up almost immediately was that the ship had been attacked by Japanese pirates, who had murdered the crew and passengers and looted the ship. Less than a decade had passed since the end of World War II, and the Japanese were still very unpopular in the islands.

Another theory was that an underwater volcanic explosion had thrown passengers and crew overboard. Just such an incident had actually taken place a few months earlier. The region in which the abandoned ship was found drifting was known for underwater explosions. None, however, had been recorded in the vicinity at the time of the disappearance.

Other theories included freak waves, or waterspouts, that swept all aboard into the sea. Either was possible, but the idea that everybody, or even a majority of those aboard, would have been swept overboard at one time seemed highly improbable.

As the investigation into the case proceeded, one thing became clear: the *Joyita* had been in very poor repair and probably should never have been allowed to go to sea in the first place.

Attention focused on the owner and captain of the *Joyita*, Thomas Henry "Dusty" Miller a former commander in the British Navy who had become a colorful south sea island character, the sort of devil-may-care, hard-drinking sea captain so often depicted in the movies. But Miller's life of late had not been like a film; he had fallen on very hard times. He lacked the money to maintain the *Joyita* properly. But he evidently hoped to recoup his losses by using the ship to carry supplies and passengers to the remote Tokelau Islands, which did not have a regular ship service and badly needed supplies. The operation might have been very profitable if Miller had been able to get it underway. But there had been one delay after another, and in the few weeks before his last voyage, Captain Miller's condition had become desperate. He had been reduced to living on his ship and picking up odd jobs just to get enough money to buy food. He confided to friends that he had sometimes gone several days with hardly anything to eat.

When Miller finally did get his boat ready for the voyage and set out, there was an explosion in the engine room shortly after the *Joyita* left port. Without a functioning engine, she drifted until an anchor was thrown out. The *Joyita* finally did make it back to port, where emergency repairs were hastily performed. The authorities were considering forbidding the *Joyita* permission to sail. If this happened, Miller knew that he was ruined, so he managed to get his ship away before a final decision was made. No one aboard the *Joyita* was ever seen alive or dead again.

After examining the *Joyita*, the commission of inquiry was able to establish certain facts: A pipe into the engine's saltwater cooling system had been badly corroded and burst, causing a serious but hard-to-locate leak. Water quickly knocked out the ship's electrical system, cutting off all power and leaving the *Joyita* to drift helplessly. All this had probably happened just a few hours after she had left port. Even the emergency radio was not working properly, for investigators found a break in the antenna lead. Signals would not have carried over two miles. All this was the result of Miller's inability to afford repairs.

The ship was listing badly, and those aboard might have feared that she would sink. Part of her superstructure had been torn away, perhaps before she was abandoned. Passengers and crew might have taken to the boats, only to be swallowed up by the sea a little later. That is a plausible theory, but it runs into some problems.

There is no dispute about the condition of the *Joyita*, the burst pipe, or the flooded electrical system. But no matter how badly damaged she was, the *Joyita* was not going to sink, and Dusty Miller knew it. During her career, the *Joyita* had once been a refrigerated fishing boat, and her hold was lined with 640 cubic feet of cork. This meant that no matter how badly damaged, she would float, well, like a cork. Miller had often boasted of his ship's unsinkability. That may have been one of the reasons that he was willing to set out on her, even though he knew she was barely seaworthy. The fact that the *Joyita* was found floating over a month after she had been abandoned was eloquent testimony to her unsinkability. Would Dusty Miller, or any sane person for that matter, abandon an unsinkable ship for a frail lifeboat in the shark-infested waters of the Pacific?

There was no doubt that the ship had been abandoned. The boats, as well as the ship's log and navigational instruments, were missing. So was everything else of value. But it is also evident that someone stayed aboard after the ship was abandoned. A piece of canvas awning had been lashed to a broken stanchion. The awning may have served to catch rainwater for drinking, shield someone from the sun, or both.

That raised other possibilities—mutiny, for example. The mystery of the *Joyita* made news around the world. It was labeled a *Mary Celeste* of the Pacific, and like the more famous case, it too was never really solved.

In 1962, a writer named Robin Maugham went to Fiji to investigate the *Joyita* mystery for an article that he was writing. He became so enmeshed with the story that he actually purchased the *Joyita*. After the tragedy, the ship had been repaired, but it quickly ran aground again. She got the reputation of being a "hoodoo ship," and it was impossible to sell her until Maugham came along. Actually, bad luck had been with the *Joyita* since she was first built. She was originally constructed as an oceangoing yacht for Hollywood film director Roland West. In 1935, actress Thelma Todd succumbed to carbon-monoxide poisoning under mysterious circumstances while aboard the *Joyita*. The ship ultimately wound up in the hands of the U.S. Navy and was at Pearl Harbor when it was bombed.

During his investigation, Maugham talked to a Commander Peter Plowman, one of those who had searched the empty ship after she had been hauled into port. Plowman had never been called to testify at the official inquiry because, after the burst pipe was discovered, officials felt that his testimony would not be necessary. But while going over the ship, Plowman had found a doctor's stethoscope, a scalpel, some needles and catgut for stitching, and four lengths of bloodstained bandages.

Maugham thought that this bit of information provided the last piece of evidence needed for a reconstruction of what had occurred aboard the *Joyita* in October 1955.

Shortly after leaving port, the ship ran into heavy seas, and the strain burst the pipe. The flooding that resulted stopped the engines and cut the power. The ship tried to radio for help, but the signals failed to carry, due to the break in the aerial lead.

The drifting ship was then hit by a large wave that tore away part of the superstructure, adding to the flooding and to panic of those aboard.

At some point while all this was going on, Dusty Miller was injured, probably as the result of a fall. He was treated by a doctor who was one of the passengers, but remained unconscious and was unable to tell the others that no matter how badly damaged she might appear, his ship would not sink. All this Maugham deduces from the medical materials Plowman found.

The rest of the crew and the passengers, now convinced that the *Joyita* was about to go down, made for the boats and were later lost in the rough seas. But someone had stayed behind, at least long enough to put up a canvas awning.

Maugham speculates that for some reason the injured Miller was not taken off the *Joyita* and that one of his crew, probably Tanni, an islander who was devoted to him, stayed behind with him. Days or weeks later, another ship encountered the drifting *Joyita*. Miller was almost certainly dead by that time. Tanni may also have been dead, or the newcomers might had killed him and thrown his body and Miller's overboard. They looted what they could from the ship and left the *Joyita* to drift without a soul on board. If they looted the ship, they would not have been likely to report ever having encountered her.

The explanation is an ingenious one, and it does cover the facts as far as we know them. But of necessity, it is made up of speculation piled upon speculation. A piece of bloodstained bandage does not prove that Dusty Miller was rendered unconscious. Chuck Simpson, another member of the crew, apparently also knew that the ship was cork lined and unsinkable. Besides, he had already survived three shipwrecks during World War II and certainly would not have panicked easily. Why did he abandon the ship or allow others to? If some ship had actually encountered the *Joyita*, even to loot her, rumors would probably have gotten around when the looters sold the stolen items. Yet there were no rumors.

The fate of the passengers and crew of the *Joyita* remains a mystery.

See also: THE *MARY CELESTE*

KING TUT'S CURSE   DEATH SHALL COME ON SWIFT WINGS
TO HIM WHO DISTURBS THE PEACE OF THE KING.

This curse, according to legend, was carved above the door of the tomb of King Tutankhamen. However, no such inscription can be found today. In another version, the curse was inscribed on a tablet found in the tomb but hidden in order not to frighten the diggers and since lost. But the extensive catalogs of the contents of the tomb have no record of such a tablet, and curses on tombs are a rarity in Egypt anyway. Yet the curse of King Tut's tomb is one of the most persistent and widely believed of all the tales of ancient Egypt. Certainly the events surrounding the discovery of the tomb are dramatic enough to inspire thoughts of the supernatural.

Tutankhamen was really a minor king. He was a successor of the heretic pharaoh Akhnaton, and despite the fact that he seemed to wish to accommodate traditional religious forces, he was never popular. He ruled for only a short time and died at the age of nineteen, perhaps murdered by his enemies.

He was buried in a relatively modest tomb (modest for an Egyptian king) in the Valley of the Kings, and his successors made an attempt to erase his memory by having his name taken out of the offical king list and hammered out of inscriptions on temple walls. There was a definite campaign to make the world forget that Tutankhamen had ever existed, and ironically this attempt probably resulted in his current fame.

The rich tombs of the kings of Egypt were magnets for tomb robbers over the centuries. Every royal tomb except that of Tutankhamen had been thoroughly plundered in antiquity. His tomb may have been overlooked because he was almost completely forgotten. Yet Tutankhamen's enemies had not been able to wipe out all traces of his existence, and his name was known to a few archaeologists. They also knew that there was no record of his tomb ever having been found, or of objects from his tomb turning up for sale, so there was some hope that the tomb might still be undiscovered.

One of those who held such a hope was Howard Carter. Carter had come to Egypt from England in 1891 when he was only seventeen years old. Over the years he became convinced that he could locate the tomb of Tutankhamen, but he was not a wealthy man and had no institutional support, and archaeology is an expensive business. So Carter teamed up with someone who did have a lot of money, Lord Carnarvon, scion of an old and extremely wealthy family, who had more than a dilettante's interest in Egyptology. Basically, Carter supervised the digging and Carnarvon supplied the money, but Carnarvon did come to Egypt regularly and followed the progress of the expeditions keenly.

For a long time there wasn't much to follow. Carter was sure that the tomb was somewhere in the Valley of the Kings, the bur-

Funerary mask of Tutankhamen
(Photography by the Egyptian Expedition, The Metropolitan Museum of Art)

ial place for all the kings of that era. Carter began digging in 1917, and by the start of the season in 1922 he had found nothing. Both he and Carnarvon were getting discouraged, and Carter knew it was to be his last season of digging in the Valley unless something turned up, and something certainly did.

On November 4, 1922, Carter's workmen uncovered a step cut into the rock. It was the first of sixteen steps that led to a sealed doorway, upon which was inscribed the name Tutankhamen. It was apparent that whatever was behind the door had not been plundered by robbers.

Carter dispatched a famous telegram to Carnarvon:

AT LAST HAVE MADE A WONDERFUL DISCOVERY IN VALLEY. MAGNIFICENT TOMB WITH SEALS INTACT. RECOVERED SAME FOR YOUR ARRIVAL. CONGRATULATIONS.

Carnarvon rushed to Egypt, and the tomb was opened on November 26. The diggers had reached another sealed door. Carter made a small hole in it. His hands were shaking so badly that he could barely hold the candle needed for light. He peered into the hole, but could see nothing. Carnarvon, who was standing impatiently behind him, asked if he saw anything. "Yes," Carter replied, "wonderful things."

Practically everyone is familiar with at least some of the wonderful things found in the tomb. In the early 1970s an exhibit of a small part of the tomb's treasures toured the world, and everywhere record-breaking crowds turned out to see the exhibit. But the original discovery created a virtual Egyptomania throughout the world.

The mood of the discoverers on that November day was one of unrestrained joy. There were no forebodings, no fears, no talk of a curse. According to the legend, the first victim of the curse was Howard Carter's canary. Carter was very fond of the bird, but a few days after the tomb was opened the bird was killed by a cobra. The cobra is one of the symbols of ancient Egyptian royalty.

But the curse stories did not really get started until March 1923.

Howard Carter (left) *working at Tutankhamen's tomb*
(Ashmolean Museum)

Lord Carnarvon himself fell ill and was taken to the hospital in Cairo, where on April 5 he died. The exact cause of death was not really known, but it seems to have been the result of an infection that spread from an insect bite.

Carnarvon was only fifty-seven when he died, but he had not been a healthy man for years. He had never fully recovered from the effects of a serious automobile accident some twenty years earlier. Indeed, he had taken up Egyptology in the first place because his poor health required him to spend the English winters in warmer climates. Still, his death was completely unexpected, and its trivial cause seemed incredible and unnatural.

The legend continues that at the exact moment of Carnarvon's death there was a brief power failure in Cairo, and all the lights went out. Back in England on the Carnarvon estate, one of the Lord's favorite dogs began to howl and then suddenly and mysteriously fell over dead.

Lord Carnarvon's death created very nearly as much of a sensation as the original discovery of the tomb. The legend of the curse of King Tut was now well launched, and every time someone who had been connected with the discovery died, the rumor went around that the curse had struck again. By 1929 eleven people associated with the discovery of Tutankhamen's tomb were dead. Among them were Carnarvon's half-brother and another relative, Lady Elizabeth Carnarvon. Astonishingly, she too died of an infected insect bite.

Carter's personal secretary, Richard Bethell, was found dead in his chair at his fashionable London club. The cause of his death was never determined, or if it was, the cause was never made public. A short time later, Bethell's father, Lord Westbury, jumped to his death from a building near Buckingham Palace. Lord Westbury left behind a note that read: "I really cannot stand any more horrors and I hardly see what good I am going to do here, so I am going to make my exit." During the funeral the hearse carrying Lord Westbury's body knocked down and killed an eight-year-old boy.

In the years that followed, there were still more deaths attributed to the curse. By 1935, the total number of "victims" of King Tut's curse was supposed to have reached twenty-one.

Howard Carter himself never believed in the curse; indeed the very mention of the subject used to infuriate him. He is really the best evidence that there was no curse. It was Carter, not Carnarvon, who found the tomb, yet Carter lived until 1939, dying at the respectable age of sixty-six of entirely natural causes. If there was a curse, its effects were delayed almost seventeen years in his case. It might be argued that the curse waited until Carter had finished all his work on the tomb before striking.

Lord Carnarvon's son and daughter, both of whom were present at the opening of the tomb, lived to extremely advanced ages.

Professional archaeologists scoff at the idea of King Tut's curse or indeed any other cursed tombs. One said that if Egyptian tombs were cursed, all archaeologists would be dead. Flinders Petrie, who was one of the greatest archaeologists ever to work in Egypt and who incidentally was Howard Carter's teacher, lived to be ninety-two. Petrie had visited Tutankhamen's tomb and most of the other tombs in Egypt, apparently without ill effect. His robust health was legendary.

Rumors of curses never discouraged tomb robbers, either. That profession has flourished in Egypt for centuries. So the legend of King Tut's curse appears to be just that, a legend—though a good one.

See also: AKHNATON

T HE *MARY CELESTE*   The famous case of the *Mary Celeste* really begins in November 1872 when she was docked in New York harbor while being loaded with a cargo of commercial alcohol, bound for Genoa, Italy.

At a nearby pier was the British ship the *Dei Gratia,* also being loaded with a cargo for a transatlantic voyage.

Benjamin Spooner Briggs, captain of the *Mary Celeste,* and David Reed Morehouse, captain of the *Dei Gratia,* were old friends, and they had dinner together on the evening of November 3. Two days later, the *Mary Celeste* set sail. The *Dei Gratia* got underway on November 11.

On December 5 the *Dei Gratia* encountered the *Mary Celeste* adrift off the coast of Portugal. Captain Morehouse and his crew were amazed to discover that the ship had been abandoned. What was even more amazing was that there seemed to be no reason for her to have been abandoned. She was a bit battered because she had been drifting but was completely seaworthy—as some members of the *Dei Gratia* crew proved by sailing her into port at Gibraltar. The *Mary Celeste*'s lifeboat and some of her navigation

Capt. Benjamin Spooner Briggs
(The Peabody Museum of Salem)

Capt. David Reed Morehouse
(The Peabody Museum of Salem)

instruments were missing, but otherwise everything, including the captain's log and all of the sailor's gear, was still on board.

The last entry in the log was dated November 24 and stated simply, "About 110 miles due west of island of Santa Maria in the Azores." There was no hint of trouble in the log. It had been eleven days and the *Mary Celeste* had covered 550 miles since that last entry was made until she was found by the *Dei Gratia*.

As soon as the *Mary Celeste* reached Gibraltar, the authorities began an investigation. A search was launched for the missing occupants of the *Mary Celeste*, but nothing turned up. At first Captain Morehouse was suspected of having had something to do with the disappearance, because by the law of salvage he could claim a substantial profit from having brought in an abandoned ship. But

269

The Dei Gratia *sights the abandoned* Mary Celeste

no evidence connecting anyone on the *Dei Gratia* to the disappearance was ever presented.

All the usual reasons for abandoning a ship—storms, pirate attack, mutiny—were considered and discarded. Any of these events would have left evidence of damage or struggle, and there was none on the *Mary Celeste*. In the end, the investigators had to admit that they didn't know what had happened.

But the case has continued to fascinate historians of the sea to the present day. A host of exotic explanations for the disappearance have been offered. They range from the suggestion that the crew ate food contaminated with a fungus that drove them to madness and mass suicide, to the even more bizarre idea that they were plucked from the ship by a passing UFO.

The most probable explanation is that there was a minor explosion among the alcohol casks in the cargo hold. The explosion was not severe enough to do any damage but it frightened the captain

270

and crew into making for the lifeboat. The lifeboat was then swamped by a wave before they could get back to their undamaged ship.

Though the explanation sounds reasonable, like everything else about the *Mary Celeste* case it is unprovable.

See also: THE *JOYITA* MYSTERY

THE MYSTERIOUS AIRSHIP   From November 1896 until about May 1897, thousands, perhaps tens of thousands, of Americans reported seeing a "mysterious airship" overhead. The sightings started in California and slowly moved eastward to Ohio and West Virginia. The airship was seen over cities like Sacramento, Omaha, and Chicago. What makes the sightings mysterious is that there were no airships in 1896–97. The Wright brothers didn't even get their flying machine off the ground until December 1903, a full eight years after the mysterious airship sightings began. There were, of course, many other inventors experimenting with the flying machine idea before the Wright brothers. And there were a variety of balloons and other than lighter-than-air craft already in use. But there is nothing in known aviation history that can account for the 1896–97 wave of sightings. They truly represent a nineteenth-century UFO case.

A fairly typical airship sighting was made by Robert Lowen of Evanston, Illinois, a suburb of Chicago. A report of his sighting was published in *The Chicago Times Herald* in April 1897.

Lowen was looking through field glasses and was "able to discern four lights a short distance apart and moving in unison. The first was a bright white light and appeared to be operated like a searchlight. Behind it was a green light and further to the rear were green and white lights strung together."

The Chicago Tribune reported: "At several points the moving wonder was observed by persons equipped with small telescopes or powerful field glasses, and those persons claim to have described the outlines of a structure bearing the lights. The consensus of judgment . . . is that the main body of the night flyer was about seventy feet in length of slender proportions and fragile construction. To this body it is reported were attached the movable headlight and other lights described. A few observers claim that they also saw, a short distance above the body, laterial structures, resembling wings or sails."

For several months the mysterious airship was a nationwide sensation. Stories about it appeared in practically every newspaper in the country, and it was news in Europe as well. The stories grew wilder, with accounts of meeting the airship inventor and his

Drawing supposedly made from a photograph of the mysterious airship when it appeared over Chicago on April 11, 1897
(Courtesy Chicago Historical Society)

crew and even tales of encounters with creatures from another planet. Then, as suddenly and mysteriously as it had appeared, the airship disappeared. Or at least the newspapers stopped printing stories about it. The whole airship excitement was completely forgotten until the 1960s, when researchers interested in UFOs began rummaging through old newspapers and came up with some of the original stories.

What caused all the excitement? At the time, there was a great deal of speculation that a mysterious inventor working somewhere in isolation had perfected an airship and was testing it out secretly. But no evidence has ever surfaced to support this theory, and it now seems highly unlikely that such an inventor ever existed.

There were some misidentifications—meteors and planets being mistaken for the lights of an airship. And there was certainly plenty of hoaxing. There are a few cases of tricksters releasing balloons. There is also some evidence that railroad telegraph operators were engaged in an informal conspiracy to spread airship stories. At the end of the nineteenth century, the railroad telegraph was the primary means of long-distance communication in the United States.

There were unquestionably newspaper hoaxes. Late nineteenth-century newspapermen regarded the journalistic hoax as a legitimate art form, and many of the readers recognized the fictional nature of the articles they were reading. Indeed, much early science fiction was presented in the form of newspaper hoaxes.

Most science fiction of the era is what might properly be called invention stories, that is, stories woven around some marvelous new invention. There were many invention stories about airships during this period, because inventors really were working on airships. The world stood on the brink of heavier-than-air flight, and it was a subject much speculated about.

But underneath all the mistakes and hoaxes, there may be some genuinely puzzling and mysterious events.

See also: ANIMAL MUTILATIONS; UFOS

THE PHILADELPHIA EXPERIMENT   An often-repeated story is that sometime during World War II the U.S. Navy conducted a successful test of teleportation. The S.S. *Andrew Fursenth* was transported instantly from its dock in Philadelphia to a dock in the Norfolk-Newport News-Portsmouth area and back again. The teleportation took only a few minutes, but the experiment had disastrous long-term results. Half the crew was lost. Many of the survivors were "mad as hatters." Others would "go blank" or "get stuck." They would seem to disappear or "freeze" on the spot.

When one of the men would "freeze," others would rush forward to lay their hands upon him; this was supposed to be the "cure." But the "cure" didn't always work. At one point, when a sailor froze and his friend ran forward to lay his hands on him, both began to smolder. They burned for "eighteen days."

This wild and incredible tale first came to light in what are known as the Allende letters. Maurice K. Jessup, an astronomer and UFO researcher, had written a book called *The Case for the UFO* in 1955. The following year, he received several letters from a man signing himself Carlos M. Allende or Carl Allen. A copy of Jessup's book, with extensive annotations in the same handwriting as that found in the Allende letters, arrived at the Office of Naval Research. The material from Allende indicated in a rambling, almost incoherent sort of way that the writer had some sort of special or secret knowledge of UFOs and of life beyond earth. Amid the ramblings is told the story of the Philadelphia Experiment.

Allende indicated that he had either witnessed the experiment or had in some other way gained firsthand knowledge of it. In this, as in practically everything else, the letters are not at all clear. He also said that there was a brief article about the experiment in a Philadelphia newspaper, but no one has ever been able to locate it.

The Navy insists that the whole story is complete nonsense and that it never had any interest in the subject of teleportation. Some UFO researchers have claimed that the Navy was very interested and spent a lot of time and money unsuccessfully trying to locate the mysterious Allende.

At first, Jessup himself did not seem to take the letters too seriously, but as time went on he talked and wrote about them more frequently. On April 29, 1959, Maurice Jessup was found dead inside his car in a Dade County, Florida, park. The verdict was suicide. Some insist that Jessup was murdered because he "knew too much." But others who were acquainted with Jessup found his death no surprise. Maurice Jessup, they say, was a deeply troubled man who had often talked of suicide.

The Allende letters, and particularly the part about the Philadelphia Experiment, did not die, however. They became part of the lore surrounding UFOs. It was frequently mentioned in books and articles on UFOs and other strange phenomena and was even the subject of a feature film.

A man who most people believe to be the real Carlos Allende actually showed up at the headquarters of the Aerial Phenomena Research Organization (APRO) in Tucson, Arizona. He confessed to this pro-UFO group that the whole thing had been a hoax, that he had written the letters, "because Jessup's writings scared me." However, he did make some rather mysterious comments about UFOs and later tried to retract his original "confession." Those who have met Allende tend to dismiss him as a harmless eccentric, hardly one to be taken seriously about the Philadelphia Experiment or anything else.

Is there any truth at all to the story of the Philadelphia Experiment? It is possible that the whole idea began with experiments in degaussing—the neutralizing of a ship's magnetism so that it could pass over magnetic mines without setting them off. A degaussed ship would, in a sense, disappear—but only magnetically; the physical body of the ship would, of course, stay where it was. Allende might have heard of these experiments and become confused.

Whatever the origin of the story, there is no truth in the rumor that the Navy was ever conducting experiments in teleportation, in Philadelphia or anywhere else.

See also: UFOS

THE PROPHECIES OF FATIMA   In 1917, three children of shepherds in Fatima, Portugal, reported that they had seen a vision of the Virgin. The Virgin promised the children that she would reappear to them several times. As word of the vision spread, crowds gathered in order to witness the appearance. At the time of what was supposed to be the final appearance of the Virgin, thousands were waiting in a field near Fatima. Though the luminous figure of the Virgin reported by the children did not appear to the multitude, there were accounts that many in the crowd saw a luminous globe in the sky and that the sun appeared to rotate wildly. The majority of the crowd, however, reported no unusual appearances.

The Virgin was said to have given the children some prophecies that were to be made public. Among them were the prediction that World War I would soon end and that under the next pope, Pius XI (1922–39), there would be a more terrible war and that if Russia did not consecrate itself to Her it would "spread its errors throughout the world" and as a result many countries would be "annihilated." The Russian Revolution had just taken place. There was also a secret prediction, one that was not to be made public. All that the children would say was that this final prophecy would bring joy to some and sorrow to others. It is this final prophecy that has been the subject of endless rumor and speculation.

Two of the children died in the great influenza epidemic that swept the world after World War I. The third, Lucia Santos, became a nun. Between 1935 and 1941, she wrote several volumes on her life and visions. It was said that during this period she wrote down the final secret prophecy and put it in a sealed envelope with instructions that it should be opened upon her death or in 1960, whichever came first. The sealed envelope was supposed to have been in the office of the bishop of Leiria in Portugal.

In 1960, Lucia Santos, now known as Sister Maria of the Immaculate Heart, was still alive in a Carmelite convent in Spain. There was a rumor that the sealed envelope was taken to Rome, where it was opened by Pope John XXIII, who cried for three days over the terrible contents of the message, but never revealed what he had read. The most persistent speculation about the message is that it predicted either the end of the Catholic Church or the end of the world.

In 1960, Catholic information agencies all over the world were swamped with requests for information about the secret Fatima prophecy. No information was forthcoming, and officially the Church has maintained an ambiguous and arm's-length relationship to the events at Fatima. Not only has the Church declined to reveal the contents of the sealed prophecy, it has not even been officially confirmed that such a prophecy even exists.

THE *TITANIC* PROPHECIES   What has been called "the most astounding instance of prophecy" is to be found in a novel. In 1898, a book called *The Wreck of the Titan,* by a virtually unknown British writer named Morgan Robertson, was published. It was what we would today call a disaster novel, about the sinking of a great ocean liner. The novel itself sank like the fictional ocean liner.

But in 1912, fourteen years after the publication of *The Wreck of the Titan,* the events described in the novel came horribly and spectacularly true. The *Titanic,* the largest, most luxurious ocean liner ever built, struck an iceberg and sank in the greatest civilian naval tragedy in history.

The parallels between the novel and the real events are truly startling. First, there are the names of the ships, *Titan* and *Titanic.*

Both were on their maiden voyages across the Atlantic. Both were triple-screw vessels, and both had an inadequate number of lifeboats, twenty-four on the *Titan* and only twenty on the *Titanic*. The *Titan* was a 70,000-ton-ship; the *Titanic* was a 66,000-ton ship. Both sank in April after striking an iceberg in the North Atlantic, with an appalling loss of life. Most of the 2300 on the *Titan*, and 1503 of the 2206 on the *Titanic*, died. Both ships had been deemed "unsinkable." In the novel, one of the characters says, "God Himself could not sink the ship." The *Titanic*'s owners, the White Star Line, had declared her to be absolutely safe. She had sixteen watertight compartments, and even if the first four were torn open she could easily stay afloat.

Prophecy? Well, perhaps, but the author, who seems to have known something about ocean liner construction, may merely have been extrapolating from known facts. Icebergs were a well-known danger to ships on the North Atlantic route, and April was a month when the iceberg danger was at its height. As for the names *Titan* and *Titanic*—they both mean huge, and the liners were meant to be that—it may just have been a lucky or unlucky guess. So instead of an example of prophecy—and the author of *The Wreck of the Titan* never appears to have claimed any prophetic powers—the way in which reality seems to have followed fiction may just have been a coincidence, though admittedly quite a remarkable one.

After the *Titanic* tragedy, there were hundreds of stories from people who said that they had had some sort of premonition of disaster. J. Connon Middleton told the Society of Psychical Research in London that ten days before he was due to sail on the *Titanic* to attend a business conference in New York, he dreamed of the vessel "floating on the sea, keel upward and her passengers and crew swimming around her." He had the same dream the next night, but this time he seemed to be "floating in the air just above the wreck." Two days later he was relieved to receive a cable telling him that the business conference had been called off. He canceled his booking on the *Titanic* immediately and spent the rest of his life thankful that he had.

Colin Macdonald, a thirty-four-year-old marine engineer, said that he was up for the position of second engineer on the *Titanic,* an enviable job. Yet Macdonald was uneasy about the ship. He had a "strong impression" that something would happen, so he refused the offer. The engineer who took Macdonald's job went down with the ship.

W. T. Stead, a journalist and *Titanic* passenger, had once written a fictional account of the sinking of an ocean liner. An editor's note on the story said, "This is exactly what might take place, if liners are sent to sea short of boats," and the *Titanic was short of lifeboats. The Wreck of the Titan* was not the only disaster story about the sinking of an ocean liner.

Stead had written another fictional piece on what would happen if a liner collided with an iceberg. He was also said to have had a dream in which he saw himself standing on the deck of the sinking *Titanic* without a lifebelt and with the last lifeboat pulling away.

A couple of London psychics claimed that the writer had consulted them shortly before his departure, and both said that they had warned him not to go. "I see more than a thousand people— yourself among them—struggling desperately in the water. They are screaming for help, and fighting for their lives. But it does none of them any good—yourself included."

Despite these warnings, Stead sailed on the *Titanic* and was lost in the disaster. But can we be sure there were really any warnings, or that Stead's dream represented anything more than normal anxiety about a long ocean voyage?

Mrs. Rene Harris, a *Titanic* survivor, said that as the ship pulled out of Southampton a man she had never seen before stepped up to her and asked abruptly, "Do you love life?" The somewhat startled woman replied that she did, and then the man replied, "Then get off this ship at Cherbourg, if we get that far. That's what I'm going to do." Mrs. Harris did not know whether the unknown man got off at Cherbourg or not, but she remembered his words for the rest of her life.

Hundreds of accounts of dreams, hunches, or other experiences that somehow foretold the sinking of the *Titanic* were collected from survivors and others. Every major tragedy stimulates such accounts, and the sinking of the *Titanic*, being a tragedy of unprecedented proportions and publicity, called forth an unprecedented number of predictions reported after the fact. Dramatic as many of them are, they are not of much use as evidence of any real forewarning of disaster. A hundred or a thousand times in an average person's life he or she may have a dream or some other vague premonition of disaster. When disaster really does strike, we tend to think it was foretold, forgetting all the times the dreams and hunches were wrong. Add to this very human response another one, a selective memory that tends to add or subtract details in order to make them conform to what actually happened, and we have the psychological conditions that create an outpouring of "I knew it was going to happen," every time some unexpected and dramatic tragedy takes place. And the sinking of the great ocean liner was surely laden with both drama and tragedy.

UFOs
Unidentified flying objects, UFOs, flying saucers, or, originally, flying disks, are a complex and long-lived worldwide phenomenon. People have reported seeing strange or unexplained things in the sky for a very long time. Many have traced UFO sighting back to ancient Egyptian times and to the biblical story of Ezekial's wheel.

More recently there was a wave of sightings of a mysterious airship at the end of the nineteenth century, a time where there were no airships. During World War I, people were reporting mysterious zeppelins in places where they couldn't possibly have been. In World War II, it was strange glowing balls called "foo fighters." After the war, people in Europe, particularly in the Scandinavian countries, were reporting strange cigar-shaped objects in the sky. These were dubbed "ghost rockets."

But all of these were relatively short-lived phenomena. What started on June 24, 1947, began a controversy that has lasted to the present day, bringing forth images and ideas that have become part of the fabric of our culture.

On that day, Kenneth Arnold, a Boise, Idaho, salesman and an experienced private pilot, was flying his plane from Chehalis to Yakima in the state of Washington. In the vicinity of Mt. Ranier, he saw what he took to be nine disk-shaped objects flying at a fantastic speed. He described them as moving "like a saucer skipping over water."

The story was picked up by newspapers all over the country, but at first it was treated as a journalistic "silly season" item and seemed destined to fade quickly. But it didn't, partly because it grabbed the interest of science fiction magazine editor Raymond A. Palmer and partly because people continued to report strange things in the sky.

In the Cold War atmosphere of 1947, there was immediate fear that the Soviets had developed some sort of "secret weapon," and the Air Force took an early interest in investigating flying saucer reports.

On January 7, 1948, Captain Thomas Mantell, an experienced Air National Guard pilot, was killed while chasing a large unidentified silvery object near Louisville, Kentucky. In October of that same year, Second Lieutenant George F. Gorman got into an aerial dogfight with a mysterious lighted object over Fargo, North Dakota. A shaken Gorman later told investigators, "I had the distinct impression that its maneuvers were controlled by thought or reason."

In both of these cases, later evidence indicated that the pilots had actually been chasing weather balloons. Mantell had no oxygen equipment in his plane, and when he tried to climb to twenty thousand feet he blacked out. The weather balloon project was secret, so the Air Force could not immediately reveal the source of the error. These well-publicized cases added to the general public

UFO photograph from McMinnville, Oregon, taken in 1950
(UPI)

hysteria that was beginning to surround the subject of flying saucers.

The Air Force, which had started out looking for Soviet secret weapons, decided early on that the Soviets were not involved and that flying saucer reports were most probably the result of misidentification or out-and-out hoaxes. A panel convened by the CIA concluded pretty much the same thing. Although the Air Force continued to investigate UFOs and some connected with the investigation believed that there might be "something" to the flying saucer phenomenon, real official investigation was minimal. The primary focus of the Air Force project was on reassuring the public that we were not under attack by aliens from other planets and that everything was just fine. But the Air Force acted clumsily and created a mood of suspicion and distrust. Thus, when flying saucer supporters charged cover-up, a lot of people were willing to believe them.

The cover-up theory was pushed most enthusiastically and successfully by Donald E. Keyhoe, a retired Marine Corps major and a writer on aviation subjects. Keyhoe's article "The Flying Saucers Are Real" was published in the January 1950 issue of *True* magazine, and it broke all sales records for that magazine.

The number of reported sightings continued to rise and reached a high point in 1952. The most dramatic incident that year and one of the most dramatic in the history of UFOs, was the "invasion" of Washington, D.C., that took place on the night of July 19. There were a few visual sightings of strange lights, but the heart of this incident was the radar detection of a group of UFOs that seemed capable of moving at fantastic speeds. A plane was sent up to track the UFOs but found nothing. The Air Force reaction to this incident was a combination of lethargy and secrecy, and it did a great deal to heighten public anxiety about UFOs, exactly the opposite of what the Air Force was trying to do.

The official explanation for the incident is that false radar readings or "ghosts" were created by the unusual weather conditions Washington was then experiencing. Today that explanation is accepted, even by many people who believe in UFOs. At the time, it seemed absurd.

Alongside the considerable number of people who thought they had seen UFOs, there was a small but growing number who said that they had not only seen the spaceships and their inhabitants but had talked to them and had even taken trips to other planets via spaceship. Such people were called "contactees."

One of the earliest and most successful of the contactees was George Adamski. Adamski had been an occultist and mystic long before he had latched onto flying saucers, and the "message" that he got from those beings he called the "space brothers" sounded very much like the occult message that he had been promulgating since 1936, except now the "masters" were not members of the Royal Order of Tibet but were space beings.

According to Adamski, the space people were part of a benevolent galaxywide organization, and they had come to earth to keep people from destroying themselves. They had been making visits for centuries, but now their task had a new urgency because, with the development of atomic weapons, the people of earth could destroy not only themselves, they could harm nearby planets as well. The task of the space people was a difficult and often thankless one, and from time to time they chose particularly worthy individuals on earth to carry their message to the rest of mankind. Jesus had been one of their chosen messengers, and for the modern age they had chosen George Adamski.

Other contactees presented equally exotic messages, and one of them, Gabriel Green, ran first for president and later for the U.S. Senate in California. His senatorial bid captured 171,000 votes.

While the majority of the contactees portrayed the aliens as benevolent "space brothers," there were those who said that their contacts were considerably less friendly or were even hostile. A number of people reported having been "zapped" by UFOs or their inhabitants. A few even had burns to prove it. But the case that really captured public attention was a "kidnapping."

Betty and Barney Hill, a couple from Portsmouth, New Hampshire, claimed that they had been kidnapped and taken aboard a UFO on the night of September 19, 1961. They also said that the memory of the entire incident had been wiped from their minds and could be recalled only with the aid of hypnosis. The Hills' story became the basis for a best-selling book and apparently inspired a number of similar "kidnapping" accounts.

Most of those who have studied the Hill case closely believe that the couple were not lying; they were telling the truth as they saw it. The experience, however, was not a real one; it was a shared dream or fantasy. This was certainly the opinion of the psychiatrist who examined the couple and who had hypnotized them. However, this rather tame conclusion was generally buried in the flood of publicity that accompanied their story.

Sightings of and public interest in UFOs rose and fell in waves over the years. After the peak of interest in 1952, there was a gradual decline until 1957, when there was another sudden upsurge. After that, there was a long gradual decline and the Air Force, which really wanted to get out of the UFO business completely, began to entertain the hope that the phenomenon would finally fade away.

Then in March 1966, a series of well-publicized sightings in Michigan caused public interest to shoot way up again. At that time, the question of the reality of UFOs was even raised in Congress. The Air Force decided that it was finally time to sponsor an outside scientific investigation of the phenomenon.

The investigation was to be carried out by the University of Colorado and was to be headed by Dr. Edward U. Condon, a physicist of international repute. The funding of $300,000 came from the Air Force. But far from settling the UFO controversy, the Condon Committee itself became the subject of controversy. Pro-UFO groups claimed that the committee was biased, and worse, part of the continuing cover-up.

The final, and very lengthy, report of the Condon Committee was issued in January 1969. It was a document more argued over than read. Ninety-one UFO cases of different types were analyzed in depth. In slightly better than two-thirds of the cases, committee felt that it had been able to identify the UFO as a known object, natural phenomenon, or hoax. One-third of the cases were left unexplained, primarily, the committee felt, because there was not enough information to come to a definite conclusion. Condon

UFO photograph from Zanesville, Ohio, taken in 1967
(UPI)

himself insisted that since there was absolutely no evidence that
UFOs were extraterrestrial spaceships or indeed anything out of
the ordinary, people should stop wasting time and money investigating them. Statements like that outraged pro-UFO groups,
which said that the report proved there were genuine unknowns
and that Condon was trying to fool the public. The controversy
became heated and bitter.

Air Force officials announced happily that the Condon Report
was good enough for them, and they promptly got out of the UFO
business.

Interest in UFOs declined steadily after 1969, not so much because people had accepted Condon's view, or in fact were even

aware of it, but because there were no sensational new sightings to stimulate interest. Without something new, the subject had become boring. People had waited too long for the saucers to land.

Even longtime UFO buffs were becoming discouraged at the lack of physical evidence for UFOs. Some began to adopt a "paraphysical" hypothesis: that the UFOs were not physical spaceships but some sort of nonphysical psychic projection, perhaps stimulated by extraterrestrials. The UFOs were real, yet not real; it was a difficult proposition to argue with but not a very satisfying one to hold.

Steven Spielberg's magnificently directed UFO film, *Close Encounters of the Third Kind* (1977), attracted huge and appreciative audiences in 1977. Yet few seemed to be changed by the film's pro-UFO message; they regarded it primarily as entertainment. The success of the film did not even generate the expected upturn in UFO sightings.

Once-vigorous pro-UFO groups have become moribund, and while there still are occasional flaps, they are rarely of more than local interest. Yet there remains today a substantial number of people who still strongly believe that the UFO "mystery" has never been adequately explained and that there may have been something unusual, possibly unearthly, about a percentage of UFO sightings and experiences. In addition, they contend, the government is still "covering up." Although UFOs are now at a very low ebb, it would be premature to suggest that a new wave of interest is impossible or even unlikely.

UFOs have become part of the general culture. Surveys indicate that a majority of people are inclined to believe in them, even if belief is not active at the moment.

See also: CRASHED SAUCERS; THE MYSTERIOUS AIRSHIP; MYSTERIOUS LIGHTS

Selected

BIBLIOGRAPHY

Despite my personal reservations about Charles Fort, all those interested in the strange should at least look at his books: *The Book of the Damned, New Lands, Lo!* and *Wild Talents.* They are available in a variety of editions. I used a single volume edition, *The Books of Charles Fort* published for the Fortean Society (Henry Holt, N.Y., 1941). This volume has an interesting introduction by Tiffany Thayer. More about Fort himself can be found in Damon Knight's biography *Charles Fort, Prophet of the Unexplained* (Doubleday, N.Y., 1970).

The best collector of anomalies of nature today is William R. Corless. He has edited and written a number of excellent books and other publications. Information on his work can be obtained through The Source Book Project, Glen Arm, Md. 21057. A couple of small publications also keep up Fort's work. The most active is *Fortean Times,* 96 Mansfield Rd. London NW3 2HX, England. In the United States there is the International Fortean Organization, which publishes the journal *INFO* rather irregularly. The address is P.O. Box 367, Arlington, VA. 22210. And there is, of course, *Fate* magazine, which publishes articles on strange topics of all sorts.

Erich von Däniken has written a series of books on the ancient astronaut theme starting with his international best seller *Chariots of the*

Gods? (Putnam's, N.Y., 1970). His books should be read for their entertainment value only.

The late Ivan Sanderson is somewhat more reliable in his *Investigating the Unexplained* (Prentice Hall, Englewood Cliffs, N.J., 1972), though Sanderson constructs his cases as much by what he leaves out as by what he puts in and one is tempted to call this book *Explaining the Uninvestigated.*

Professor Charles Hapgood's *Maps of the Ancient Sea Kings* (Chilton, Philadelphia, 1963) is a work of unorthodox, but not uninteresting scholarship. *The Crystal Skull* by Richard Garvin (Doubleday, N.Y., 1973) is a popular exploration of all the stories surrounding that strange object.

Atlantis: The Antediluvian World, by Ignatius Donnelly, which is available in many editions may be the most influential work of crank scholarship of modern times. Lewis Spence's books *Atlantis in America* (Brentano's, N.Y., 1925), *The Problem of Atlantis* (Brentano's, N.Y., 1925) and *The Problem of Lemuria* (David McKay, Philadelphia, 1933) are less well known and considerably more difficult to obtain.

Stonehenge has been written about in scores of books, but the absolute best popular treatment is *Stonehenge Complete* by Christopher Chippindale (Cornell University Press, Ithaca, N.Y., 1983). Robert Silverberg thoroughly dissects the mound builder myth in *Mound Builders of Ancient America* (N.Y. Graphic Society, Greenwich, CT, 1968). Walker Chapman's *The Search for El Dorado* (Bobbs Merrill, N.Y., 1967) is a good popular exploration of that ghastly era in history.

Geoffrey Ashe is the world's number one hunter for Camelot and other traces of Arthurian Britain. Any of his books, starting with *King Arthur's Avalon* (Dutton, N.Y., 1955), make fascinating reading.

L. Sprague de Camp explains how some of the puzzling ancient monuments were built in *The Ancient Engineers* (Doubleday, N.Y., 1973). In *Lost Continents* (Dover, N.Y., 1970) he explores the Atlantis theme.

The Secrets of the Great Pyramid by Peter Tompkins (Harper, N.Y., 1971) is a beautifully produced, well-written book; unfortunately the author tends to believe too much. Also far too ready to believe is Charles M. Ballard. However, his *They All Discovered America* (Doubleday, N.Y., 1961) still makes amusing reading.

The Fire Came (Doubleday, N.Y., 1976) by John Baxter and Thomas Atkins gives a full history of the great Siberian explosion, but the explanations lean toward the bizarre.

The Hollow Earth (University Books, N.Y., 1969) by Raymond Bernard is a classic of pseudoscience.

Secret Societies (Holt, Rinehart and Winston, N.Y., 1967) provides a nice overview of a variety of fascinating and sometimes sinister organizations. The modern witch phenomena really started with Margaret Murray's *The Witch Cult in Western Europe* (Oxford Press, London, 1921). A more scholarly look at what witchcraft really was is given in *Europe's Inner Demons* (Basic Books, N.Y., 1975) by Normal Cohn. Any book by Frances Yates is bound to be interesting and thought-provoking. *The Rosicrucian Enlightenment* (Routledge & Keegan Paul, London, 1972) might be of greatest interest.

Few can really read Helena Petrovena Blavatsky's massive book *The Secret Doctrine,* which is available in several editions, but it does give an idea of the ideas of one of the great occultists of modern times. Colin Wilson writes on occult subjects better than most. Of his numerous books, *Mysteries* (Putnam's, N.Y., 1978) would probably appeal most to the readers of this book.

The Roswell Incident by Charles Berlitz and William Moore (Grosset & Dunlap, N.Y., 1980) tries to make a real mystery out of the crashed saucer legend.

Mute Evidence by Ian Summers and Dan Kagen (Bantam, N.Y., 1984) is an excellent and responsible exposition of this unpleasant subject.

And finally let me modestly recommend my own, *The Great Airship Mystery* (Dodd, Mead, N.Y., 1981), as the best (and only) book on that story.